Y0-BJY-454

JUDICIAL INTERPRETATION OF
INTERNATIONAL LAW IN
THE UNITED STATES

THE MACMILLAN COMPANY
NEW YORK · BOSTON · CHICAGO · DALLAS
ATLANTA · SAN FRANCISCO

MACMILLAN & CO., LIMITED
LONDON · BOMBAY · CALCUTTA
MELBOURNE

THE MACMILLAN CO. OF CANADA, LTD.
TORONTO

JUDICIAL INTERPRETATION
OF INTERNATIONAL LAW
IN THE UNITED STATES

BY

CHARLES PERGLER, D.C.L., LL.D.

DEAN OF THE NATIONAL UNIVERSITY SCHOOL OF ECONOMICS
AND GOVERNMENT; FORMERLY COMMISSIONER IN
THE UNITED STATES AND MINISTER TO JAPAN
FROM CZECHOSLOVAKIA

New York
THE MACMILLAN COMPANY
1928
All rights reserved.

COPYRIGHT, 1928,
BY THE MACMILLAN COMPANY.

Set up and printed.
Published August, 1928.

SET UP BY BROWN BROTHERS LINOTYPERS
Printed in the United States of America by
THE FERRIS PRINTING COMPANY, NEW YORK

PREFATORY NOTE

The primary purpose of this work is to present to the student, especially the lawyer, a survey of the principles of international law governing the relations of states in times of peace, as interpreted by the judiciary in the United States. The title indicates sufficiently, it is assumed, the limits the writer desired to place upon his endeavors.

Needless to say, those branches of international law, the exposition and application of which are wholly in the hands of the political departments of the government, are not dealt with in this volume, except incidentally and as they may have been touched upon by the courts in cases appropriately before them.

The laws of war and neutrality are not dealt with in this volume. For one thing, the still recent conflict has brought much confusion into this branch of jurisprudence, and it may be well, therefore, to deal with problems arising therefrom when we shall have achieved something of a perspective, making objective, and therefore scientific, treatment easier of accomplishment than it can be at the present stage of affairs; for another thing, many, if not most, of the cases decided by the courts turn upon questions of statutory construction, and, strictly speaking, are not an exposition of principles of international law. Furthermore, if, as Kant expresses it, war is a cessation of juridical relations between the states involved, and the statement seems undoubtedly correct, then there is grave doubt in the writer's mind whether laws of war should be treated as a branch of international law. That is not to say that there are no rules regulating the conduct of states in times of war, but a question is thus fairly raised whether they should not be presented independently. In any event, the author hopes to do so in the near future.

The plan originally was to limit the survey to decisions of the United States Supreme Court, and, on the whole, this intention has been adhered to. It was found, however, that certain questions of international law have never been presented to the highest American judicial tribunal, and therefore a number of decisions of state courts of last resort, as well as of the lower federal courts, have been cited. For similar reasons, reference is also made to several general works on international law by standard writers.

As far as the writer is aware, there is no work on international law written wholly from the standpoint of American judicial interpretation, and certainly not one as extensive as the present attempt.

The fact that the United States judiciary, both federal and state, in practical litigation, has been called upon to deal so often with questions of international law, and to apply this law to actual controversies, may come as a surprise to many. This is evidence sufficiently supporting the claim that international law is a branch of jurisprudence meriting study and attention not only by students of political science, but by practical lawyers as well.

CHARLES PERGLER.

Washington, D. C.

CONTENTS

CHAPTER I

INTERNATIONAL LAW: ITS ACCEPTANCE AND ENFORCEMENT IN THE UNITED STATES

		PAGE
1.	International law as part of the common law	1
2.	International law in the Federal Constitution	3
3.	Judicial decisions, after adoption of the Constitution, declaring international law part of the law of the land	8
4.	Federal legislation and international law	10
5.	The several states of the Union and international law	18
6.	The nature and sources of international law	24

CHAPTER II

INDEPENDENCE AND SOVEREIGNTY

7.	The American Union as a state in international law.—States as persons	28
8.	The nature of sovereignty	34
9.	Recognition of states and governments and of sovereignty over territory.—By whom determinable and its effects	40
10.	The nature of belligerency and its effects	48
11.	Kinds of governments and their powers	57
12.	Rights and duties of states and their responsibility	74
13.	The continuing personality of states	85
14.	Acquisition and loss of sovereignty: Effects and results	88

CHAPTER III

JURISDICTION OF STATES

15.	Territorial limits of state jurisdiction	101
16.	Jurisdiction over vessels	107
17.	Legal effects of territorial supremacy	109
18.	Exemptions from territorial jurisdiction	116
19.	Extraterritorial jurisdiction	124
20.	Extradition	129

[vii]

Contents

CHAPTER IV
CITIZENSHIP AND ALIENAGE

	PAGE
21. Citizenship and its sources	135
22. Expatriation	143
23. Aliens, their rights and privileges	147
24. Aliens, their duties	150
25. Aliens, their disabilities	151

CHAPTER V
TREATIES

26. Treaties and the treaty-making power in the United States	156
27. Enforcement and interpretation of treaties	169
28. Termination of treaties	178

CHAPTER VI
REMEDIAL MEASURES FALLING SHORT OF WAR

29. Arbitration	188
30. Nonintercourse and embargo	190
31. Retaliation and reprisals.—Display of force	191
LIST OF AUTHORITIES CITED	195
TABLE OF CASES CITED	199
INDEX	213

JUDICIAL INTERPRETATION OF INTERNATIONAL LAW IN THE UNITED STATES

JUDICIAL INTERPRETATION OF INTERNATIONAL LAW IN THE UNITED STATES

CHAPTER ONE

INTERNATIONAL LAW: ITS ACCEPTANCE AND ENFORCEMENT IN THE UNITED STATES

§ 1. *International law as part of the common law.*—In a case decided in 1761 Lord Mansfield quoted with approval an even earlier opinion of Lord Talbot (1736) to the effect that "the law of nations, in its full extent, was part of the law of England." [1] When, therefore, Blackstone in his Commentaries declared that in England the law of nations is "adopted in its full extent by the common law, and is held to be a part of the law of the land" [2] he had sufficient judicial precedent for the pronouncement.

The foundation of the jurisprudence of all the American states is the English common law,[3] the only exception being Louisiana where the civil law is applied in con-

---

[1] Triquet vs. Bath, Burrage: Reports, vol. III., p. 1478; Stowell & Munro, International Cases; Houghton Mifflin Co., Boston, 1916, vol. I., p. XXI.; James Brown Scott, Cases on International Law, West Publishing Co., St. Paul, 1922, p. 2.

[2] Blackstone, William, Sir, Commentaries on the Laws of England, Callaghan & Co., Chicago, 1899, Book IV., Chapter IV. (Cooley's Blackstone).

[3] Pattillo vs. Alexander, 96 Ga., 60; 29 L. R. A., 616.

Judicial Interpretation of International Law

troversies of a civil nature; but even in that state the common law prevails in criminal matters.[4] It is generally held that the common law was brought to America by the English settlers on the settlement of the colonies,[5] and it is assumed that the Constitution of the United States was framed by the Constitutional Convention of 1787 and ratified by the colonies in contemplation of the continued existence of this legal system in each state, subject to such modification as necessarily followed from the delegation of enumerated powers granted to the central government.[6] The government of the Union being merely one of powers delegated directly or by necessary implication, the ruling was perfectly logical, and, indeed, inevitable, that there is no common law of the United States in the sense of a national customary law, or distinct from the common law as it prevails in the several states.[7] It is true, of course, that the federal courts are frequently called upon to enforce the common law in municipal matters, but they do this because it is the law of the state, not federal law.[8] It is equally true that the federal courts, in proper cases, determine what is, or what is not, the common law applicable to a particular cause by following federal precedents,[9] though, where the question is new, weight is given to the decisions of the state courts,[10] but the following of federal precedents, when

[4] Note, 22 L. R. A., 502.
[5] Gatton vs. Chicago R. I. & P. C. R. Co., 95 Iowa, 112; 28 L. R. A., 566; Rhode Island vs. Massachusetts; 12 Peters, p. 657.
[6] Smith vs. Alabama, 124 U. S., 465; 31 L. Ed., 508
[7] Smith vs. Alabama, *supra*.
[8] Pennsylvania vs. Wheeling, etc., Bridge Co., 13 Howard, 518; 14 L. Ed., 518.
[9] Farmer's National Bank vs. Sutton Mfg. Co., 52 Fed. Rep., 191; Faulkner vs. Hart, 82 N. Y., 413.
[10] Farmer's National Bank vs. Sutton Mfg. Co., *supra*.

they are found, is not due to the existence of any national common law, but is resorted to on the theory that judicial precedents do not constitute the rule, but are simply evidence of what the common law rule is.[11]

§ 2. *International law in the Federal Constitution.*—Nevertheless, while the common law is the legal system of the several states of the Union, and while international law as part of the common law is also the law of the several states, the fact remains that the necessity of meeting obligations imposed by international law had much to do with bringing about the formulation and adoption of the Federal Constitution, and that the rules of international law, particularly of public international law, have been primarily expounded by the federal, not the state, courts. A short review of the situation, with reference to fulfillment of international obligations, following the treaty of peace with Great Britain, but prior to the Constitutional Convention of 1787, may prove interesting.

The extent to which the former colonies at one time regarded themselves as sovereign and independent is now seldom realized. The condition is thus summarized by a recognized student of American constitutional development:

A few contemporary instances are enlightening. Thus, Connecticut, in its statute adopting a declaration of rights and privileges in 1776, declared itself a "Republic" which "shall forever be and remain a free, sovereign and independent state"; Massachusetts, in its Constitution of 1780, declared itself "a free, sovereign and independent body politic by the name of the Commonwealth of Massachusetts." Samuel Adams used to write of the "Republic of Massachusetts Bay."

[11] Franklin vs. Twogood, 25 Iowa, 529.

Judicial Interpretation of International Law

The booksellers advertised for sale in the newspapers copies of "The Constitutions of the several independent States of America." General Henry Knox (a most ardent Federalist), in drafting the frame for the Society of the Cincinnati in 1783, spoke of the war as having resulted in the establishment of the colonies as "Free, Independent and Sovereign States." In the treaty of peace, Great Britain acknowledged the United States, naming each state separately, to be "free, sovereign and independent states." The state courts, and later the early federal courts, used similar language. The Pennsylvania legislature recited, in a statute of December 3, 1782, that "whereas by the separation of the thirteen United States from Great Britain, the Commonwealth of Pennsylvania hath become a sovereign and independent state, and in consequence of such separation, a government established solely on the authority of the people had been formed." [12]

Under the Articles of Confederation there was no executive, beyond the committees the Congress of the Confederacy might see fit to establish, and conditions were such that the decisions of this body were little more than recommendations, to be observed or ignored by the states as they might deem proper or merely expedient.[13] It is not surprising that it has been remarked: "Without authority to require the states to regard the principles of international law, and incompetent even to punish piracy or felony on the high seas, it was truly a pitiable spectacle that the United States presented.[14]

In the Constitutional Convention, in discussing the defects of the Articles of Confederation, Randolph pointed out, among other things, that under them the

[12] Warren, Charles, The Supreme Court and the Sovereign States, Princeton University Press (1924).

[13] Farrand, Max, The Framing of the Constitution, Yale University Press (1923), pages 4-5.

[14] Farrand, Max, The Framing of the Constitution, *supra*.

[4]

International Law; Its Acceptance and Enforcement

United States "could not cause infractions of treaties or of the law of nations to be punished," [15] and James Madison, in his speech in the Convention, against the New Jersey Plan, asked, "Will it prevent the violations of the law of nations and treaties, which, if not prevented, must involve us in the calamities of foreign wars? The tendency of the states to these violations has been manifested in sundry instances. . . ." [16] It is again James Madison who gives us a glimpse of the care with which the phraseology and terminology of the Constitution was considered, with reference to questions of international law. In defending what was, until ratification, the Philadelphia project, in the Virginia convention, Madison explains the use of the expression "piracy" and says that "piracy is a word which may be considered as a term of the law of nations. Felony is a word unknown to the law of nations, and is to be found in the British laws, and from thence adopted in the laws of these states. It was thought dishonorable to have recourse to that standard. A technical term of the law of nations is therefore used, that we should find ourselves authorized to introduce it into the laws of the United States." [17]

The Convention was a body of practical men and did not go, nor, probably, would it have been permitted to go, beyond the necessities of the case. Those necessities required uniformity with regard to crimes committed on the high seas and uniformity concerning definition of offences against international law. Said Madison again:

[15] Farrand, Max, Records of the Federal Convention, Yale University Press (1911), p. 19.
[16] Elliott, J., Debates on the Adoption of the Federal Constitution, J. B. Lippincott Co. (1891), vol. IV., pp. 207-210.
[17] Farrand, Max, Records of the Federal Convention, *supra*, vol. III., p. 332.

[5]

"if the laws of the states are to prevail on this subject, the citizens of different states will be subject to different punishments for the same offence at sea. There will be neither uniformity nor stability in the law." [18] Hence section eight of article one of the Federal Constitution gives Congress power "to define and punish Piracies and Felonies committed on the high Seas, and Offences against the Law of Nations." Since international law is not, and cannot be, the creation of any one nation, the Convention could give Congress no more than the power of definition and punishment, and even the grant of this power of definition gave rise to certain apprehensions. Mr. Wilson remarked that "to pretend to define the law of nations which depended on the authority of all Civilized nations of the world, would have a look of arrogance that would make us ridiculous"; but Gouverneur Morris responded that "the word define is proper when applied to offences in this case, the law of nations being often too vague and deficient to be a rule." [19]

Even more important than uniformity in observance of the rules of customary international law was the necessity of enforcement of treaty obligations. While the Revolutionary War was in progress some of the states enacted laws providing that debts due British creditors should be paid into the local treasury and that such payment could be pleaded in bar to any future action for the recovery of these debts. As a result there was embodied in the treaty of peace with Great Britain an article according the creditors the usual judicial remedies;

[18] Madison's Journal, G. P. Putnam's Sons (1908), vol. II., p. 186.
[19] Farrand, Max, Records of the Federal Convention, *supra*, vol. II., p. 6151.

International Law; Its Acceptance and Enforcement

but the state courts refused to enforce this treaty provision, deeming themselves bound by state enactments, and, consequently, the treaty in this respect became a mere scrap of paper. It was this situation that brought about the constitutional provision declaring treaties the supreme law of the land, binding judges in every state, anything in the Constitution or laws of any state to the contrary notwithstanding.[20]

Again, the judicial power of the United States extends not only to all cases, in law and equity, arising under the Constitution and the laws of the United States, but under "treaties made, or which shall be made, under their authority; to all cases affecting ambassadors, other public ministers and consuls; to all cases of admiralty and maritime jurisdiction," and "to controversies . . . between a state, or the citizens thereof, and foreign states, citizens or subjects." [21]

Thus, under the Constitution, Congress has considerable powers within the sphere of international law and the federal courts have extensive jurisdiction whenever cases under it arise. But it is well to remember that the great body of international law which concerns itself with the rights of private individuals, and is generally called private international law, does not come within the scope of federal legislation, except as it may be brought there by proper exercise of the treaty-making power. Article three, section two, paragraph one of the Federal Constitution is jurisdictional and simply makes the federal courts the proper forum in a certain class of cases, while paragraph ten, of section eight, article one of the Constitution,

[20] Federal Constitution, Article six, section two; Ware vs. Hylton (1796), 3 Dallas, 199.
[21] Federal Constitution, Article three, section two, par. one.

concerning felonies and piracies committed on the high seas and offences against the law of nations, relates wholly to acts of a criminal nature. This is so not only by reason of the rule that where general words follow a designation of particular subjects or classes of persons, the meaning of the general words will ordinarily be presumed to be restricted by the particular designation, and to include only things or persons of the same kind, class or nature as those specifically enumerated, unless there is a clear manifestation of a contrary purpose,[22] but also because the term offence is applied to breaches of laws enacted for the protection of the public as distinguished from an infringement of mere private rights,[23] and the expression relating only to punishable violations of law, either felonies or misdemeanors.[24]

§ 3. *Judicial decisions, after adoption of the Constitution, declaring international law part of the law of the land.*—The courts of the United States lost no time in affirming the principle that international law is part of the law of the land. Before the end of the century, the last quarter of which saw the establishment of American independence and the adoption of the Constitution, Mr. Justice Wilson laid down the principle that "when the United States declared their independence, they were bound to receive the law of nations in its modern state of purity and refinement."[25] This was followed by a declaration of Chief Justice Marshall, in 1804, that an act of Congress ought never to be construed to violate

---

[22] United States vs. Bevans, 3 Wheaton, 336, 4 L. Ed., 404; Caminetti vs. United States, 242 U. S., 470, 61 L. Ed., 442.
[23] 29 Cyc, pp. 1351-52, and cases cited.
[24] Com. vs. Rowe, 112 Ky., 482, 66 S. W., 29.
[25] Ware vs. Hylton, 3 Dallas, 199, 1 L. Ed., 568.

the law of nations if any other possible construction remains.[26] Later, in 1815, the Chief Justice reaffirmed this position and held that until an act of Congress has been passed "the court is bound by the law of nations, which is a part of the law of the land." [27]

The position proclaimed so early in the history of the Supreme Court this tribunal has consistently maintained. Indeed, in some instances it has chosen to adopt language even stronger than that of John Marshall. Thus in 1895, speaking for the court, Mr. Justice Gray holds that international law, in its widest and most comprehensive sense, is a part of the law of the land, and must be ascertained and administered by the courts of justice as often as questions involving international law are presented in litigation between man and man and duly submitted for the decision of the courts. The Justice emphasizes that he has in mind not only questions of right between nations when he speaks of international law, but questions of what international jurists call private international law, or the conflict of laws, as it is otherwise frequently called, and concerning the rights of persons within the territory and dominion of one nation, by reason of acts, private or public, done within the dominion of another nation.[28] In a still later case, and one which has become a leading decision in the latter-day history of international law, it is again Mr. Justice Gray who holds that "international law is a part of our law, and must be ascertained and administered by the courts of justice of appropriate jurisdiction, as often as questions of right depending upon it are duly presented for

[26] The Charming Betsy, 2 Cranch, 64, 2 L. Ed., 208.
[27] The Nereide, 9 Cranch, 388, 3 L. Ed., 769.
[28] Hilton vs. Guyot, 159 U. S., 677, 40 L. Ed., 95.

their determination."[29] In administering this law the court does not consider itself "at liberty to inquire what is for the particular advantage or disadvantage of our own or another country."[30]

Enforcement of international law by the courts, whenever proper and possible, undoubtedly makes for progress in orderly international relations, but, from the point of view of the practicing lawyer, it has also the important and practical result that the law of nations, unlike foreign municipal law, does not have to be proved as a fact and is taken judicial notice of by the courts.[31]

§ 4. *Federal legislation and international law.*—A declaration that international law is law of the land, is, of course, a broad and sweeping statement and under certain circumstances, standing alone, might even prove misleading, since it is susceptible of being understood as meaning that the law of nations must prevail, and does prevail, in the courts of the United States, under all circumstances. Obviously, simple reflection will show that this cannot be so.

What the decisions mean, and are intended to mean, is, that when international law can be applied without running counter to a statutory provision, of Congress or of a state legislature, and when it is also not in conflict with an executive act or declaration governing the case, international law will be given effect and the courts will notice judicially what the international law is in a particular instance. This position is evident enough from the force-

[29] The "Paquette Habana," 175 U. S., 677, 44 L. Ed., 320; The Lusitania, 251 Fed. Rep., 715.
[30] The Peterhoff, 5 Wallace, 28, 18 L. Ed., 564.
[31] The Scotia, 14 Wallace, 170, 20 L. Ed., 822; The New York, 175 U. S., 187, 44 L. Ed., 126.

ful language of Marshall, who clearly concedes that if an act of Congress violates the law of nations, it is the act of Congress which must be enforced; no other construction can be placed upon a statement that *until an act of Congress has been passed* the court is bound by the law of nations. Expressed affirmatively, the rule is that when an act of Congress has been passed, the courts have no option but to enforce it, regardless of the rules of international law. The injured party would have a remedy, if any, in the usual diplomatic procedure. If a treaty must yield to the provisions of a congressional enactment passed subsequently to the treaty,[32] a different rule certainly cannot prevail with regard to the frequently less certain obligations of customary international law. The courts in such case will and must enforce the statute, leaving the violation of international law, if any, to adjustment through the usual channels of international intercourse.

The problem we are dealing with here is not so much one of superiority or inferiority of any branch of law, but of its enforceability in courts that derive their jurisdiction and all their power from constitutions, state and federal, and laws enacted under these constitutions. One may well believe that international law is superior to constitutions and municipal law in the sense that it is the law of all nations and stands above all other laws in moral weight, and yet realize that international law cannot be given effect by municipal courts where it clashes with provisions of municipal law. Theoretical considerations may lead us to desire a different rule, but it requires no pro-

---

[32] See "Treaties," Chapter V., The Chinese Exclusion Case, 130 U. S., 581, 32 L. Ed., 1068.

Judicial Interpretation of International Law

phetic gift to say that no court, federal or state, will ever declare a statute invalid on the sole ground that it is contrary to international law.

"International law forms an important part of the law of civilized states. To what extent and in what manner its rules are recognized by the law of any given state is a question which depends on the municipal law of the particular state." [33] Within the state nothing can be recognized as law by the courts except that which is commanded by the state.[34] This may seem a statement of the obvious, but it appears appropriate to enter into some consideration of what appears axiomatic, if for no other reason, because of the fact that only recently the contention has been advanced that treaties as well as customary international law are superior to municipal law and that in cases of conflict the latter should yield to the former. The theory is thus summarized:

The conclusion here drawn is that not only are treaties and customary international law of authority superior to national statutes and the Constitution of the United States, but also that national courts in the United States are bound in observing sound principles of law to act upon this fact. This position is denied today by the courts with respect to treaties and statutes, in reliance entirely upon an old and badly reasoned decision from an inferior court; it is in dispute with reference to statutes and customary international law, with a preponderance of authority in support of the conclusion here drawn; it is well recognized with reference to the Constitution and treaties or customary international law, although not as well recognized as it should be. Eventually the doctrine set forth

[33] W. S. Holdsworth, A History of English Law, Methuen & Co., Ltd., London (1925), vol. IV., page 25.
[34] But see sec. 6, *infra*, on "Nature and sources of international law."

International Law; Its Acceptance and Enforcement

here must prevail all along the line, in the interests of sound jurisprudence and practical convenience as well.[35]

It may be well worth while to examine the cases the author relies upon. The first case[36] is one of the French Spoliation Claims and involved an action of the administrator against the United States, a fact in itself quite suggestive of the nature of the case, the question presented being whether an American vessel convoyed by a British privateer in 1798 was liable to condemnation.

One of the bases of the claim for compensation was the contention that a statute of the United States authorized resistance of American merchantmen to French visitation and search. The court in an *obiter dictum* remarked that "no single state can change the law of nations by its municipal regulations." The aside, correct in itself, has no bearing, however, upon the question we are discussing, viz., the enforceability of international law as municipal law, and does not support the author's theory, for the simple reason that the court was dealing not with a problem of municipal law of the United States, but an alleged claim of an American citizen, or, rather, his descendants, against the French government, and, manifestly, the only law applicable was international law.

The second case[37] is another of the French Spoliation cases and it resulted from the resistance of the vessel to search by a French cruiser in 1799, the resistance causing an action lasting 2½ hours, and the court said that "the municipal law in the absence of a treaty must be subordi-

[35] Pitman B. Potter, International Law and National Law in the United States, American Journal of International Law, April, 1925, vol. 19, No. 2.
[36] The Schooner Nancy (1892), 27 Court of Claims, 99.
[37] The Ship Rose, 36 Court of Claims, 290.

nated to international law when they come in antagonism, *as that is the law common to both parties.*" The sentence italicized shows sufficiently that the question was one of applicability of a given law, a situation common enough in all litigation, and therefore not of the superiority or inferiority of any branch of the law.

But who were the parties the opinion speaks of? The tribunal answers this by saying that "this court in making the investigation contemplated by the act of our jurisdiction is sitting in the character of an international tribunal, *to determine the diplomatic rights of the United States as they existed against France prior to the ratification of the treaty of September 30, 1800.*" The parties, therefore, were two international law persons, the United States and France, and, again, the question was not one of international law as municipal law.

The author of the study referred to relies upon two other Court of Claims cases, but what has been said as to the first two applies to the remaining with equal force, for these, also, are of the group of French Spoliations,[38] the parties being two states, and in the last case the court declaring that "the statutes to which we have referred respecting the authority of Congress to authorize American merchant vessels to defend against French depredations did not change the law of nations or *impose a new international obligation* upon France as was held in the case of the Ship Rose, supra, page 283."

In the French Spoliation cases the Court of Claims acted under a special act of Congress, as appears from the opinions clearly enough; without an act of Congress

[38] The Schooner Jane, 37 Court of Claims 24· The Schooner Endeavor, Court of Claims, 242.

[14]

International Law; Its Acceptance and Enforcement

the Court of Claims would have had no jurisdiction; and in all cases the findings, with the opinions rendered, were simply certified to Congress, in the nature of recommendations, a fact in itself constituting a recognition of the power of the national legislature to carry out, or not to carry out, obligations imposed upon states by international law.

A direct ruling upon the question under consideration by the United States Supreme Court does not exist, but there is a statement from competent judicial authority to the effect that "it goes without saying that mere international comity not incorporated in any convention between the United States and a foreign power must yield to a statute with which it is in conflict." [39] This ruling was followed in a much later case, where the question was directly involved, and where, while the court reveals an underestimation of international law as a rule of conduct between states, the decision still is "that the rules of international law, like those of existing treaties or conventions, are subject to the express acts of Congress, and the courts of the United States have not the power to declare a law unconstitutional, if it be within the authority given to Congress as to legislation, even though the law itself be in contravention of the so-called law of nations." [40] A ruling made still later contains the declaration that "we make no question of the power of Congress to enact this law, for neither existing treaties, nor international law, could divest Congress of the power, if it chose to exercise it, of requiring military service of such resident aliens, as international law is not in itself binding

[39] The Kestor, 110 Fed. Rep., 432.
[40] United States vs. Bell, 248 Fed. Rep., 992.

Judicial Interpretation of International Law

upon Congress, and treaties stand upon no higher plane than statutes of the United States." [41]

Only recently it has been conceded that "it is quite true that in case of conflict between municipal and international law, the courts and executive authorities are bound by the former rather than the latter," and "that a state is entirely free to enact such legislation and may compel its own courts to apply it, its executive authorities to enforce it and its subjects to obey it," but "that the international responsibility of the state cannot be altered in the slightest by such contravening legislation." [42] The second contention is of course also true, but the fact remains that international law is not law between a state and the persons subject to its jurisdiction unless the state recognizes it as such.[43]

In an *obiter dictum* the Supreme Court has indicated that article one, section eight, of the Federal Constitution, authorizing Congress "to define and punish piracies and felonies on the high seas, and offences against the law of nations" does not permit Congress, however, to bring within the shelter of this clause any offence not recognized by international law by arbitrarily declaring it to be one. An act of Congress of April 30, 1790, declared

[41] United States, vs. Siem, 299 Fed. Rept., 582.
[42] Garner, James W., Presidential Address before The American Political Science Association, December 29, 1924, The American Political Science Review, February, 1925.
[43] Burgess, John W., Political Science and Comparative Constitutional Law, Ginn & Co. (1913), vol. I., pp. 54-55.

See also United States vs. Thompson, 257 U. S., 432, 66 L. Ed., 299. Mr. Justice Holmes declares in this opinion that "there is no mystic over law to which even the United States must bow. When a case is said to be governed by foreign law or by general maritime law, that is only a short way of saying that, for this purpose, the sovereign power takes up a rule suggested from without, and makes it part of its own rules."

International Law; Its Acceptance and Enforcement

murder as well as robbery on the high seas to be piracy, but the Supreme Court points out that murder and piracy are things so essentially different in their nature that even Congress cannot confound or identify them. If, by calling murder piracy, Congress might assert jurisdiction over that offence committed by a foreigner on a foreign vessel, what offence might not be brought within their power by the same device? the court properly asked.[44] Pirates, of course, are subject to punishment in any jurisdiction into which they may be brought, and piracy is well understood to be robbery on the high seas,[45] and if Congress could by definition declare anything else to be piracy, it is obvious it could bring within American jurisdiction almost any conceivable offence as long as it was committed on the high seas. But this is primarily a question of constitutional, not international, law, and if Congress does not possess the power thus questioned by the Supreme Court, the limitation is one imposed by the Constitution and not by reason of the superior authority of international law. As a rule of constitutional law the opinion would seem to be sound, for when the framers of the Constitution gave Congress power to punish piracies and felonies on the high seas and other offences against international law, they clearly had in mind such offences as were and are taken cognizance of by the latter, and they did not confer and did not intend to confer power to create new offences, committed abroad, or to change the very nature of any recognized offence, perhaps for the sole purpose of obtaining jurisdiction which otherwise could not be acquired. The usual canon of con-

[44] United States vs. Pirates, 5 Wheaton, 184, 5 L. Ed., 163.
[45] Life of Sir Leoline Jenkins, see Stowell & Munro, International Cases, Houghton Mifflin Co., Boston (1916), vol. I, p. 425.

struction, that the expression of one thing in a constitution involves the exclusion of other things not expressed,[46] is also to be borne in mind, and from this point of view the Constitution excludes from the power of Congress anything more than punishment and definition of international offences. Congress may provide for the punishment of crimes on the high seas whether the acts penalized are felonies or crimes of a lesser degree.[47] However, an act of Congress need not expressly declare that its object is to punish or define an international offence if in fact it does so.[48]

Under the provision in question there exists a considerable body of legislation, mostly designed to safeguard the neutrality of the United States in case of conflicts with other countries. Just how far Congress could go in "defining and punishing" piracies and felonies on the high seas and offences against the law of nations is of course an interesting question for the constitutional as well as the international jurist.

§ 5 *The several states of the Union and international law.*—Once the view is taken that international law has been "adopted in its full extent by the common law" it logically follows that it is a part of the law of every American state where the common law system prevails as the foundation of its jurisprudence. Judicial decisions to this effect are not lacking, though it must be remembered that questions of international law as such are relatively seldom presented to state courts for determination, and that more often the problem is to ascertain the particular jurisdiction of which the law should be applied

[46] Brown vs. Maryland, 12 Wheaton, 419, 6 L. Ed., 678.
[47] United States vs. Rodgers, 150 U. S., 249, 37 L. Ed., 1071.
[48] United States vs. Arjona, 120 U. S., 479, 30 L. Ed., 728.

International Law; Its Acceptance and Enforcement

to a given set of facts. Consequently the matter is usually treated under the title of conflict of laws.

Before the adoption of the Federal Constitution the Philadelphia court of oyer and terminer tried, convicted and sentenced at common law a French citizen for an assault on the secretary of the French legation, committed in the minister's residence, on the ground that the "crime in the indictment is an infraction of the law of Nations. This law, in its full extent, is part of the law of this state, and it is to be collected from the practice of different nations, and the authority of the writers." [49] Other state courts have taken it for granted that international law is a part of the law of their states,[50] one of the latest state decisions (1919) holding that "international law is a part of the law of the United States, and must be administered whenever involved in causes presented for determination," though in a state court.[51]

What if an act of one of the state legislatures, and not of Congress, violates an established principle of international law? As the situation stands at the present time, clearly there would be only one course open to the courts, viz., to enforce the state statute, always assuming its constitutionality and that it does not contravene any valid federal enactment, or any treaty within the power of the central government and therefore the law of the land. This conclusion is inescapable if we proceed on the theory, as we must, in view of the decisions, that international law is a part of the common law, and no more, and if we bear in mind that the common law prevails in the states "except as modified, changed or repealed by statute

[49] Respublica vs. DeLongchamps, 1 Dallas, 111, 1 L. Ed., 59.
[50] Heirn vs. Bridault, 37 Miss., 209.
[51] Riddell vs. Fuhrman, 233 Mass., 69, 123 N. E., 237.

Judicial Interpretation of International Law

or in so far as it is not inconsistent with the constitution, or the statutes, or the institutions of the state."[52]

As between the state and persons and property subject to its jurisdiction, international law is subject to the same rules as other common law principles. This conclusion would in any event follow from the provision of the Tenth Amendment to the Constitution providing that "the powers not delegated to the United States by the Constitution, nor prohibited by it to the States, are reserved to the States respectively, or to the people," and from the fact that the states are sovereign except to the extent to which they have surrendered certain powers to the federal government.

The power of the separate states even in matters involving questions of international law and having a bearing on foreign relations has been illustrated a number of times, for instance in the New Orleans lynching cases and in the way the federal government thought it necessary to proceed in its attempts to dissuade California from passing enactments considered anti-Japanese; but perhaps never has it been quite so strikingly exemplified as in what are known as the *McLeod* and *The Caroline* cases. In view of some of the contentions already referred to,[53] and to avoid even the slightest possibility of confusion of thought, it may be worth while to give here the material facts in these cases, and since they are succinctly given in a work on American foreign policy, for the sake of brevity the statement therein appearing is adopted here:

[52] Horace Watters & Co. vs. Gerard, 189 N. Y., 302, 82 N. E., 143; Harris vs. Powers, 129 Ga., 74, 58 S. E., 1038.
[53] See section on "Federal Legislation and International Law," *supra*.

International Law; Its Acceptance and Enforcement

During the Canadian rebellion of 1837 Americans along the border expressed openly their sympathy for the insurgents who secured arms and munitions from the American side. In December a British force crossed the Niagara river, boarded and took possession of *The Caroline*, a vessel which had been hired by the insurgents to convey their cannon and other supplies. The ship was fired and sent over the falls. When *The Caroline* was boarded one American, Amos Durfee, was killed and several others wounded. The United States at once demanded redress, but the British government took the position that the seizure of *The Caroline* was a justifiable act of self-defense against people whom their own government either could not or would not control.

The demands of the United States were still unredressed when in 1840 a Canadian named Alexander McLeod made the boast in a tavern on the American side that he had slain Durfee. He was taken at his word, examined before a magistrate, and committed to jail in Lockport. McLeod's arrest created great excitement on both sides of the border. The British minister at Washington called upon the government of the United States "to take prompt and effectual steps for the liberation of Mr. McLeod." Secretary of State Forsythe replied that the offense with which McLeod was charged had been committed within the state of New York; that the jurisdiction of each state of the United States was, within its proper sphere, perfectly independent of the federal government; that the latter could not interfere. The date set for the trial of McLeod was the fourth Monday in March, 1841. Van Buren's term ended and Harrison's began on the fourth of March, and Webster became secretary of state. The British minister was given instructions by his government to demand the immediate release of McLeod. This demand was made, he said, because the attack on *The Caroline* was an act of a public character; because it was a justifiable use of force for the defense of British territory against unprovoked attack by "British rebels and American pirates"; because it was contrary to the principles of civilized nations to hold individuals responsible for acts done by order of the constituted authorities of the state; and because His Majesty's Government could not admit the doctrine that the federal government had no power to interfere and that the decision must rest with the state of New York. The relations of foreign powers were with the federal government. To admit that the federal government had no control over a state would lead to the dissolution of the Union so far as foreign powers are concerned, and to the accrediting foreign diplomatic agents, not to the federal government, but to each separate state. Webster received the note quietly and sent the attorney general to Lockport to see that McLeod had competent counsel. After considerable delay, during which Webster replied to the main arguments of the British note, McLeod was acquitted and released.[54]

British remonstrances, and all endeavors of the federal government, were not only fruitless, but the Supreme Court of the State of New York gave its own interpretation of the law governing the case, and, in the words of an American writer, "held that a subject of a foreign state was liable to be proceeded against individually, and tried on an indictment in the criminal courts for arson and murder, notwithstanding the acts for which the indictment was made had been subsequently avowed by his government, and it, consequently, refused to discharge him from custody. The opinion of the court was delivered by Mr. Justice Cowen and is of great length. So far as the question of national law is concerned, the opinion rests upon the proposition that, till war is declared by the war-making power, the officers or citizens of a foreign government, who enter our territory, are as completely obnoxious to punishment by our law as if they had been born and always resided in this country; that while two nations are at peace with each other, the acts of hostility

[54] Latané, John H., From Isolation to Leadership, Doubleday, Page & Co. (1918), pp. 103-105.

International Law; Its Acceptance and Enforcement

by individuals must be regarded as private and not public acts, and that the courts will hold the parties individually responsible, notwithstanding the avowal of such acts by their government." [55]

Even though McLeod was finally acquitted by the jury on proof of an alibi, the fact that he was actually tried [56] only emphasizes the absolute control of the state authorities. In case of conviction the federal government would have been helpless, though undoubtedly Great Britain could have insisted upon the responsibility of the United States under international law. The situation was an inevitable result of the American constitutional system.

Congress, following the McLeod incident, passed the act August 29, 1842, giving the federal courts jurisdiction over aliens claiming immunity for acts done under authority of their state, "the validity and effect whereof depend upon the law of nations." But does this act define an offence against the law of nations? Hardly, because the claim is that in such cases there is no offence on the part of the individual; but if the statute does not define an international offence, then it may be of doubtful constitutionality, though, probably, such cases could be reached by a proper treaty and legislation in pursuance thereof.[57]

Congress is not given exclusive power "to define and punish piracies and felonies committed on the high seas, and offences against the law of nations," and the states

---

[55] Halleck, H. W., International Law, H. H. Bancroft & Co. (1861), pp. 303-304, Nov. 19; People vs. McLeod, 1 Hill, 377; 37 Am. Dec., 328.
[56] Stowell & Munro, International Cases, Houghton Mifflin Co., Boston (1916), vol. I., p. 123.
[57] See chapter on Treaties, *infra*.

[23]

may legislate on the subject, unless and until the United States has assumed jurisdiction.[58]

Political developments have served to obscure the importance and power of state legislatures, but it is well to remember that within their constitutional sphere they are as supreme as any parliamentary body can be; that, as a matter of fact, state legislation deals with the life of an individual in all its possible phases, and that Congressional legislation, under the present system, can never be, from the point of view of the individual, as all-embracing as that of the law-giving bodies of the separate states of the American Union. Bearing this fact in mind, we shall the better realize that state legislatures, too, have their international responsibilities, and that upon them, also, depends the observance of, and respect for, international law.

§ 6. *The nature and sources of international law.*—In the last analysis all law is the result of the experiences and needs of community life,[59] and international law is primarily derived from the practice of civilized states,[60] its test being usage. "That which has received the assent of all must be the law of all." [61]

The nature of what Chief Justice Marshall called "the test of usage" is forcefully set forth in a case already cited.[62] In rendering one of his best known opinions (The Young Jacob and Johanna, 10 Rob. 20), involving the legality of capture of small fishing vessels, Lord

[58] Thorpe, F. N., The Essentials of American Constitutional Law, G. P. Putnam's Sons, New York (1917), pp. 44-45.
[59] Lee, Guy Carleton, Historical Jurisprudence, The Macmillan Co., New York (1911).
[60] Thirty Hogsheads of Sugar vs. Boyle, 9 Cranch, 191, 3 L. Ed., 701.
[61] The Antelope, 10 Wheaton, 66, 6 L. Ed., 268.
[62] The Paquette Habana, 175 U. S., 694, 44 L. Ed., 320.

International Law; Its Acceptance and Enforcement

Stowell said that "in former wars, it has not been usual to make captures of these small fishing vessels; but this was a rule of comity only, and not of legal decision. . . ." In discussing the expression Mr. Justice Gray observed that "assuming the phrase 'legal decision' to have been there used in the sense in which the courts are accustomed to it, as equivalent to 'judicial decision,' it is true that, so far as appears, there had been no such decision on the point in England. The word 'comity' was apparently used by Lord Stowell as synonymous with courtesy and good will. But the period of a hundred years which has since elapsed is amply sufficient to have enabled what originally may have rested in custom or comity, courtesy or concession, to grow, by the general assent of civilized nations, into a settled rule of international law."

From this it logically follows that when changes in international law have occurred by common consent and practice of civilized nations, the courts will take judicial notice of the fact and in a proper case apply to controversies the law so newly expressed.[63] In other words, international law is a living thing, evolving and developing, and, it is to be hoped, improving.

Works of commentators and jurists, "who, by years of labor, research and experience, have made themselves peculiarly well acquainted with the subjects of which they treat," are resorted to as evidence of what the international law is,[64] but the Supreme Court of the United States will not change its rulings to conform to the opinions of foreign writers as to what they believe the existing law to be on any particular subject,[65] and the

[63] The Scotia, *supra*.
[64] Hilton vs. Guyot, *supra*.
[65] The Adula, 176 U.S., 361, 44 L. Ed., 505.

Judicial Interpretation of International Law

decisions of the federal government upon problems of international law and international relations, which, by the Constitution, are entrusted to the federal government, are obligatory upon every citizen of the United States,[66] and where there is a controlling executive or legislative act, or judicial decision, such act or decision will be followed by the courts.[67]

Judicial decisions in a degree give stability to international law, and, therefore, while not accepting them as authority, the Supreme Court does receive, and does consider, the decisions of courts of other countries in adopting rules prevailing in the United States.[68]

In a general way it has been said that international law is partly unwritten and partly conventional,[69] and in ascertaining the unwritten part the court will also resort to principles of reason and justice, and evidence of these is found in the works of learned jurists and in judicial decisions. In one of the earlier cases in the United States, involving questions of international law, Mr. Justice Chase said that "the law of nations may be considered of three kinds, to wit, general, conventional, or customary. The first is universal, or established by the general consent of mankind, and binds all nations. The second is founded on express consent, and is not universal, and only binds those nations that have assented to it. The third is founded on tacit consent, and is only obligatory on those nations who have adopted it." [70]

The decisions of American courts, not only as to recog-

[66] Kennett vs. Chambers, 14 Howard, 38, 14 L. Ed., 316.
[67] Hilton vs. Guyot, *supra*.
[68] Thirty Hogsheads of Sugar vs. Boyle, *supra*.
[69] Thirty Hogsheads of Sugar vs. Boyle, *supra*.
[70] Ware vs. Hylton, *supra*.

International Law; Its Acceptance and Enforcement

nition of international law in the United States, but also concerning its nature and sources, should end, at least for the practicing and practical lawyer, the perennial and rather unprofitable debate as to whether or not there is such a thing as international law. The courts apply this law whenever they can and they are clear concerning its nature and sources. At times it may be difficult to ascertain the rule applicable in a given case, but this is so even in our own day in many branches of municipal law. Instances of what are known as cases of first impression arise with a frequency not always realized.

Law is a rule of conduct, and this is true of international, as well as of municipal, law; and while municipal law has back of it the mighty enforcing arm of the state, international law finds its most effective sanction to be what we might call automatic, that is to say, it is found in the needs of civilized states. To secure them the observance of certain rules in their relations with other states is unavoidable and hence obligatory. In maintaining international law as a part of the common law, American courts have gone far in making of this law not only a rule of conduct for sovereign states, but for citizens as well.

CHAPTER TWO

INDEPENDENCE AND SOVEREIGNTY

§ 7. *The American Union as a State in International Law. States as Persons.*—While from the inception of the Union international law has been applied and interpreted, and its origin and nature discussed, there hardly exists a satisfactory judicial definition of international law, certainly not by the Supreme Court of the United States. But it has been said that "the law of nations is a system of rules, which reason, morality, and custom, have established among civilized nations as their public law," [1] and that "international law is a term which has not as yet, perhaps, been fully and accurately defined, or rather the specific matters to which it may extend its scope may not be fully settled. It includes the entire body of obligations which one nation owes to another in respect to its own conduct or the conduct of its citizens toward other nations, or their citizens." [2] However, whatever variations exist in definitions of international law, all of these agree that this law comprises those rules of conduct that govern the society of states, or nations.[3] To avoid possible confusion, it should be added that "the terms state

[1] Heirn vs. Bridault, 37 Miss., 209.
[2] United States vs. White, 27 Federal Reporter, 200.
[3] Westlake, J., International Law, Cambridge University Press (1904); Hall, W. E., A Treatise on International Law, 7th Ed., Oxford University Press (1917).

Independence and Sovereignty

and nation are used in the law of nations, as well as in common parlance, as importing the same thing, and imply a body of men, united together, to procure their mutual safety and advantage by means of their union." [4] What, then, in international law, as expounded by the American judiciary, is the state, or nation?

The term "State," as used in American Constitutions, and American constitutional law, applies and refers to a state of the Union,[5] but, of course, so many attributes of sovereignty are lodged in the several states of the American nation that the language of the courts, in regard to these, frequently is useful in considering the nature of states in the international sense of the term. In one of the most famous cases of American constitutional law and history, Mr. Justice Wilson said that "by a state I mean a complete body of free persons united together for their common benefit, to enjoy what is their own, and to do justice to others. It is an artificial person. It has its affairs and its interests. It has its rules: It has its rights: And it has its obligations. It may acquire property, distinct from that of its members. It may incur debts to be discharged out of the public stock, not out of the private fortunes of individuals. It may be bound by contracts, and for damages arising from the breach of contracts. In all our contemplations, however, concerning this feigned and artificial person, we should never forget, that, in truth, and nature, those who think and speak and act, are men." [6]

As a result of the war of secession, the United States Supreme Court acquired jurisdiction in a number of con-

[4] Cherokee Nation vs. Georgia, 5 Peters, 1; 8 L. Ed., 25.
[5] Hepburn vs. Elzey, 2 Cranch, 445; 2 L. Ed., 332.
[6] Chisholm vs. Georgia, 2 Dallas, 456; 2 L. Ed., 453.

Judicial Interpretation of International Law

troversies which necessitated a discussion of the nature of the state, and, in one of the most important of these, Mr. Justice Chase said:

Some not unimportant aid, however, in ascertaining the true sense of the Constitution, may be derived from considering what is the correct idea of a state, apart from any union or confederation with other states. The poverty of language often compels the employment of terms in quite different significations; and of this hardly any example more signal is to be found than in the use of the word we are now considering. It would serve no useful purpose to attempt an enumeration of all the various senses in which it is used. A few only need be noticed.

It describes sometimes a people or community of individuals united more or less closely in political relations, inhabiting temporarily or permanently the same country; often it denotes only the country, or territorial region, inhabited by such a community. The people, in whatever territory dwelling, either temporarily or permanently, and whether organized under a regular government, or united by lower and less definite relations, constitute the state.

In the Constitution the term state most frequently expresses the combined idea just noticed, of people, territory and government. A state in the ordinary sense of the Constitution is a political community of free citizens, occupying a territory of defined boundaries, and organized under a government sanctioned and limited by a written constitution, and established by the consent of the governed. It is the union of such states, under a common constitution, which forms the distinct and greater political unit, which that Constitution designates as the United States, and makes of the people and states which compose it one people and one country.[7]

It is this "one people and one country," however, which is the State in international law, and the government of

[7] *State of Texas vs. White et al,* 7 Wall, 700; 19 L. Ed., 227.

Independence and Sovereignty

the Union is the only one which other nations recognize and deal with.[8]

Since we are considering the state as a concept of international law, probably the most satisfactory and comprehensive judicial definition of a state, for our purposes, viz., as the term is used in international law, is the one holding it to be "a people permanently occupying a fixed territory, bound together by common laws, habits and customs, into one body politic, exercising, through the medium of a common government, independent sovereignty and control over all persons and things within its boundaries, capable of making war and peace, and of entering into international relations with other communities."[9]

While it has never formulated a definition of its own, the United States Supreme Court has quoted with approval Vattel's statement "that nations or states are bodies politic, societies of men united together for the promotion of their mutual safety and advantage of the joint efforts of their combined strength. Such a society has her affairs and her interests. She deliberates and takes resolutions in common, thus becoming a moral person who possesses an understanding and a will peculiar to herself, and is susceptible of obligations and rights. Law of Nations, sec. 1."[10]

The Supreme Court has very emphatically declared that "the United States is not only a government, but it is a national government, and the only government in this country that has the character of nationality. It is

[8] The Chinese Exclusion Cases (Chae Chang Ping vs. United States), 130 U. S., 581; 32 L. Ed., 1068.
[9] Rocke vs. Washington, 19 Ind., 53; 81 Am. Dec., 376.
[10] Keith vs. Clark, 97 U. S., 454; 24 L. Ed., 1071.

invested with power over all foreign relations of the country, war, peace and negotiations and intercourse with other nations; all which are forbidden to the state governments."[11] In an even earlier case it was said that "the United States form, for many, and for most important purposes, a single nation. . . . In war we are one people. In making peace, we are one people. In all commercial regulations, we are one and the same people. In many other respects, the American people are one; and the government which is alone capable of controlling and managing their interests in all these respects is the government of the Union. It is their government, and in that character they have no other. America has chosen to be in many respects, and to many purposes, a nation; and for all these purposes her government is complete; to all these objects it is competent. The people have declared that in the exercise of all powers given for these objects it is supreme. It can then, in effecting these objects, legitimately control all individuals or governments within the American territory. The Constitution and laws of a state, so far as they are repugnant to the Constitution and laws of the United States, are absolutely void. These states are constituent parts of the United States. They are members of one great empire—for some purposes sovereign, for some purposes subordinate."[12]

States are the persons whose relations are governed by international law,[13] this consideration of states as persons being necessitated by the fact that observance of, and

[11] Knox vs. Lee (Legal Tender Cases), 12 Wallace, 455; 20 L. Ed., 313.

[12] Cohens vs. Virginia, 5 Wheaton, 264; 5 L. Ed., 257; see also Lane County vs. Oregon, 7 Wallace, 76; 19 L. Ed., 101.

[13] Hall, W. E.. A Treatise on International Law, 7th Ed., Oxford University Press (1917).

Independence and Sovereignty

obedience to, law, can be rendered only by persons.[14] Like any other person they may prosecute civil actions in American courts,[15] though they may not be sued themselves, or their property attached, since "a free, sovereign, and independent state, was [is] not suable according to the law of nations." [16]

British courts have held that the United States may bring action before them in its own name, and it need not have, or appoint, an officer to prosecute the action on its behalf.[17] Where a state law provides for a security for costs, to be furnished where the plaintiff is "a person residing without the state," or "a foreign corporation," an independent foreign state, appearing in the state court as plaintiff, comes within the provisions of the statute, for the word "person" is "used in its enlarged sense, as comprising all legal entities," and "in that sense it embraces moral persons having legal rights, capable of entering into contracts and incurring obligations, as well as natural persons." [18] The New York court cites in this case a federal decision, quoting Vattel, to the effect that "every nation that governs itself, under what form soever, without any dependence on a foreign power, is a sovereign state. Its rights are naturally the same as those of any other state. Such are moral persons who live together in a natural society, under the law of nations." [19]

[14] Republic of Mexico vs. De Arangoiz, 12 N. Y. Super Ct., 634.
[15] The Sapphire, 11 Wallace, 164; 20 L. Ed., 127.
[16] Nathan vs. Virginia, 1 Dallas, 77; 1 L. Ed., 44; Beers vs. Arkansas, 20 Howard, 527; 15 L. Ed., 991.
[17] United States of America vs. Wagner, L. R., 2 Chancery Appeals, 582.
[18] Republic of Honduras vs. Soto, 112 N. Y., 310; 19 N. E., 845.
[19] Cherokee Nation vs. State of Georgia, 5 Peters, 52; 8 L. Ed., 25.

§ 8. *The nature of sovereignty.*—Perhaps the most controversial problem of political science is the nature of sovereignty. An attempt to deal with the question from the point of view of theory is not within the scope of this treatise. Yet, even for practical reasons, it may not be amiss to point out that in actual international life there is no such thing as absolute sovereignty if by this term we mean freedom of action regardless of the rights of others. From one point of view the history of international relations is the history of a gradual, progressive limitation upon the freedom of action of independent states.

States being the persons governed by international law, it may be said that, as in the case of natural persons, the liberty of an individual ceases where the rights of another commence, so is the freedom of conduct of an international law person, viz., the state, limited by the rights of other persons, viz., of other states. There can be no license for the state in international society, any more than there is, or can be, license for the individual within the association of men which we know as the state.

It may well be contended that limitations upon sovereignty, imposed by the necessities of practical international life, are not a limitation of independence of states, for the reason that these limitations, in a legal sense, are accepted and not imposed by any superior. There is the additional reason that the limitations being of an equal character and extent with regard to all independent states, and since they take no more from one than another once they are accomplished, the relative position of the members of the society of nations remains unchanged. In other words, if powers are equally limited, the situation in effect remains the same, and, at least from one point of view, as a matter of fact and as regards the relative powers of the states involved, no limitation has taken place.

In considering sovereignty in a work of this nature, for our purpose it is almost inevitable that the theory must be accepted that to the problem of sovereignty there are two different sides and that one of these is the international, or external, while the other is purely internal.[20] "External sovereignty relates to the position of the state among other states," and it is of course this sovereignty that we have in mind when discussing sovereignty as a problem of international law, though it is just as well to interpose here a *caveat* to the effect that international law imposes upon states obligations also in matters that at first blush seem purely domestic, such as the treatment of aliens, etc. Internal sovereignty, on the other hand, concerns "the relation between the state and all other persons or associations within its territory."

This brings up the dispute between two groups of political scientists as to the divisibility of sovereignty. But is there, of necessity, a conflict? And is it not the function of the thoughtful practical lawyer to reconcile the two apparently rival theories, if this can be done, even as the lawyer in court frequently must harmonize two apparently conflicting principles of law? Such harmonization has, indeed, been attempted in an essay from which the following passages merit quotation:

The preceding discussion of the two great political theories, in which is found asserted, in the one the indivisibility of

[20] Merriam, C. E., History of the Theory of Sovereignty since Rousseau, pp. 214-216; Columbia University Studies in History, Economics and Public Law, vol. XII., No. 4.

sovereignty, in the other its divisibility, leads to the conclusion that the two theories are entirely congruous, in spite of their use of the same terms with different signification.

The applicability of the principles of each theory is confined to a distinct sphere. The analytical theory determines the nature of the internal organization of the state, of its municipal, including its constitutional, law; the international theory explains the nature of the mutual relations of states, the nature of the international law. The analytical theory with its "sovereignty" and kindred concepts affords no explanation of international law, nor the international theory with its "independence" any explanation of constitutional law.

Thus it is plainly necessary to keep distinct the concepts of each theory, and there are a number of minor concepts the significance of which for the one theory or the other, for international or constitutional law, or for both, it is essential to determine.[21]

Legal theories, like many other theories, frequently are nothing more than an attempt to provide rational, or philosophic, justification for a certain condition of things. It has been shown conclusively, it is believed, that the Austinian conception of law, still dominant among the Bench and Bar of America, is valid if applied to a certain stage of legal development, but is fallacious if the claim is made that always and under any and all conditions that only is law which is the command of the sovereign.[22] It is not the function of the judiciary, as judiciary, however, to formulate new legal theories, any more than it is the judge's function to devise new laws. That is the lawmaker's task, though it is undeniable that

[21] Crane, R. T., The State in Constitutional and International Law, pp. 7-11; Johns Hopkins University Studies in Historical and Political Science, series XXV., Nos. 6-7.
[22] Lawrence, T. J., Some Disputed Questions in Modern International Law, Deighton, Bell & Co., Cambridge (1884), Essay I., Is There a True International Law?

Independence and Sovereignty

occasionally judges face new situations and must apply to them old rules, or, following accepted canons of legal reasoning, must announce what perhaps does appear to be a new rule, which, however, always may be changed or modified by legislative power. But if we bear in mind that pioneering is not the duty, or even the right, of the judge, in his official capacity, it is the more readily understood why the American judiciary, when discussing sovereignty at all, gave expression to views prevalent at the time the various cases came for adjudication before it and why it adopted what by some has been called the older, and by others the classical, conception of sovereignty. It is perhaps more accurate to say that the American judiciary has expounded the constitutional theory of sovereignty, as was really unavoidable, since the judiciary is wholly a creation of municipal law, including in that term the state and federal constitutions.

Justice Story defined sovereignty, in its largest sense, as the "supreme, absolute, uncontrollable power; the *jus summi imperii;* the absolute right to govern." [23] John Marshall said: "The jurisdiction of the nation within its own territory is necessarily exclusive and absolute. It is susceptible of no limitation not imposed by itself. Any restriction upon it, deriving validity from an external source, would imply a diminution of its sovereignty to the extent of the restriction, and an investment of that sovereignty to the same extent in that power which could impose such restriction. All exceptions, therefore, to the full and complete power of a nation within its own territories must be traced up to the consent of the

[23] Cherokee Nation vs. Southern Kansas R. R. Co., 33 Federal Reporter, 900.

nation itself. They can flow from no other legitimate source." [24]

Marshall's statement is a perfect description of the nature of sovereignty from the constitutional point of view, and it is not necessarily inconsistent with the theory of external sovereignty which deals with the relation of states. These relations do impose certain obligations upon the various members of the family of nations.

Occasionally the courts have failed to distinguish between the state and the government and have not realized that the government is no more than an organ of sovereignty. Thus in one of the decisions we find this statement: "The sovereignty of a nation, or state, may, in all respects, be absolute and unconditional, except the limitations it chooses to impose upon itself, but the sovereignty of the government organized within the state may be of a very limited nature, extending to few or many objects—unlimited as to some, but restrained as to others. The people comprising a state may divide its sovereign powers among various functionaries, and each, in the limited sense, would be sovereign in respect to the powers confided to each." [25] But, on the whole, such confusion is fortunately rare, as is indicated by the following language: "There is a distinction between the government of a state and the state itself. In common speech and apprehension they are usually regarded as identical, and as ordinarily the acts of the government are the acts of the state, and because within the limits of its delegation of power the government of the state is generally confounded with the state itself. The state itself, however,

---

[24] The Exchange vs. McFaddon, 7 Cranch, 136; 3 L. Ed., 287.
[25] Union Bank vs. Hill, 3 Caldw. (Tenn.), 325.

Independence and Sovereignty

is an ideal person, intangible, invisible, immutable. The government is an agent and within the sphere of its agency a perfect representative; but outside of that it is a lawless usurpation. The constitution of the State is the limit of the authority of its government, and both government and state are subject to the supremacy of the Constitution of the United States and of the laws made in pursuance thereof." [26]

The founders of the republic realized that government is an agency. "The federal and state governments are, in fact, but different agents and trustees of the people, constituted with different powers and designated for different purposes." [27] An attempt to differentiate between the state and its people proved unsuccessful early in the history of the republic. "A distinction was taken at the bar between a state and the people of the state. It is a distinction I am not capable of comprehending. By a state forming a republic (speaking of it as a moral person) I do not mean the legislature of the state, the executive of the state, or the judiciary, but all the citizens which compose that state, are, if I may so express myself, integral parts of it; all together forming a body politic." [28]

In days that have witnessed the rise of new states, it is not an academic question only to ask when the independence of a country commences. For instance, the Czechoslovak republic claimed a right to reparations from Germany as one of the allied belligerent powers and in

[26] Poindexter vs. Greenhow, 114 U. S., 270; 29 L. Ed., 185; Grunert vs. Spaulding, 78 N. W. (Wis., 1899), 606.
[27] Madison, James, The Federalist, The Central Law Journal Co. (1917), vol. I., p. 321.
[28] Penhallow et al. vs. Doane's Administrators, 3 Dallas, 54; 1 L. Ed., 507.

order to determine the right it was necessary to decide when the country became an independent state. The question was not without its difficulties, since before the republic was declared there was a *de facto* Czechoslovak government abroad, which was recognized by a number of powers, one of them being the United States, on September 3, 1918. However, independence having been proclaimed on Czechoslovak soil on October 28, 1918, the Reparations Commission held that Czechoslovakia is to be considered independent from the latter date. In the United States there is a judicial decision to the effect that "the several states which composed this Union, so far at least as regarded their municipal regulations, became entitled, from the time when they declared themselves independent, to all the rights and powers of sovereign states. . . . The treaty of peace contained a recognition of their independence, not a grant of it." [29]

§ 9. *Recognition of states and governments and of sovereignty over territory.—By whom determinable and its effects.*—The establishment of a new state, and its right to exist, is a domestic question;[30] for internal purposes a state does not require recognition from other states.[31] As respects its own government a nation becomes independent from the declaration thereof;[32] but if it desires intercourse with other states and wishes to be considered and treated as a member of the family of nations, recognition is the necessary preliminary step;[33]

[29] McIlvaine's Coxe's Lessee, 4 Cranch, 212; 2 L. Ed., 207.
[30] Woolsey, Theodore D., Introduction to the Study of International Law, Scribner, Armstrong & Co. (1875), par. 40, page 54.
[31] Twiss, Travers, The Law of Nations, Longman, Green, Longman & Roberts (1861), par. 20, page 19.
[32] United States vs. Hutchings, 26 Federal Cases, No. 15,429.
[33] Twiss, Travers, The Law of Nations, *supra*.

Independence and Sovereignty

indeed, as regards other nations it is considered independent only when recognized by them.[34] Recognition is the act which gives a *de facto* state international status.[35]

Within the whole range of international relations there is probably no duty more solemn, nor one calling for more thoughtful consideration, from the point of view of international order and continuity of international life, than the one requiring recognition, or denial thereof, to new states and new governments. Recognition is an act of the political department of the government,[36] and, it might be added, a very delicate political act, demanding, frequently, the highest order of statesmanship. Manifestly it is, and can only be, the function of that department of government entrusted with the conduct of foreign relations, and the decisions and policies of this department must be accepted by all other governmental branches. In the United States "no doctrine is better established than that it belongs exclusively to governments to recognize new states, in the revolutions which may occur in the world," [37] and this is of course true not only of new states, but of new governments as well.[38] If the courts undertook to determine whether a nation had in fact become an independent sovereign state, before recognition by the branch entrusted with the conduct of foreign affairs, they would take upon themselves "the exercise of political authority for which a judicial tribunal is wholly unfit, and which the constitution has

[34] United States vs. Hutchings, *supra*.
[35] Wulfson vs. Russian Socialist Soviet Government, 234 N. Y., 372; 138 N. E., 24.
[36] Wulfson vs. Russian Socialist Soviet Government, *supra*.
[37] Gelston vs. Hoyt, 3 Wheaton, 324; 4 L. Ed., 381; The Nueva Anna, 6 Wheaton, 193; 5 L. Ed., 239.
[38] Kennett vs. Chambers, 14 Howard, 38; 14 L. Ed., 316.

conferred exclusively upon another branch of the government." [39]

Not only recognition of new states and governments, but also "who is the sovereign, *de jure* or *de facto*, of a territory, is not a judicial, but a political question, the determination of which by the legislative and executive departments of any government conclusively binds the judges, as well as all other officers, citizens and subjects of that government." [40]

In cases involving the validity of grants by Spain in disputed territory, after the cession of Louisiana to the United States, the question being one of interpretation of the treaty of cession, the court declined to consider the merits of the treaty, and, considering itself bound by the decision of the political department of the government, whose province it is to deal with foreign relations, declared, per Chief Justice Marshall:

> In a controversy between two nations concerning national boundary, it is scarcely possible that the courts of either should refuse to abide by the measures adopted by its own government.
>
> There being no common tribunal to decide between them, each determines for itself on its own rights, and if they cannot adjust their differences peaceably, the right remains with the strongest. The judiciary is not that department of the government to which the assertion of its interests against foreign powers is confided; and its duty commonly is to decide upon individual rights, according to those principles which the political departments of the nation have established. If the course of the nation has been a plain one, its courts would hesitate to pronounce it erroneous.

[39] Kennett vs. Chambers, *supra*.
[40] Jones vs. United States, 137 U.S., 202; 34 L. Ed., 691.

Independence and Sovereignty

We think then, however individual judges might construe the treaty of St. Ildefonso, it is the province of the court to conform its decisions to the will of the legislature, if that will has been clearly expressed.

After the acts of sovereign power over the territory in dispute, asserting the American construction of the treaty by which the government claims it, to maintain the opposite construction in its own courts would certainly be an anomaly in the history and practice of nations. If those departments which are entrusted with the foreign intercourse of the nation, which assert and maintain its interests against foreign powers, have unequivocally asserted its right of dominion over a country of which it is in possession, and which it claims under a treaty; if the legislature has acted on the construction thus asserted, it is not in its own courts that this construction is to be denied. A question like this respecting the boundaries of nations, is, as has been truly said, more a political than a legal question; and in its discussion the courts of every country must respect the pronounced will of the legislature."[41]

The date on which California became territory of the United States is a question that came before the courts, and it was held that the authority and jurisdiction of Mexican officers in California terminated on the 7th of July, 1846, because "the political department of the government has designated that day as the period when the conquest of California was completed, and the Mexican officers displaced, and in this respect the judiciary follows the action of the political department."[42]

The famous controversy over the title to the Falkland

[41] Foster vs. Neilson, 2 Peters, 253; 7 L. Ed., 415; Garcia vs. Lee, 12 Peters, 511; 10 L. Ed., 226.
[42] United States vs. Yorba, 1 Wallace, 412; 17 L. Ed., 635; United States vs. Pico, 23 Howard, 326; 116 L. Ed., 464.

Judicial Interpretation of International Law

Islands gave rise to a case which well illustrates how this question of recognition may occur in actual litigation. The government of the United States always insisted that the Falkland Islands did not constitute any part of the dominions within the sovereignty of what then was known as Buenos Ayres, and that the seal fishery at those islands is a trade free and lawful to American citizens, and that the Buenos Ayres government is not competent to regulate, prohibit, or punish it. However, an American sealing vessel, insured on a sealing voyage, was ordered by an official of the government of Buenos Ayres to leave the Falkland Island waters and not to catch seals off this territory. Upon refusal of the master to comply with the order, the vessel was seized and condemned under authority of that government. The United States Supreme Court held that the master, in refusing to obey orders to leave, acted within the scope of his duty and in vindication of American rights, and was not bound to abandon the waters under a threat of illegal capture; therefore the insurers were liable to pay for the loss of the vessel and its cargo. "When the executive branch of the government, which is charged with the foreign relations of the United States, shall, in its correspondence with a nation, assume a fact in regard to the sovereignty of any island or country, it is conclusive on the judicial department." [43] In this case Mr. Justice McLean further said that "it is not material to inquire, nor is it the province of the court to determine, whether the executive be right or wrong. It is enough to know that, in the exercise of his constitutional functions, he had decided the question. Having done this, under the

[43] Williams vs. Suffolk Ins. Co., 13 Peters, 415; 10 L. Ed., 226.

Independence and Sovereignty

responsibilities which belong to him, it is obligatory on the people and government of the Union. If this were not the rule, cases might often arise in which, on the most important question of foreign jurisdiction, there would be an irreconcilable difference between the executive and judicial departments."

Facts of an entirely different nature, arising in a case much more recent, illustrate the same rule and its applications as well. The syllabus is sufficient for our purposes:

> The question whether Algeria is a part of France and within the scope of the President's proclamation of May 30, 1898, putting in force a reciprocal commercial agreement between France and the United States, as authorized by section 5 of the tariff act of 1897, or is merely a colony, and not affected by such agreement, is one which must be determined solely by the laws of France, and when the French minister of foreign affairs and the diplomatic and consular representatives of that country in the United States unite in stating that since the decree of October, 1870, abolishing the colonial government of Algeria, dividing it into departments and adding them to the departments of European France, it has been an integral part of the republic of France, their statement should be accepted as conclusive by a court of this country in the administration of its custom laws, and in giving effect to the agreement between the two nations, entered into in a spirit of amity, with desire to improve their commercial relations.[44]

Until recognition is accorded, either by the government of the United States, or by the government to which the new state belonged, courts will consider the old order as unchanged;[45] but recognition is retroactive

---

[44] Tartar Chemical Co. vs. United States, 116 Federal Reporter, 726.
[45] Rose vs. Himely, 4 Cranch, 239; 2 L. Ed., 608; Gelston vs. Hoyt, 3 Wheaton, 324; 4 L. Ed., 381; The Nueva Anna, 6 Wheaton, 193; 5 L. Ed., 239.

Judicial Interpretation of International Law

and validates all actions and conduct of a government from the commencement of its existence."[46]

Courts will take judicial notice of the territorial extent of the jurisdiction of their government, or of its recognition or denial of sovereignty of any foreign power, and this judicial notice may be based upon public acts of the legislature and executive and it is not necessary that these acts be formally offered and admitted in evidence. The acts of the State Department in legal contemplation are the acts of the President, and the determination of the President that certain territory belongs to the United States, or is a part thereof, may be declared through the State Department. In determining what shall be taken notice of judicially, judges may not only refresh their memories from sources they consider reliable, but may even make inquiries of the State Department.[47]

[46] Oetjen vs. Central Leather Co., 246 U. S., 297; 62 L. Ed., 726; Ricaud vs. American Metal Co., 264 U. S., 304; 62 L. Ed., 733. Lately it has been said, however, that only acts within the territory of the newly recognized government can be validated by the retroactive effect of recognition, and that "acts therefore performed outside its own territory cannot be validated by recognition." Lehigh Valley Railroad Company vs. State of Russia, 21 Fed. (2d) 396. See also Cornell Law Review for February, 1928, note by James D. Hurley, "International Law: Recognition: Retroactive Effect." The author of the note cites a number of cases and in conclusion declares: "Outside of its own territory a government has no authority or jurisdiction. There its standing and the legality of its acts depend upon the will and the law of the territorial sovereign in question. A determination by such sovereign, at one time, as to the status of a foreign government, as such determination affects rights and liabilities within its own territory, should not be retroactively reversed by subsequent recognition. So acts which are illegal because done by or in aid of an unrecognized foreign government do not become legal by subsequent recognition of the government, nor does the lack of the right of an unrecognized foreign government to sue become retroactively cured so that, by recognition, it may claim to have had the right to sue from the time when it came into power within its own territory."

[47] Jones vs. United States, *supra*.

Independence and Sovereignty

Obviously, individuals may act (indeed, have performed acts) under authority of unrecognized governments for which, but for such authority, they could be held liable, in certain instances even criminally. Facing a situation of this sort, what are the courts to do? An answer has been found in the following language:

> When a civil war rages in a foreign nation, one part of which separates itself from the old established government, and erects itself into a distinct government, the courts of the Union must view such newly constituted government as it is viewed by the legislative and executive departments of the government of the United States.
>
> If that government remains neutral, but recognizes the existence of a civil war, the courts of the Union cannot consider as criminal those acts of hostility which war authorizes, and which the new government may direct against its enemy.
>
> The same testimony which would be sufficient to prove that a vessel or person is in the service of an acknowledged state, is admissible to prove that they are in the service of such newly erected government. Its seal cannot be allowed to prove itself, but may be proved by such testimony as the nature of the case admits; and the fact that a vessel or person is in the service of such government may be established otherwise, should it be impracticable to prove the seal.[48]

The language of the court in the last case would seem to indicate that a recognition of the existence of a civil war is necessary, even if otherwise the insurgent government has not been recognized. But there may be cases of rebellion, the result of which is the erection of a new government, where conditions enabled the United States government to maintain complete passivity, even to the extent of taking no notice of the rebellion and civil war

[48] United States vs. Palmer, 3 Wheaton, 610; 4 L. Ed., 471; The Divina Pastora, 4 Wheaton, 52; 4 L. Ed., 512.

Judicial Interpretation of International Law

and foregoing any proclamation of neutrality. The language of at least one case seems general enough to cover this contingency. "The seal to the commission of a new government, not acknowledged by the government of the United States, cannot be permitted to prove itself; but the fact that the vessel, cruising under such commission, is employed by such government, may be established by other evidence, without proving the seal." [49]

While the question of recognition of new states and governments is not a judicial one, but one for the department of foreign affairs, there exist established rules of international law, generally observed, which govern such recognition. The student desiring to familiarize himself with these rules, is referred to standard works on international law in all its phases.

§ 10. *The nature of belligerency and its effects.*—The nature of belligerency ordinarily is not discussed in this connection. But recognition of belligerency is governed by virtually the same rules as recognition of states and governments: such recognition does confer certain rights possessed by sovereign states, and certain legal consequences follow therefrom. It has not seemed improper, therefore, to set forth under this general title the judicial conception of belligerency and its effects.

Recognition of belligerency is a political act, just as the recognition of a new state, or government, and is therefore also determinable only by the political department of the government.[50] But the subject is a comparatively new one, and the governing principles are an outgrowth of the development of the modern rules of

---

[49] The Estrella, 4 Wheaton, 298; 4 L. Ed., 574.
[50] See, however, The Three Friends, 166 U. S., 1; 41 L. Ed., 897.

Independence and Sovereignty

neutrality.[51] Belligerency may become, and frequently has become, a fact requiring recognition, although conditions are not ripe for a recognition of that state, or government, which one of the belligerents, or insurgents, is seeking to establish.[52] There is a distinction between a condition of political revolt, an actual state of war, on the one hand, and a state of war in the legal sense on the other hand,[53] and a recognition of belligerency is no more than an acknowledgment of a fact, but not of a legal state of war.[54]

The neutrality laws of the United States from an early date recognized the distinction between a legal state of war and hostilities not yet so recognized. Indeed, conditions have demanded provision for the preservation of neutrality during struggles at a time when one of the parties could not even be recognized as a belligerent. Thus the act of 1794 made it a penal offence "if any person shall, within the territory or jurisdiction of the United States, . . . hire or retain another person to go beyond the limits or jurisdiction of the United States, with intent to be enlisted or entered in the service of any foreign prince or state," but it was soon found that this wording was insufficient to meet all situations, particularly in view of conditions then prevailing in South America, and accordingly the act of 1817 adds to the words "any foreign prince or state" the expressions "or of any colony, district, or people," and this wording also appears in § 5283 of the Revised Statutes.

[51] Moore, John Bassett, A Digest of International Law, vol. I., par. 59, p. 164.
[52] Moore, John Bassett, A Digest of International Law, *supra*.
[53] The Three Friends, *supra*.
[54] Moore, John Bassett, A Digest of International Law, *supra*.

Judicial Interpretation of International Law

The neutrality laws now in force observe the distinction,[55] and the Supreme Court has held that "any insurgent or insurrectionary body of people acting together, undertaking and conducting hostilities, although its belligerency has not been recognized, is included in the terms 'colony, district, or people' as used in United States Revised Statutes § 5283, making it an offence to fit out a vessel to be employed "in the service of any foreign prince or state, or of any colony, district or people, to cruise or commit hostilities against the subjects, citizens, or property of any foreign prince or state, or of any colony, district, or people, with whom the United States are at peace." [56]

When does the necessity of recognition of belligerency arise? The answer is that "belligerency is recognized when a political struggle has attained a certain magnitude and affects the interests of the recognizing power; and in the instance of maritime operations recognition may be compelled, or the vessels of the insurgents, if molesting third parties, may be prosecuted as pirates." [57]

What are the effects of recognition of belligerency and what are the rights conferred thereby? "The recognition of belligerency involves the right of blockade, visitation, search and seizure of contraband articles on the high seas, and abandonment of claims for reparation on account of damages suffered by our citizens from the prevalence of warfare." [58]

It should be remembered, of course, that recognition of belligerency confers upon the government recognized

[55] United States Statutes at Large, vol. 35, p. 1088.
[56] The Three Friends, *supra*.
[57] The Three Friends, *supra*.
[58] The Three Friends, *supra*.

Independence and Sovereignty

the rights and imposes upon it the duties of an independent state in relation to the hostilities, but no more, and especially that it does not accord the rights of an independent state generally.[59] The rule embodied in the decisions quoted has been stated to be that recognition of belligerency "does not confer upon the community recognized all the rights of an independent state; but it grants to its government and subjects the rights and imposes upon them the duties of an independent state in all matters relating to the war. It follows from this that the powers which give such recognition are bound to submit to lawful captures of their merchantmen made by the cruisers of the community recognized or those of the mother country. They must also respect effective blockades carried on by either side, and treat the officers and soldiers of the rebels as lawful combatants, no less than the officers and soldiers of the established government."[60]

Cases arising from the American Civil War, and its effects upon individual rights, have given the courts a number of opportunities to discuss what is belligerency and what are its tests. Probably the most famous of these are those known as The Prize Cases; their importance, and the consideration they gave to the question, justify the following rather extended quotation:

Insurrection against a government may or may not culminate in an organized rebellion, but a civil war always begins by insurrection against the lawful authority of the government. A civil war is never solemnly declared; it becomes such by its accidents—the number, power, and organization of the persons

[59] The Three Friends, *supra*.
[60] Lawrence, T. J., The Principles of International Law, par. 162, p. 303, Macmillan & Co., London and New York (1895).

Judicial Interpretation of International Law

who originate and carry it on. When the party in rebellion occupy and hold in a hostile manner a certain portion of territory; have declared their independence; have cast off their allegiance; have organized armies; have commenced hostilities against their former sovereign, the world acknowledges them as belligerents, and the contest a war. They claim to be in arms to establish their liberty and independence, in order to become a sovereign state, while the sovereign party treats them as insurgents and rebels who owe allegiance, and who should be punished with death for their treason.

The laws of war, as established among nations, have their foundation in reason, and all tend to mitigate the cruelties and misery produced by the scourge of war. Hence the parties to a civil war usually concede to each other belligerent rights. They exchange prisoners, and adopt the other courtesies and rules common to public or national wars.

"A civil war," says Vattel, "breaks the bands of society and government, or at least suspends their force and effect; it produces in the nation two independent parties, who consider each other as enemies, and acknowledge no common judge. Those two parties, therefore, must necessarily be considered as constituting, at least for a time, two separate bodies, two distinct societies. Having no common superior to judge between them, they stand in precisely the same predicament as two nations who engage in a contest and have recourse to arms.

"This being the case, it is very evident that the common laws of war—those maxims of humanity, moderation and honor—ought to be observed by both parties in every civil war. Should the sovereign conceive he has a right to hang up his prisoners as rebels, the opposite party will make reprisals, etc.; the war will become cruel, horrible, and every day more destructive to the nation."

As civil war is never publicly proclaimed, *eo nomine*, against insurgents, its actual existence is a fact in our domestic history which the court is bound to notice and to know.

The true test of its existence, as found in the writings of the sages of the common law, may thus be summarily stated:

Independence and Sovereignty

"When the regular course of justice is interrupted by revolt, rebellion or insurrection, so that the courts of justice cannot be kept open, civil war exists and hostilities may be prosecuted on the same footing as if those opposing the government were foreign enemies invading the land." [61]

The nature of belligerent rights finds elucidation in another of the cases originating in the Civil War:

When a rebellion becomes organized, and attains such proportions as to be able to put a formidable military force in the field, it is usual for the established government to concede to it some belligerent rights. This concession is made in the interests of humanity, to prevent the cruelties which would inevitably follow mutual reprisals and retaliations. But belligerent rights, as the terms import, are rights which exist only during war; and to what extent they shall be accorded to insurgents depends upon the considerations of justice, humanity, and policy controlling the government. The rule stated by Vattel, that, the justice of the cause between two enemies being by the law of nations reputed to be equal, whatsoever is permitted to the one in virtue of war is also permitted to the other, applies only to cases of regular war between independent nations. It has no application to the case of a war between an established government and insurgents seeking to withdraw themselves from its jurisdiction or to overthrow its authority. Halleck's Int. Law, c. 14, sec. 9. The concession made to the Confederate government in its military character was shown in the treatment of captives as prisoners of war, the exchange of prisoners, the recognition of flags of truce, the release of officers on parole, and other arrangements having a tendency to mitigate the evils of the contest. The concession placed its soldiers and military officers in its service on the footing of those engaged in lawful war, and exempted them from liability for acts of legitimate warfare.[62]

[61] The Prize Cases, 2 Black, 635; 17 L. Ed., 459.
[62] Williams vs. Bruffy, 96 U. S., 176; 24 L. Ed., 716; see also Ford vs. Surget, 97 U. S., 594; 24 L. Ed., 1018.

Judicial Interpretation of International Law

Granting of belligerent rights to the Southern States was not, however, an abandonment of the sovereign rights of the Union, and, in the language of one of the courts, "by no means precluded us from treating them in other respects as rebels."[63] It is for the sovereign, endeavoring to overcome a rebellion, to judge whether he shall choose to exercise the rights of sovereignty or of belligerency and this election must be determined by the nature of his act. "If as a legislator he publishes a law ordaining punishments for certain offences, which law is to be applied by the courts, the nature of the law, and of the proceedings under it, will decide whether it is an exercise of belligerent rights or exclusively of his sovereign power."[64]

The reader will of course remember that Civil War cases, while often clearly discussing the general nature of belligerent rights, necessarily always considered the status of the Confederacy under the Constitution, and that they do not invariably present the point of view which a third party, merely witnessing a contest and maintaining a neutral attitude, would or could adopt. Nevertheless, and with this caution in mind, the Civil War cases are frequently helpful to the international jurist.

When a recognition of belligerency has been accorded by the government of the United States, the courts will treat as lawful those acts of the belligerents which a state of war permits and authorizes. When the American government found it possible to recognize as belligerents the revolted South American colonies, captures by them

[63] The Lilla, 2 Spr., 177; Federal Cases No. 8, 348.
[64] Rose vs. Himely, 5 Cranch, 239; 2 L. Ed., 608.

Independence and Sovereignty

at sea were regarded as other captures made by virtue of a state of war and under the laws thereof, and the American courts would not undertake to determine their legality, since they were judicial organs of a neutral country.[65]

The legal consequences of acts of unrecognized insurgents present something of a problem, more serious, naturally, in their possible criminal, than civil, phases. The practice has been described as follows:

> When, however, piratical acts have a political object, and are directed solely against a particular state, it is not the practice for states other than that attacked to seize, and still less to punish, the persons committing them. It would be otherwise, so far as seizure is concerned, with respect to vessels manned by persons acting with a political object, if the crew, in the course of carrying out their object, committed acts of violence against ships of other states than that against which their political operation was aimed; and the mode in which the crew were dealt with would probably depend on the circumstances of the case.[66]

This rule is laid down by an eminent writer on international law. Nevertheless, there exists judicial authority to the effect that in the absence of recognition, insurgents, operating on the high seas, are pirates, and in the case in question an insurgent vessel in revolt against the government of Colombia, although it had not attacked ships of other nations, was held to have been lawfully seized by a United States gunboat.[67] In this instance the court ruled that it is a question solely

[65] The Divina Pastora, 4 Wheaton, 52; 4 L. Ed., 50; The Santissima Trinidad, 7 Wheaton, 337; 5 L. Ed., 280.
[66] Hall, W. E., A Treatise on International Law, The Clarendon Press, London (1917), par. 81, p. 274.
[67] United States vs. The Ambrose Light, 25 Federal Reporter, 408.

for the executive department whether a nation shall exercise its rights only when an injury is threatened, or after it is inflicted, but that when the executive branch has acted, claiming its extreme rights, the courts must apply the strict technical rules of international law. "The right here asserted," said the court, "may be rarely enforced; the very knowledge that the right exists tends effectually, in most cases, to prevent any violation of it, or at least any actual interference by insurgents with the rights of other nations. But if the right itself were denied, the commerce of all commercial nations would be at the mercy of every petty contest carried on by irresponsible insurgents and marauders under the name of war."

But, whatever the technical rule may be, if strictly construed, it may safely be said that as a matter of practice a vessel will not be dealt with as a pirate, even if it operates under the orders of non-recognized insurgents, provided it does not injure the interests of other states and conducts its operations wholly against the government it seeks to overthrow, or against the government of the state which it seeks to dismember. There is no direct American judicial authority for this statement and cases that occasionally have been cited in support of the contention are not in point, for the reason that they arose under municipal legislation, chiefly § 5283 of the Revised United States Statutes, forbidding the fitting out and arming a vessel with intent that it shall be employed by any foreign state or people against any state or people with whom the United States is at peace, and because the attempted libel was not on the ground that the vessel in question was depredating upon the high seas, without

Independence and Sovereignty

authority from any sovereign power.[68] However, whether a vessel shall or shall not be seized, and a prosecution for piracy against the crew initiated or not, is a question for the executive authorities and these for obvious reasons would be governed by the prevailing practice of states as hereinbefore set forth. In any event, seizure and prosecution are not likely unless the crew of a vessel acts in bad faith, without any commission or documents whatever,[69] or unless insurgents deliberately go out of their way to assail interests of neutral powers.

When acknowledgment of insurgents by the political department has not taken place, proclamations and messages of the President are sufficient to give the courts judicial information of the existence of an actual conflict.[70]

§ 11. *Kinds of governments and their powers.*—In the eyes of international law, the question of a state's right to exist being an internal one, the only inquiry proper for other states is, whether the new state can enter into and fulfill reciprocal obligations,[71] or, we may add in view of recent international events, whether it is willing to do so. Nor is international law concerned with the form of governments and the nature of constitutions, provided, again, these do not stand in the way of fulfillment of

[68] The Itata, 56 Federal Reporter, 505. The opinion carefully distinguishes this case from the Ambrose Light Case See also United States vs. Weed, 5 Wallace, 62; 18 L. Ed., 531; and The Watchful, 6 Wallace, 91; 18 L. Ed., 763.
[69] United States vs. Smith, 5 Wheaton, 153; 5 L. Ed., 57.
[70] The Three Friends, *supra*.
[71] Woolsey, Theodore D., Introduction to the Study of International Law, par. 40, p. 54, Scribner, Armstrong & Co., New York (1875).

international obligations.[72] Therefore, once a government obtains recognition, either as a government *de jure* or *de facto*, it obtains a standing in the courts of other countries enabling it to enforce certain rights and obligations.[73] However, there have been governments, or at least bodies claiming the authority of governments, which have not been accorded full *de facto,* much less *de jure* recognition, but which have exercised authority over large territories where life went on in many respects as usual and where transactions, affecting private rights, have taken place, the validity and legality of which had to be passed upon with a view both to justice and stability of organized society. The Southern Confederacy is the most famous of these, as well as the most important, and the duration of its rule has given the courts ample opportunity to discuss various kinds of governments and their powers.

De facto governments vary in degree and kind. The government of the Commonwealth under Cromwell was certainly *"de facto* in the most absolute sense,"* and to have upset all acts done under its authority would have resulted in confusion worse confounded. A *de facto* government—an actual government—in its highest degree partakes in many respects of the nature of a lawful government. "This is when the usurping government expels the regular authorities from their customary seats and functions, and establishes itself in their place, and so becomes the actual government of the country. The distinguishing characteristic of such a government

[72] Woolsey, Theodore D., Introduction to International Law, *supra*.
[73] See sec. 7, States as persons; and sec. 9, Recognition of states and governments and of sovereignty over territory, *supra*.

Independence and Sovereignty

is that adherents to it in war against the government *de jure* do not incur the penalties of treason; and under certain limitations, obligations assumed by it in behalf of the country, or otherwise, will, in general, be respected by the government *de jure* when restored." Thus the Supreme Court in discussing such governments as was that of Oliver Cromwell. The Southern Confederacy was not a government of this nature and was never recognized by the United States as a *de facto* government in this sense. What sort of a government, then, was it?

But there is another description of government, called also by publicists a government *de facto*, but which, perhaps, can be more aptly denominated a government of paramount force. Its distinguishing characteristics are (1), that its existence is maintained by active military power within the territories, and against the rightful authority of an established and lawful government; and (2), that while it exists, it must necessarily be obeyed in civil matters by private citizens who, by acts of obedience, rendered in submission to such force, do not become responsible, as wrongdoers, for those acts, though not warranted by the laws of the rightful government. Actual governments of this sort are established over districts differing greatly in extent and conditions. They are usually administered by military authority, but they may be administered, also, by civil authority, supported more or less directly by military force.

It is true that the authority of the government of the Confederate States "did not originate in lawful acts of regular war, but it was not, on that account, less actual or supreme." Therefore the court continues:

And we think it must be classed among the governments of which these are examples. It is to be observed that the rights and obligations of a belligerent were conceded to it, in its military character, very soon after the war began, from motives of humanity and expediency by the United States. The whole territory controlled by it was thereafter held to be enemies' territory, and the inhabitants of that territory were held, in most respects, for enemies. To the extent, then, of actual supremacy, however unlawfully gained, in all matters of government within its military lines, the power of the insurgent government cannot be questioned. That supremacy did not justify acts of hostility to the United States. How far it should excuse them must be left to the lawful government upon the re-establishment of its authority. But it made obedience to its authority in civil and local matters not only a necessity but a duty. Without such obedience, civil order was impossible.[74]

In any event, in the Confederacy "the existence of a state of insurrection and war did not loosen the bonds of society, or do away with civil government or the regular administration of the laws. Order was to be preserved, police regulations maintained, crime prosecuted, property protected, contracts enforced, marriages celebrated, estates settled, and the transfer and descent of property regulated, precisely as in time of peace. No one, that we are aware of, seriously questions the validity of judicial or legislative acts in the insurrectionary states touching these and kindred subjects, where they were not hostile in their purpose or mode of enforcement to the authority of the national government, and did not impair the rights of citizens under the Constitution."[75]

The whole question of the status of the Confederacy

[74] Thorington vs. Smith, 8 Wallace, 1; 19 L. Ed., 363.—Cromwell's government, while no more than *de facto* for the Stuarts, was actually a *de jure* one and had diplomatic relations with other countries.

[75] Horn vs. Lockhart, 17 Wallace, 570; 21 L. Ed., 657; Williams vs. Bruffy, 96 U. S., 176; 24 L. Ed., 716.

Independence and Sovereignty

came up in still other cases and the Supreme Court adhered to the views so expounded. It upheld transactions in territory controlled by the Confederate Government "except when proved to have been entered into with actual intent to further invasion or insurrection," and it was further declared that "judicial and legislative acts in the respective states composing the so-called Confederate States should be respected by the courts if they were not hostile in their purpose or mode of enforcement to the authority of the national government, and did not impair the rights of citizens under the constitution."[76]

The acts of the states in rebellion, in the ordinary course of administration, had to be upheld in the interests of organized society to which such a government—some government—was a necessity."[77] Accordingly, a contract for the payment of Confederate notes, made during the rebellion between parties residing within the Confederate States, could be enforced in the courts of the United States.[78] But a purchaser of cotton from the Confederate States, who knew that the money he paid for it went to sustain the rebellion, could not in the Court of Claims recover its proceeds,[79] and bonds issued by authority of the Convention of Arkansas, which attempted to carry the state out of the Union, for supporting the war, were not a valid consideration for a promissory note, since these bonds did not constitute any forced currency and were not the only circulat-

[76] Baldy vs. Hunter, 171 U. S., 388; 43 L. Ed., 208.
[77] Sprott vs. United States, 20 Wallace, 459; 22 L. Ed., 371.
[78] Thorington vs. Smith, *supra*.
[79] Sprott vs. United States, *supra*.

ing medium.[80] The rule was that all acts done in aid of the rebellion were illegal and void.[81]

Cases arising from the war between the states have been dealt with at some length despite the fact that they present situations not again likely to occur and in many of their phases involve problems of constitutional, not of international, law. Principles enunciated in these cases may indicate how the courts can solve various questions originating in conditions such as Russia at the present writing presents, with its unrecognized government, without doing violence to the necessary and proper rule that all matters of recognition are for the political departments of the government.

That an unrecognized government cannot be permitted to sue in the courts of the nonrecognizing country, or to make use of the governmental machinery of the latter for any purpose, seems to be too clear to require extended argument or citation of authorities.[82] To permit the appearance of a nonrecognized government as plaintiff or petitioner in United States courts would not only be running counter to the policy and decisions of that department of government charged with the conduct of foreign relations, but conceivably, indeed probably, might lead to anomalous and even ludicrous situations. Thus it has been held, and unavoidably so, that the ambassador of the Russian provisional government, established following the downfall of the

[80] Hanauer vs. Woodruff, 15 Wallace, 439; 21 L. Ed., 224. The opinion distinguishes the case from Thorington vs. Smith, *supra*.
[81] Dewing vs. Perdicaries, 96 U. S., 193; 24 L. Ed., 654.
[82] The Penza, 277 Federal Reporter, 91; The Rogday, 278 Federal Reporter, 294; The Rogday, 279 Federal Reporter, 130.

monarchy and which functioned immediately prior to the Communist *régime*, had the capacity to commence actions for that government despite the notorious fact that his government had fallen, if at the time the action was commenced he was the accredited representative to the United States, which recognized the government he represented.[83] Certainly the courts cannot permit themselves to be placed in a position of being forced to decide who is the proper plaintiff, whether the recognized or unrecognized government; there can be, and is, but one rule, viz., to follow, in this regard, the decision of the Department of State. It should be equally obvious that an unrecognized government cannot be permitted to avail itself of American courts of justice by a subterfuge, and that, therefore, it is perfectly proper and logical to rule that if the Russian Socialist Federated Republic has no capacity to sue in American courts, the individual members of a body subordinate to the government thereof cannot be permitted to do what the principal cannot do; in other words, that agents cannot obtain and exercise better or greater rights than their principals.[84]

It has been held also that an unrecognized foreign *de facto* government, even when its existence is admitted, cannot be sued in the tribunals of a nonrecognizing country, and that any question of redress from a foreign government is a political one, not confided to the courts, but to another department of the government.[85] The

[83] Russian Government vs. Lehigh Valley R. R. Co., 293 Federal Reporter, 133; ib. 135. For later citation, see 21 Fed. (2d) 396.
[84] Preobrazhenski *et al.* vs. Cibrario *et al.*, 192 N. Y. S., 275.
[85] Wulfson vs. Russian Socialist Federated Soviet Republic, 234 N. Y., 378; 138 N. E., 25.

rule is that a recognized foreign government cannot be sued in the courts of this country without its consent.[86] But is this necessarily true, or should it be so, when the courts are dealing with a nonrecognized government? Is nonsuability of nonrecognized governments a necessary corollary of their lack of capacity to sue?

As the situation now is, courts cannot grant redress against a nonrecognized government because governments cannot be sued without their consent, this rule being applied even to unrecognized governments which may have property within the jurisdiction of the court that but for the rule could be resorted to for satisfaction of just claims; but the political department cannot obtain redress through the usual diplomatic channels because it has no diplomatic relations with the government in question. What may be the result in many meritorious cases and to many an injured party? Public policy and justice would point to the conclusion that a nonrecognized foreign government should not be permitted to take advantage of its culpability both in international relations and with reference to the injured party, by the application of what is a rule of comity to which the unrecognized government has not been admitted and is not deemed fit to be admitted by recognition.

A foreign government may sue in American courts even in the absence of treaty provisions to that effect as a matter of comity, the rules of which come into opera-

---

[86] The American Union as a State in International Law.—States as persons.—Sec. 7, *supra*.—A foreign nation at war which makes contracts in the United States for supplies for its armies does not thereby divest itself of its sovereign character and become subject to suit. Roumania vs. Guaranty Trust Co., 250 Federal Reporter, 341.

Independence and Sovereignty

tion only when the government has been recognized by the United States. Comity has been defined as "that reciprocal courtesy which one member of the family of nations owes to others at peace with it."[87] But since privilege to sue is one granted for reasons of comity, and since immunity from suit is granted by one sovereign to another with whom he is at peace and whom he has recognized as being entitled to all the privileges of a member of the international family, does it not follow that this privilege does not and should not shelter a nonrecognized *de facto* government? Is not immunity from suit one of the very privileges it is not entitled to by reason of its failure to comply with conditions making recognition proper and possible? Surely, these questions should seem weighty enough to warrant a reconsideration of the rule as broadly laid down and broadly applied.

The difficulty in the way of reconsideration, as suggested, or of any modification, lies in the danger of an action against a nonrecognized government being construed as a species of recognition by the judicial department. But this is largely a technical obstacle which should not prove insurmountable. Actions against an unrecognized foreign government can have little or no practical utility unless the government has property within the jurisdiction of the court, and this would necessitate, in all probability, an action *in rem*. The question of notice, and its nature, would certainly arise, but this, too, should not be impossible of solution. An exception to nonexercise of jurisdiction over foreign states seems

[87] Russian Socialist Federated Soviet Republic vs. Cibrario, 235 N. Y., 255; 139 N. E., 259.

to exist where the action concerns local real estate.[88] There is no reason in principle why property of non-recognized states, both real and movable, should not be resorted to where both justice and public policy demand it.

The decrees of an unrecognized revolutionary government are of no force and effect in the United States, and accordingly, in an action for accounting, decrees of confiscation by the Soviet Government have not been recognized,[89] and so have the courts declined to recognize decrees of nationalization and to apply them to problems of property rights brought for adjudication before them.[90] However, whatever the ultimate fate of the Soviet *régime,* it is obvious that its methods and measures will have a profound effect upon all phases of Russian life and cannot be without influence upon the rights of many individuals and groups. The successors of this government, should it have any, will not be able to upset everything it has done, and, probably, will not desire to do so lest chaos be reintroduced. In France, following the Revolution, no later government questioned the validity of titles to land acquired during the great upheaval.[91] Can courts of other countries ignore everything that has been done, and will be done, in Russia, unless the Soviet Government is recognized? This might often prove

---

[88] Borchard, Edwin M., The Diplomatic Protection of Citizens Abroad, sec. 72, p. 175; The Banks Law Publishing Co., New York (1916).

[89] Bourne vs. Bourne, 204 N. Y. S., 866.

[90] James & Co. vs. Second Russian Insurance Co., 239 N. Y., 248; 146 N. E., 369. Russian Reinsurance Company vs. Stoddard, 240 N. Y., 149; 147 N. E., 703.

[91] Macy and Gannaway, Comparative Free Government, page 554, The Macmillan Co. (1919).

Independence and Sovereignty

flying in the face of unalterable facts and conceivably tantamount to a denial of justice. For instance, to use an extreme example, could the courts refuse to recognize the validity of a marriage contracted under the Soviet laws? Would not a second marriage, entered into in the United States, be bigamous? The fact is that in deciding cases, into the disposal of which the effects of non-recognition enter, courts always must be governed by considerations of public policy."[92]

In the Civil War cases the courts were confronted by a more difficult situation because they had to deal with the laws of an authority that actually sought the dismemberment of the Union, and which, from the Northern point of view, was not only unrecognized, but treasonable. Yet the courts took the position that "while there was no validity in any legislation of the Confederate States, so far as the acts of the several states did not impair the supremacy of the national authority, or the just rights of citizens under the Constitution, they are, in general, to be treated as valid and binding,"[93] and that "transactions between persons actually residing within the territory dominated by the Government of the Confederate States were not invalid for the reason only that they occurred under the sanction of the laws of that Government or of any local government recognizing its authority."[94] That the Civil War cases have not escaped the notice of the courts, and that the courts will seek to reconcile logic of juridical conceptions with inexorable facts, has lately become quite evident, to the satisfaction

[92] James & Co. vs. Second Russian Insurance Co., *supra*.
[93] Williams vs. Bruffy, 96 U. S., 176; 24 L. Ed., 716.
[94] Baldy vs. Hunter, 171 U. S., 388; 43 L. Ed., 208.

Judicial Interpretation of International Law

of all who would not reduce logic to absurdity and who see in the courts not only tribunals for elucidation of law, but also instruments of practical life and living justice.

Juridically a government that is unrecognized may be viewed as no government at all, if the power withholding recognition chooses thus to view it. In practice, however, since juridical conceptions are seldom, if ever, carried to the limit of their logic, the equivalence is not absolute, *but is subject to self-imposed limitations of common sense and fairness*, as we learned in litigation following our Civil War. In those litigations acts or decrees of the rebellious governments, which, of course, had not been recognized as governments *de facto*, were held to be nullities, when they worked injustice to citizens of the Union, or were in conflict with its public policy. On the other hand, acts or decrees that were just in operation and consistent with public policy were sustained not infrequently to the same extent as if the governments were lawful. These analogies suggest the thought that, subject to like restrictions, effect at times be due to the ordinances of foreign governments which, though formally unrecognized, have notoriously an existence *de facto*. Consequences appropriate enough when recognition is withheld on the ground that rival factions are still contending for mastery, may be in need of readjustment before they can be fitted to the practice, now a growing one, of withholding recognition whenever it is thought that a government, functioning unhampered, is unworthy of a place in the society of nations.[95]

In a later case it was said that a decree of the Russian Soviet Government had no effect in the United States, unless, possibly, *"to such an extent as justice and policy require,"* and it did not relieve from liability a Russian insurance company, which had qualified to do business in New York. "Neither comity nor public policy require

[95] Sokoloff vs. National City Bank, 239 N. Y., 158; 145 N. E., 917.

Independence and Sovereignty

enforcement of a mandate of another government, confiscating assets of nationalized insurance companies for its benefits, *to the prejudice of citizens of the United States, or any friendly power,* especially where it has been denied recognition." [96]

Those parts of the opinion of the court which have been italicized here, indicate fairly clearly the position the courts in all probability will take when a case arises necessitating a direct decision of the question, especially when we bear in mind the significant sentence, appearing in one of the opinions, that "we do not say that a government unrecognized by us will always be viewed as nonexistent." For that matter, a still later case brings out even more clearly the points touched upon in the precedents just referred to.

The fall of one governmental establishment and the substitution of another governmental establishment which actually governs, which is able to enforce its claims by military force and is obeyed by the people over whom it rules, must profoundly affect all the acts and duties, all the relations of those who live within the territory over which the new establishment exercises rule. Its rule may be without lawful foundation; but, lawful or unlawful, its existence is a fact, and that fact cannot be destroyed by juridical concepts. The State Department determines whether it will recognize its existence as lawful, and until the State Department has recognized the new establishment, the court may not pass upon its legitimacy or ascribe to its decrees all the effect which inheres in the laws or orders of a sovereign. The State Department determines only that question. *It cannot determine how far the private rights and obligations of individuals are affected by acts of a body not sovereign, or with which our government will have no dealings. That question does not concern our*

[96] Fred S. James & Co. vs. Second Russian Insurance Co., 239 N. Y., 248; 146 N. E., 369.

foreign relations. It is not a political question, but a judicial question. The courts in determining that question assume that until recognition these acts are not in full sense law. *This conclusion must depend upon whether these have nevertheless had such an actual effect that they may not be disregarded. In such case we deal with result rather than cause. We do not pass upon the right or wrong of what it has done; we consider the effect upon others of that which has been done, primarily from the point of view of fact rather than of theory.*[97]

In the case last cited a Russian insurance corporation had been nationalized by a decree of the Soviet Government and prohibited by this Government from holding directors' and stockholders' meetings, as well as from doing business in Russia as a corporation. The directors of the corporation, however, after going into exile, continued holding meetings in Paris and brought action against a New York trust company to recover money and securities originally deposited with the New York institution to comply with a law for the protection of policyholders and creditors as a condition precedent to engaging in business in that state. Obviously, had the court chosen to adopt the position dictated by extreme logic and disregarded completely the Soviet decrees, a recovery from the trust company would have resulted. However, when the case reached the court of last resort, this tribunal ruled that under the circumstances a New York court could not assume jurisdiction, chiefly because the courts were not able to protect the trust company, if they permitted recovery in the pending litigation, against a recovery in the tribunals of some country where

[97] Russian Reinsurance Company vs. Stoddard, 240 N. Y., 149; 147 N. E., 703. (Italics are author's.)

the Soviet *régime* has been recognized, a contingency the occurrence of which neither public policy nor sound sense permitted.[98]

While the courts will be undoubtedly always reluctant to give any effect to the decrees of an unrecognized government, and while the quotations just set forth are largely in the nature of *dicta*, it may be safely assumed that the judiciary will take cognizance of laws and decrees of such governments as facts and to be dealt with as facts, where to do otherwise would not be consonant with public policy or justice. It may not be wise, of course, to lay down generally what are the exceptions to the rule sometimes too sweepingly expressed, viz., that unrecognized governments are to be considered as nonexistent, in matters arising within the jurisdiction of the government refusing recognition, and therefore probably preferable to consider each case as it arises; but that common sense will not be abandoned for the sake of strict adherence to formula seems fairly clear. Nor will it be necessary, in applying such common sense, to trench upon the province of the political department of the government.

Primarily, recognition is conferred for reasons of international policy, and questions of private right are, usually, simply judicial questions and nothing else. Their settlement is the province of the courts. Should a problem be inextricably involved with that of foreign policy, and judicial decision impossible without running counter to the attitude adopted by the proper branch of the gov-

---

[98] Dickinson, Edwin D., The Russian Reinsurance Company Case, The American Journal of International Law, October 1925, page 753; see also "Recent Recognition Cases" by the same author, The American Journal of International Law, April, 1925, page 263.

ernment, then naturally the larger consideration must prevail even at the cost of sacrificing a legitimate private interest. It may be surmised, however, that the number of cases where this can be avoided will prove comparatively large.

Rule of military authorities by virtue of conquest and occupation is one whose mandates cannot be resisted by those living within the territory concerned and is certainly a government of paramount force. Therefore, subsequent evacuation of this territory by the occupying troops, and resumption of government by the lawful sovereign, cannot undo past transactions or change their character. Thus, when the British in September, 1814, occupied Castine, established a custom house and proceeded to levy import duties, new duties could not be imposed by the United States authorities when the latter re-entered the territory following the treaty of peace. "By the surrender the inhabitants passed under a temporary allegiance to the British Government, and were bound by such laws, and such only, as it chose to recognize or impose. From the nature of the case, no other laws could be obligatory upon them, for where there is no protection, or allegiance, or sovereignty, there can be no claim to obedience. Castine was therefore, during this period, so far as respected revenue laws, to be deemed a foreign port, and goods imported into it by the inhabitants were subject to such duties only as the British Government chose to require." [99] The conquering power may displace, and has the right to displace, the pre-existing authority, and to assume all governmental functions and power.[100] But when, during the

[99] United States vs. Rice, 4 Wheaton, 246; 4 L. Ed., 562.
[100] New Orleans vs. Steamship Co., 20 Wallace, 387; 22 L. Ed., 354.

Independence and Sovereignty

war with Mexico, the port of Tampico was occupied by American military authorities, the port remained a foreign one within an act of Congress of July 30, 1846, and goods shipped from Tampico to the United States were subject to the usual tariff. Military occupation did not make Tampico a part of the Union, and it never was recognized as such by the administrative authorities, or by Congress, the latter consideration being evidently the decisive one with the court.[101] Also, despite military occupation and military government appointed by, and representing, the President of the United States, where this was done with the object of assisting the inhabitants to establish a government of their own, a country remained foreign territory within an act of Congress providing for extradition of persons violating the laws of a foreign territory occupied by, or under the control of, the United States. More specifically, Cuba was foreign territory during the American occupation, following the war with Spain, and extradition could not be prevented on the ground that it was not a foreign country.[102]

The formation of a civil government in conquered territory is lawful exercise of belligerent rights and properly continues until the legislative branch of the government ordains otherwise, even after cession of the territory to the conqueror by a treaty of peace. When a suit was brought to recover from a collector of the port of San Francisco, by virtue of appointment by the military governor, certain tonnage duties and imposts paid by plaintiff upon ships which had arrived in San Francisco and upon foreign merchandise landed there from them

[101] Fleming vs. Page, 9 Howard, 603; 13 L. Ed., 276.
[102] Neely vs. Henkel, 180 U. S., 109; 45 L. Ed., 448.

Judicial Interpretation of International Law

in 1848 and 1849, the action failed.[103] The executive authority may properly establish a provisional government, to ordain laws and institute a judicial system, all of which continues in force after the termination of the war and until modified by Congress.[104]

Judgments of proper tribunals, acting under the authority of *de facto* governments, so far as they affect the private rights of the parties thereto, are valid. Thus a judgment of a Spanish tribunal in Louisiana, having jurisdiction of the cause, was upheld although rendered after cession of the territory, but prior to its actual surrender to the United States.[105] On the other hand the courts have declined to uphold grants of land made by a *de facto* government, ruling over territory which did not properly belong to it, against the government to which the territory actually belonged.[106] This conclusion was reached in litigation involving titles to land in territory which had been the subject matter of a boundary dispute.

§ 12. *Rights and duties of states and their responsibility.*—The world—the society of nations—is composed of distinct sovereignties, possessing equal rights and independence.[107] This problem of the equality of states has been the subject of much valuable discussion, both from the standpoint of theory as well as actual international conditions.[108] However, the courts have nothing

---

[103] Cross vs. Harrison, 16 Howard, 190; 14 L. Ed., 899.
[104] Leitensderffer vs. Webb, 20 Howard, 176; 15 L. Ed., 891.
[105] Keene vs. McDonough, 8 Peters, 308, 8 L. Ed., 955.
[106] Coffee vs. Groover, 123 U. S., 1; 31 L. Ed., 51.
[107] The Exchange vs. McFaddon, 7 Cranch, 116; 3 L. Ed., 287.
[108] Dickinson, Ed., The Equality of States in International Law, Cambridge, Harvard University Press, 1920. Lawrence, T. J., Essays on Some Disputed Questions of Modern International Law, Cambridge, Deighton, Bell and Co. (1884).

[74]

Independence and Sovereignty

to do with formulation of international policies and their enforcement, and it is almost entirely in this political sphere that the question of equality of states is controversial.

Equality of states is a legal principle, and it "consists in the fact that in the received principles and rules of international law, other than those of a ceremonial nature, no distinction is made between great states and small, . . ."[109] and no legal principle is better established, or more universally recognized, than the one of equality of nations. "Russia and Geneva have equal rights."[110] From this principle of equality certain practical results follow, the most important one being that one nation cannot impose a rule upon another nation rightfully, each nation legislating for itself and this legislation operating only upon itself. The law of nations results from the consent of all and no one state can change it.[111] Again, one sovereign being bound to respect the independence of other sovereigns, his legal equals, the courts of one country refuse to sit in judgment on the acts of another government done within the latter's territory.[112] "Sovereignty means that the decree of the sovereign makes law, and foreign courts cannot condemn the influences persuading the sovereign to make the decree."[113] The acts of a military commander, acting under orders of the erstwhile Mexican Govern-

[109] Westlake, John, International Law, Peace, p. 308.
[110] The Antelope, 10 Wheaton, 66; 6 L. Ed., 268.
[111] The Antelope, *supra*.
[112] Underhill vs. Hernandez, 168 U. S., 250; 42 L. Ed., 456. Hewitt vs. Speyer, 250 Federal Reporter, 367. Ricaud vs. American Metal Co., 246 U. S., 304; 62 L. Ed., 733.
[113] American Banana Co. vs. United Fruit Co., 213 U. S., 347; 53 L. Ed., 826.

ment of Carranza, who had seized the property of a Mexican citizen as a military contribution, were not subject to re-examination and modification by American courts though the property came within their jurisdiction.[114]

Members of the society of nations, recognizing international law as a body of rules to be observed by them and enforced within their territory, may and do require of each other the performance of certain international obligations, and these are reciprocal in their nature. "A right secured by the law of nations to a nation, or its people, is one the United States, as the representatives of the nation, are bound to protect," and in the protection of such rights due diligence is required. Therefore, the courts have upheld a statute to prevent counterfeiting of foreign money within its territory and punishing the offence when committed on the ground that in the sphere of foreign relations exclusive authority is conferred upon the national government, which is thus "made responsible to foreign nations for all violations by the United States of their international obligations," the Constitution for this reason granting the power "to define and punish . . . offences against the law of nations,"[115] and the right to coin money being an essential of sovereignty, and counterfeiting of foreign money being an offence against international law. Nor was it necessary that the statute expressly declare the crime to be an offence against the law of nations, the fact being sufficient, and appearing upon the face of the act, that it was passed for the protection of an international interest. Indeed, while a refusal to protect the rights of other states, such

[114] Oetjen vs. Central Leather Co., 246 U. S., 297; 62 L. Ed., 726.
[115] Constitution of the United States, Article 1, second 8, cl., 10.

Independence and Sovereignty

as the right to coin money, "may not, perhaps, furnish sufficient cause for war, it would certainly give just ground of complaint and thus disturb that harmony between the governments which each is bound to cultivate and promote." [116]

The principle of responsibility of states has been stated in sweeping language:

> It is an established principle of international law that a nation is responsible for wrongs done by its citizens to the citizens of a friendly power. Ordinarily this responsibility is discharged by a government rendering to a resident alien the same protection which it affords to its own citizens and bringing the perpetrators to trial and punishment. This responsibility of a nation for the acts of its individual members is so well established and regulated by international law that it falls little short of being a natural right. [117]

Where a treaty provided for guaranties to the citizen of either nation in the territory of the other, "the most constant protection and security for their persons and property," and that "they shall enjoy in this respect the same rights and privileges as are or shall be granted to the natives on their submitting themselves to the conditions imposed upon the natives," it was held that these provisions conferred upon alien residents rights enjoyed by American citizens, but no more. [118]

Within the territories of the American Union states are the organs of sovereignty for the protection of life and personal liberty within the respective states, and under the Constitution power for that purpose rests

---
[116] United States vs. Arjona, 120 U. S., 479; 30 L. Ed., 728.
[117] Jonathan Brown vs. United States and Brulé Sioux, 32 Ct. Cl., 432.
[118] City of New Orleans vs. Abbagnato, 62 Federal Reporter, 240.

Judicial Interpretation of International Law

exclusively with them.[119] At times occurrences in certain of the states have embarrassed the government of the nation and made fulfillment of international obligations difficult and even impossible. Of course, from the standpoint of international law, and international duty, such situations, due to the federal constitutional system, do not relieve the nation from responsibility and liability.[120]

Claims and grievances of one country against the government of another can be advanced and prosecuted only through diplomatic channels, by negotiations of one government with another. "Redress of grievances by reason of such acts must be obtained through the means open to be availed of by sovereign powers, as between themselves."[121] The principle of action, or non-action, in such cases has been stated broadly as follows:

One nation treats with the citizens of another only through their government. A sovereign cannot be sued in his own courts without his consent. His own dignity, as well as the dignity of the nation he represents, prevents his appearance to answer a suit against him in the courts of another sovereignty, except in performance of his obligations, by treaty or otherwise, voluntarily assumed. Hence, a citizen of one nation wronged by the conduct of another nation, must seek redress through his own government. His sovereign must assume the responsibility of presenting his claim, or it need not be considered. If this responsibility is assumed, the claim may be prosecuted as one nation proceeds against another, not by suit in the courts, as of right, but by diplomacy, or, if need be, by war. It rests with the sovereign against whom the demand is made to determine for himself what he will do in respect to it. He may pay or reject it, he may submit it to

[119] United States vs. Cruikshank, 92 U. S., 542; 23 L. Ed., 588.
[120] See Chap. I, par. 5, The several states of the Union and international law, *supra*.
[121] Underhill vs. Hernandez, 169 U. S., 250; 42 L. Ed., 456.

Independence and Sovereignty

arbitration, open his own courts to suit, or consent to be tried in the courts of another nation. All depends upon himself.[122]

Before citizens approach their governments for intercession on their behalf, against other governments, it is wise, and may be stated to be a requirement, to exhaust all direct methods of redress, if any, afforded by the government against which complaint is made, for there is no rule of international law making it obligatory upon the government of one nation to enforce claims against another nation if the citizens themselves are afforded means of satisfaction without the intervention of their government. Interference by the government of a nation should be resorted to only under exceptional circumstances, and, obviously, exceptional circumstances do not arise where proper claims can be satisfied without bringing into operation the weighty apparatus of a government.[123]

In the American Union the relation of a state with its citizens is not that of an independent sovereign state, because a state of the Union cannot resort to war against another state upon refusal of the latter to extend redress to the citizens of the former, a power and right a state internationally sovereign does possess and may exercise. Therefore, the Eleventh Amendment to the Constitution of the United States prohibits action by one state against another on behalf of its citizens where the prosecuting state has no direct interest of its own, and this interest cannot be created by a legislative assumption of the rights of citizens.[124]

[122] United States vs. Diekelman, 92 U. S., 520; 23 L. Ed., 742.
[123] New Hampshire vs. Louisiana, 108 U. S., 76; 27 L. Ed., 656.
[124] New Hampshire vs. Louisiana, *supra*.

Judicial Interpretation of International Law

Citizens of a country against which claims are made are not permitted to participate in an award made by an international commission at the instigation, and on behalf of, citizens of the intervening country. Thus a claim of a French citizen against the United States, for cotton taken during the Civil War, was submitted by the widow and administratrix for adjudication to a commission functioning under a treaty between the two countries. Upon a favorable finding on the merits, one-sixth of the award was withheld because it was ascertained that one of the three heirs of the deceased claimant was an American citizen, and when the latter sued the United States Government, the action of the commission was upheld by the courts on the ground that he had no cause of action, since, if any did exist, it accrued to the administratrix, and the cause of action was not against the French Government, for it received no money for the plaintiff's benefit.[125] Again, where the property of a French subject was occupied by United States troops and the claimant's executor presented claims by virtue of the provisions of a convention between the two countries, only French legatees were entitled to be represented before the Claims Commission and they only were entitled to participate in the distribution.[126] Nor will the American government intervene against another government unless the claimant's citizenship is affirmatively established. Thus in the case of a schooner seized by the French on March 7, 1800, sailing from Norfolk to Mattinico, it did not appear that the owners of the vessel and cargo were citizens of the United States, or

[125] Bodemueller vs. United States, 39 Federal Reporter, 437.
[126] Burthe vs. Denis, 133 U. S., 514; 33 L. Ed., 768.

Independence and Sovereignty

that the schooner was a registered vessel. Upon its condemnation by a French prize tribunal it was held that this condemnation could not be considered illegal because neither the American registry nor the citizenship of the owners was established.[127] But a certificate issued under the authority of a government showing the nationality of a vessel, or the citizenship of her owners, can be questioned by foreign powers only by application to the government that issued the certificate. Therefore, where a vessel carried an American register, a decree of condemnation was illegal although it appeared therefrom that the supercargo, who was one of the owners, was a native of Germany without any proof of American naturalization, since the register of an American vessel in the eighteenth century was conclusive evidence in French prize courts of her American character and of her owners' nationality.[128]

Where a Claims Commission makes an award for damages and injuries, its decision, within the scope of its authority, is conclusive and final as between the parties claiming the property and may not be re-examined before any judicial tribunal.[129] A claim is an assignable property right, but if a prior assignee gives no notice of the assignment until a second assignee prosecutes a claim before a Claims Commission to a reward in his favor, the equities of the parties are equal and the possessor of the legal title will prevail.[130] Again, so long as money received as a result of an international award, by a Claims Commission, or other tribunal agreed upon, is

[127] The Vandeput, 37 Ct. Cl., 396.
[128] The Conrad, 37 Ct. Cl., 459.
[129] Comegess vs. Vasse, 1 Peters, 193; 7 L. Ed., 108.
[130] Judson vs. Corcoran, 17 Howard, 611; 15 L. Ed., 231.

Judicial Interpretation of International Law

still in the possession of a government, it is its moral obligation as a sovereign to inquire, if occasion arises, as to its duty with respect to the fund, not only toward the citizen for whom the award was received, but toward the government from which it was obtained and it may at any time institute investigation of the good faith of the claim. If it is then found that the award was made as the result of fraud or perjury, or either, the parties may be barred from all claims upon the award and the money returned to the Government by which it was paid.[131]

When a citizen demands a recognition and adjustment of his claim against a foreign power, he subjects himself to the jurisdiction of such a court as Congress may designate for the purpose, and when a statutory recognition of a claim to an international award is made, the award being in the custody of the government, it is impressed with the character of a right susceptible of a judicial determination and ceases to be a mere appeal to the grace of the sovereign, and a judicial proceeding to determine the *bona fides* of the claim not only does not conflict with the diplomatic authority of the President, vested in him by the Constitution, but is one calculated to carry out the international obligations and moral duties of the claimant's government.[132]

The United States Government has accorded British subjects, if otherwise entitled, the right to recover by process in the American Court of Claims the proceeds of captured and abandoned property. This privilege is based upon reciprocity and is accorded only to the citi-

---

[131] United States vs. La Abra Silver Mining Co., 29 Ct. Cl., 432.
[132] United States vs. La Abra Silver Mining Co., *supra*.

Independence and Sovereignty

zens or subjects of such foreign governments as grant American citizens the right to prosecute claims against these governments in their courts. The British proceeding, known as a "petition of right" is one that accords to United States citizens the right to prosecute claims against the British Government, and, therefore, as between these countries the rule of reciprocity in this respect is in operation.[133] However, a British citizen who never resided in the United States, but committed acts which would have rendered him liable to punishment for treason had he owed allegiance to the United States, was excluded from the benefits of an act of March 12, 1863, conferring the right, within two years after the close of the Civil War, to maintain a suit in the Court of Claims for recovery of proceeds of the sale of property captured from the enemy which were paid into the treasury, and sale of cotton to the Confederate Army constituted aid to the enemy within the prohibitory terms of the statute.[134]

Of the rule that a foreign government cannot be sued in the courts of another state certain modifications should be registered in this connection. It has been held, for instance, that a suit *in rem* may be maintained against the property of a foreign government, although this property is destined for public use, where recovery is sought for salvage services rendered while it was in the possession of a lightering company and where the property was still in the possession of the latter when libeled and seized by the marshal. In this case the company had contracted to transport the property from a railroad

[133] United States vs. O'Keefe, 11 Wallace, 178; 20 L. Ed., 131. United States vs. Carlisle, 16 Wallace, 147; 21 L. Ed., 426.
[134] Young vs. United States, 97 U. S., 39; 24 L. Ed., 992.

Judicial Interpretation of International Law

terminal to a vessel, but had no other connection with the foreign government.[135] It has also been held that a claim for damages exists against a United States public vessel guilty of a maritime tort as much as if the vessel belonged to a private citizen. Reasons of public policy prevent enforcement by a direct proceeding against the vessel, but where the property itself is subjected to the jurisdiction of the courts by affirmative governmental action, a claim will be entertained and recovery permitted. This situation arose in the case of a prize ship which ran into and sank another vessel while on the way to a place of adjudication in charge of a prize master and crew. The captured vessel, in proceedings instituted by the government, was condemned as a lawful prize and the proceeds of its sale paid into the registry. The owners of the sunken vessel intervened by petition and asserted a claim upon the proceeds for damages caused by the collision. The claim was sustained and the damages ordered paid out of the proceeds before their distribution.[136] However, an attempt to impress custom revenues in the hands of American bankers with a charge in complainant's favor, the controversy growing out of a contract with the republic of Ecuador and where it would have been necessary to pass upon the validity of acts of a foreign nation, was not sustained.[137]

Since governments can conduct business only through representatives, where a public agent acts within the scope of his authority and in performance of his duty, he cannot be held to personal liability and his contracts are public, not personal.[138]

[133] Hodgson vs. Dexter, 1 Cranch, 345; 2 L. Ed., 130.
[135] The Johnson Lighterage Co., No. 24; 231 Federal Reporter, 365.
[136] The Siren, 7 Wallace, 152; 19 L. Ed., 129.
[137] Hewitt vs. Speyer, 250 Federal Reporter, 367.

Independence and Sovereignty

The rules governing presentation of claims against foreign governments and the procedure in such cases, owing to the non-suability of governments as a rule are not a subject of judicial interpretation, and the student and lawyer must therefore consult works devoted to this phase of international law generally.[139]

§ 13. *The continuing personality of states.*—One of the causes of the rise and growth of international law is the need of stability in the relations of states that compose the society of nations. It is for this reason that the principle of continuity of states, regardless of changes of government, or its internal organization, is one of the most fundamental in the law of nations. A state may undergo changes in its population and territory, it may be subjected to upheavals in its constitutional structure, unless the changes in territory are such as to deprive it of its unitary character, in contemplation of international law it still retains the same international personality.[140] When the State of Tennessee by a constitutional amendment adopted in 1865 declared null and void notes issued by the Bank of Tennessee, an institution functioning under a charter containing a clause by which the State agreed to receive the bank's notes in payment of taxes, and a controversy arose by reason of a refusal of the State to comply with this provision, the United States Supreme Court, when the case reached this tribunal, took occasion to declare:

Cicero and other public jurists define a State to be a body political or society of men united together for the purpose of promoting their mutual safety and advantages by their com-

---

[139] See especially Borchard, Edwin M., The Diplomatic Protection of Citizens Abroad, The Banks Publishing Co., New York (1916).

[140] Fenwick, Charles G., International Law, The Century Co., New York & London (1924), p. 111.

bined strength. Wheaton, International Law, sect. 17. Such a body or society when once organized as a state by an established government, must remain so until it is destroyed. This may be done by disintegration of its parts, by its absorption into and identification with some other state or nation, or by the absolute and total dissolution of the ties which bind the society together. We know of no other way in which it can cease to be a state. No change of its internal polity, no modification of its organization or system of government, nor any change in its external relations short of entire absorption in another state, can deprive it of existence or destroy its identity.

The political society which in 1796 became a State of the Union, by the name of a State of Tennessee, is the same which is now represented as one of those States in the Congress of the United States. Not only is it the same body politic now, but it has always been the same. There has been perpetual succession and perpetual identity. There has from that time always been a State of Tennessee, and the same State of Tennessee. Its executive, its legislative, its judicial departments have continued without interruption and in regular order. It has changed, modified, and reconstructed its organic law, or State Constitution, more than once. It has done this before the rebellion, during the rebellion, and since the rebellion. And it was always done by the collective authority and in the name of the same body of people constituting the political society known as the State of Tennessee.[141]

An action brought against an American vessel, *The Sapphire,* as a result of a collision with a French transport in the harbor of San Francisco, in the name of Napoleon III, did not abate upon the latter's deposition. "The reigning sovereign represents the national sovereignty, and that sovereignty is continuous and perpetual, residing in the proper successors of the sovereign for the time being." The person or party in power is no more than an agent of the national sovereignty. A suc-

[141] Keith vs. Clark, 97 U. S., 454; 24 L. Ed., 1071.

cessor of an overthrown government, recognized by the government of the United States, is competent to prosecute an action already pending and entitled to the fruits thereof. How and by what methods governmental changes are accomplished is immaterial, and the rights and liabilities of the state are not changed thereby.[142]

It is well to remember in this connection that this question of continuing duties and liabilities of states, regardless of changes of government and no matter how accomplished, goes to the very roots of international relations, and that upholding the principle spells the difference between orderly development on the one hand and chaos on the other. The matter goes far beyond a mere question of debts or payment of obligations, only as such: The distinction is one between an organized society or, in the last analysis, none at all.

An extradition treaty with Prussia was not terminated by the formation of the German Empire in 1871. The Supreme Court placed its decision on the ground that the German Government continued to recognize the treaty, as did the American Government, and that from a memorial of 1889, transmitted by the German Government to the American *chargé* at Berlin it was apparent that the states of the German Empire were not hindered from independently regulating problems of extradition, by treaty or by special legislative enactment,[143] but no doubt the decision was also sound from the standpoint of the German Empire's succession to the international rights and duties of Prussia.[144]

Title to property held by an insurgent government, if

[142] The Sapphire, 11 Wallace, 164; 20 L. Ed., 227; Agency of Canadian Car & Foundry Co. vs. American Can Co., 258 Federal Reporter, 363.
[143] Terlinden vs. Ames, 184 U. S., 270; 46 L. Ed., 534.
[144] Fenwick, Charles G., International Law, *supra*, p. 116.

Judicial Interpretation of International Law

the rebellion fails, and upon its suppression, vests absolutely in the victor.[145] However, since governments must protect their citizens, where the defeated government was a *de facto* one, British courts have held that the victor takes the property subject to such rights as may have accrued to citizens of foreign states when he seeks to assert his title in the foreign court.[146]

§ 14. *Acquisition and loss of sovereignty: Effects and results.*—In the course of litigation of various kinds American courts have passed upon titles acquired by discovery and occupation,[147] settlement,[148] accretion,[149] cession,[150] conquest,[151] and prescription.[152]

It was perhaps natural that during the period of exploration and discovery, accompanied by a race for the acquisition of new territories, the great powers of Europe considered discovery sufficient to confer absolute title to land previously unknown, and the echoes of the struggle and the resultant theory are found in some of the adjudi-

[145] United States vs. Huckabee, 16 Wallace, 434; 22 L. Ed., 457. Whitfield vs. United States, 93 U. S., 165; 23 L. Ed., 400. Titus vs. United States, 20 Wallace, 475; 22 L. Ed., 400.

[146] United States vs. Prioleau, 2 Hem. & M., 559. Scott, James Brown, Cases on International Law, West Publishing Co., St. Paul (1922), p. 90. United States vs. McRae, L. R., 8 Eq., 69, Scott's Cases, p. 92.

[147] Johnson vs. McIntosh, 8 Wheaton, 543; 5 L. Ed., 681. Jones vs. United States, 137 U. S., 202; 34 L. Ed., 691. Shively vs. Bowlby, 152 U. S., 1; 38 L. Ed., 331.

[148] Mortimer vs. New York Elevated R. R. Co., 6 N. Y. Supp., 898. Ketchum vs. Buckley, 99 U. S., 188; 25 L. Ed., 473.

[149] Nebraska vs. Iowa, 143 U. S., 359; 36 L. Ed., 186. New Orleans vs. United States, 223 U. S., 268; 56 L. Ed., 432.

[150] American Insurance Co vs. Canter, 1 Peters, 511; 7 L. Ed., 242. Mormon Church vs. United States, 136 U. S., 1; 34 L. Ed., 481.

[151] American Insurance Co. vs. Canter, *supra*. More vs. Steinbach, 127 U. S., 70; 32 L. Ed., 51.

[152] Rhode Island vs. Massachusetts, 4 Howard, 591; 11 L. Ed., 1116. Indiana vs. Kentucky, 136 U. S., 479; 34 L. Ed., 329.

Independence and Sovereignty

cated cases. It has been said, for instance, that the English possessions in America were claimed by the right of discovery and not by the right of conquest and that "absolute rights of property and dominion were held to belong to the European nation by which any particular portion of the country was first discovered." [153]

Titles to lands, derived from Indian tribes solely, have not been recognized by the courts and while the Indians concededly were the rightful occupants of the soil, the principle that discovery conferred absolute title upon the power whose agent the discoverer happened to be, was tantamount to a denial of their right to convey the soil according to their own will.[154] So the City of New York, despite the one-time Dutch occupation, is deemed to have continuously remained British territory,[155] prior to the American Revolution, of course. However, in discussing title by discovery, Justice Marshall remarked that this title "might be consummated by possession," [156] and in a modern case, in a concurring opinion, it has been pointed out that Roman law did not recognize title by discovery unless followed by occupation, or unless intention to take possession was given to the world. The latter opinion proceeds to say that "it must be conceded that modern diplomatists and publicists incline to the opinion that mere transient discovery amounts to nothing unless followed in a reasonable time by occupation and settle-

[153] Hall, W. E., A Treatise on International Law, The Clarendon Press (1917), pp. 104-105. Martin vs. Waddell, 16 Peter, 367; 10 L. Ed., 997.
[154] Johnson vs. McIntosh, *supra*.
[155] Mortimer vs. New York Elevated R. R. Co., *supra*.
[156] Johnson vs. McIntosh, *supra*.

ment, under the sanction of the state,"[157] Where occupancy by a nation's citizens is continuous and useful, although only for a special purpose, such as working mines or catching fish, and is in the name of the state, or with its assent, that state may exercise jurisdiction over the territory thus acquired for such a period as it sees fit.[158]

Acquisition of title by accretion is familiar in private law and is no less just when applied to public, than to private rights.[159] The rule is also an ancient one, for in the Institutes of Justinian occurs the following passage: "Moreover, the alluvial soil added by a river to your land becomes yours by the law of nations. Alluvion is an imperceptible increase, and that is added by alluvion which is added so gradually that no one can perceive how much is added at any one moment of time."[160]

A river continues to be the boundary between states, whatever changes may occur on either bank by reason of "invisible accession or abstraction of particles" and "one country may, in process of time, lose a little of its territory, and the other gain a little, but the territorial relations cannot be reversed by such imperceptible mutations in the course of the river."[161] But it seems that the rule as to alluvial increase differs in the case of lakes and ponds and the sea from that applied to rivers,[162] a matter, however, that ordinarily can concern only private rights as distinguished from public rights; a deposit on one shore

[157] Mortimer vs. New York Elevated R. R. Co., *supra*, concurring opinion of Mr. Justice Freedman.
[158] Jones vs. United States, *supra*.
[159] New Orleans vs. United States, *supra*.
[160] County of St. Clair vs. Livingston, 23 Wallace, 46; 23 L. Ed., 59.
[161] Nebraska vs. Iowa, *supra*.
[162] Ker & Co. vs. Couden, 223 U. S., 268; 56 L. Ed., 432.

Independence and Sovereignty

of a lake, or sea, cannot very well concern the state owning the other shore.

During a conflict still unconcluded by a treaty conquered territory is held merely as a military occupation until its status is determined by such treaty, when it may become a part of the victorious state if the agreement confirms the acquisition.[163] Over acquired territories the power of Congress is general and plenary and is based upon the power of the Government to declare war and conclude treaties of peace.[164]

Title by adverse possession, under claim of right or color of title, in private law, finds its analogy in the rule that where a state for a long time acquiesces in the possession of territory by another state, and the latter exercises sovereignty and dominion over it, such possession is conclusive of the title and rightful authority of that state.[165] "For the security of rights, whether by states or individuals, long possession, under a claim of title, is protected. And there is no controversy in which this great principle may be invoked with greater justice and propriety, than in a case of disputed boundary." [166]

A new sovereignty may of course arise, and frequently has been established, as the result of a successful revolution, and as has been pointed out the commencement of such sovereignty is considered to date from the time independence is declared.[167] In any event, the American view of the treaty of peace of 1783 was always of one recognizing pre-existing rights and not a grant of inde-

---

[163] American Insurance Co. vs. Canter, *supra*.
[164] Mormon Church vs. United States, 136 U. S., 1; 34 L. Ed., 481.
[165] Indiana vs. Kentucky, 136 U. S., 479; 34 L. Ed., 329.
[166] Rhode Island vs. Massachusetts, 4 Howard, 591; 11 L. Ed., 1116.
[167] McIlvaine vs. Coxe's Lessees, 4 Cranch, 209; 2 L. Ed., 207.

pendence.[168] Each state became sovereign when the Revolution took place.[169]

Title to territory may be abandoned by a state.[170]

Problems resulting from changes of sovereignty, and from the rise of new sovereignties, were never so complex and difficult as following the Great War when the Peace Conference was confronted with the apportionment of obligations and duties of destroyed or dismembered states. The results reached and payments imposed by the Versailles treaties upon the new nations of Europe to a large extent were dictated by political and economic considerations, this being particularly true of contributions to the cost of the alleged liberation of territories which prior to the war formed a part of the Austro-Hungarian Empire.[171]

In the United States, in what was called a "quasi-international difference," replying to an argument that the debt of Virginia, liability for which was in question, was incurred for local improvements and that therefore apportionment thereof should be according to the territory in which the money was expended, the Supreme Court took the position that where a debt is created for expenditures benefiting the entire state, the whole state should equally bear the burden and not merely the locality where the improvements actually were made, and that upon dis-

---

[168] Harcourt vs. Gaillard, 12 Wheaton, 527; 6 L. Ed., 716. Henderson vs. Poindexter's Lessee, 12 Wheaton, 530; 6 L. Ed., 718. See also United States vs. Repentigny, 5 Wallace, 211; 18 L. Ed., 627. Ely's Adm. vs. United States, 171 U. S., 220; 43 L. Ed., 142.

[169] Mumford vs. Wardwell, 6 Wallace, 423; 18 L. Ed., 756.

[170] Jones vs. United States, 137 U. S., 202; 34 L. Ed., 691.

[171] 13 American Journal of International Law Supplement (1919), 151-386; 14 American Journal of International Law Supplement (1920), 1-83, 344-355.

Independence and Sovereignty

memberment division of the liability should be made in accordance with this principle.[172]

Following a cession of territory, the most important problem usually concerns the laws remaining in force. The rule as to public laws differs from that relating to private laws, those concerning individuals and their rights. Public, or political, laws, are necessarily changed in so far as they vary from those of the new sovereignty,[173] for the reason that when a nation acquires territory, whether by treaty or any other method, it can hold it only in accordance with its own constitution and public laws, and because such possession cannot be subject to the laws of the government which had parted with the territory.[174] Any other rule would be an impairment and diminution of the new sovereignty.[175] Public policy of states frequently differs with regard to various problems, and, manifestly, a new sovereignty cannot permit continued administration of laws which are in conflict with its own public policy, or its constitution and institutions. A number of cases illustrates the necessity of this rule to avoid what would be equivalent to fraud perpetrated in view of the possible, or probable change.

Thus it has been held that grants of land within American territory made *flagrante bello* by a British governor (on January 24, 1777) were void and that such grants could derive validity only from treaty provisions,

[172] Commonwealth of Virginia vs. State of West Virginia, 220 U. S., 1; 55 L. Ed., 353.
[173] American Insurance Company vs. Canter, *supra*. Vilas vs. City of Manila, 220 U. S., 345; 55 L. Ed., 491.
[174] Pollard vs. Hagan, 3 Howard, 212; 11 L. Ed., 565.
[175] United States vs. D'Auterive et al., 10 Howard, 609; 13 L. Ed., 560. United States vs. Montault, 12 Howard, 47; 13 L. Ed., 887.

but which in this case did not exist.[176] Except for municipal purposes and maintenance of order, the sovereignty of the ceding power is extinguished even before actual delivery of the territory and following the signing of the treaty.[177] Power to grant land or franchises is one of the attributes of sovereignty and ends with the transfer of territory.[178] The authority of Mexican governors to alienate public domain came to an end on July 7, 1846, the date fixed by Congress as completing the conquest of California.[179] The extinction of Spanish sovereignty in Cuba also extinguished such property rights as may have been possessed in connection with a heritable office in that island which had been abolished by the Spanish rulers, but whose holder, pending compensation for its condemnation, was receiving the emoluments pertaining to one of the perquisites of that office.[180] But the new sovereign may continue the functions of local officials and where this is done their acts, within the scope of their authority, are valid, and a sale made by such an official, who turned the proceeds into the new treasury, has been upheld.[181]

Following the war with Spain and the resulting acquisition of Porto Rico and the Philippine Islands, the courts were confronted with the question whether terri-

[176] Harcourt vs. Gaillard, 12 Wheaton, 523; 6 L. Ed., 716.

[177] Davis vs. The Police Jury of Concordia, 9 Howard, 279; 13 L. Ed., 138. United States vs. Reynes, 9 Howard, 127; 13 L. Ed., 74.

[178] More vs. Steinbach, 127 U. S., 70; 32 L. Ed., 51. Alexander vs. Roulet, 13 Wallace, 386; 20 L. Ed., 564.

[179] Stearns vs. United States, 6 Wallace, 589; 18 L. Ed., 843. U. S. vs. Pico, 23 Howard, 326; 16 L. Ed., 464. U. S. vs. Yorba, 1 Wallace, 422; 17 L. Ed., 635.

[180] O'Reilly de Camara vs. Brooke, 209 U. S., 45; 52 L. Ed., 676.

[181] Ely's Administrator vs. United States, 171 U. S., 220; 43 L. Ed., 142.

Independence and Sovereignty

tory ceded to the United States can be considered for any purpose a "foreign country." In one of the previous cases, decided by the Supreme Court, there appeared a *dictum* which indicated the possibility of such a theory.[182] A ruling to that effect, where the question was decisive of the issue, was, however, clearly impossible and as a matter of fact the *dictum* was repudiated in a somewhat later case.[183] The difficulties in the Insular cases did not arise from doubt as to the principles of international law, but rather as a problem of American constitutional law. The view finally prevailed that the term "United States" has a broader meaning when the Government is dealing with foreign sovereignties than when considered as a term of constitutional law and that it includes all territories subject to the jurisdiction of the Federal Government, wherever located.[184] A foreign country was defined as one exclusively within the sovereignty of a foreign nation,[185] and therefore with the ratification of the Treaty of Peace between the United States and Spain, April 11, 1899, the Island of Porto Rico ceased to be a foreign country within the meaning of the tariff laws,[186] and the same rule was applied to the Philippine Islands.[187] But duties upon imports from the United States to Porto Rico, exacted by the military commander prior to the ratification of the peace treaty and after the commencement of the occupation, were

---

[182] Fleming vs. Page, 9 Howard, 603; 13 L. Ed., 276.
[183] Cross vs. Harrison, 16 Howard, 164; 14 L. Ed., 889.
[184] Downes vs. Bidwell, 182 U. S., 244; 45 L. Ed., 1088. Geofroy vs. Riggs, 133 U. S., 258; 33 L. Ed., 642.
[185] De Lima vs Bidwell, 182 U. S., 1; 45 L. Ed., 1041.
[186] De Lima vs. Bidwell, *supra*.
[187] Fourteen Diamond Rings vs. United States, 183 U. S., 176; 46 L. Ed., 138.

within the war power of the military authorities and it was immaterial that in the particular case the imports were from New York. The situation was not the same as after ratification of the treaty when different considerations were necessary.[188] An act of Congress, requiring exports from the United States into Porto Rico to pay a duty of 15% of the amount of duties paid upon merchandise imported from foreign countries was not contrary to the constitutional provision declaring that no tax or duty shall be laid on articles exported from any state,[189] since that provision is limited to merchandise exported to foreign countries and has no application to Porto Rico which was held not to be a foreign country within the general tariff law.[190]

Under the common law of England, as expounded by the British courts, which, in turn, have been followed by the courts of the United States, the rights and relations of inhabitants of conquered or ceded territory *inter se* continue to be governed by the laws and usages in force at the time of the transfer,[191] and the rule of international law is to the same effect. An inclusive statement of the general rule has been made in the following language:

It is a general rule of public law, recognized and acted upon by the United States, that whenever political jurisdiction and legislative power over any territory are transferred from one nation or sovereign to another, the municipal laws of the

[188] Dooley vs. United States, 182 U. S., 222; 45 L. Ed., 1074.
[189] Article I, sec. 9, par. 5.
[190] Dooley vs. United States, 183 U. S., 151; 43 L. Ed., 128.
[191] H. W. Halleck, International Law, H. H. Bancroft & Co., San Francisco (1861), pp. 830-833.

Independence and Sovereignty

country, that is, laws which are intended for the protection of private rights, continue in force until abrogated or changed by the new government or sovereign. By the cession, public property passes from one government to the other, but private property remains as before, and with it those municipal laws which are designed to secure its peaceful use and enjoyment. As a matter of course, all laws, ordinances and regulations in conflict with the political character, institutions and contitution of the new government are at once displaced. Thus, upon a cession of political jurisdiction and legislative power—and the latter is involved in the former—to the United States, the laws of the country in support of an established religion, or abridging the freedom of the press, or authorizing cruel and unusual punishments, and the like, would at once cease to be of obligatory force without any declaration to that effect; and the laws of the country on other subjects would necessarily be superseded by existing laws of the new government upon the same matters. But with respect to other laws affecting the possession, use and transfer of property, and designed to secure good order and peace in the community, and promote its health and prosperity, which are strictly of a municipal character, the rule is general, that a change of government leaves them in force until, by direct action of the new government, they are altered or repealed. . . .[192]

Private rights of inhabitants of conquered or ceded territory are usually protected by treaty stipulations, but these rights would be held inviolate, under the law of nations, even in the absence of treaty provisions,[193] and a construction of a treaty, which would be contrary to this principle, will be avoided as far as possible.[194]

[192] Chicago, Rock Island & Pac. Ry. Co. vs. McGlinn, 114 U. S., 542; 29 L. Ed., 270. United States vs. Percheman, 7 Peters, 51; 8 L. Ed., 604.
[193] Strother vs. Lucas, 12 Peters, 410; 9 L. Ed., 1137.
[194] Strother vs. Lucas, *supra*.

Judicial Interpretation of International Law

Thus a treaty by which Spain ceded to the United States in full property and sovereignty in East and West Florida was not construed as affecting the property of individuals.[195] In interpreting rights of inhabitants of transferred territory, and in being guided by international law, usages and customs of the former government, as well as the principles of equity, the courts will not insist upon every legal formality,[196] and whenever necessary to proper adjudication, will take judicial notice of laws in force prior to the cession.[197] However, where stipulations in a treaty exist, they must be observed,[198] so that where a preliminary treaty of the cession of Canada, of November 3, 1762, authorized the sale of all property, movable and immovable, within eighteen months, and a royal proclamation extended complete protection to persons and property of inhabitants who should remain and become British subjects, property of a French citizen, who did not take advantage of the treaty provisions, and did not sell his property, nor become a British subject, remaining on the contrary in French military service, was abandoned to the conqueror.[199]

The term "property," as applied to lands and which the courts will protect by virtue of the principles of international law, includes all species of title, inchoate or complete, and embraces executory as well as executed rights.[200]

---

[195] United States vs. Clarke, 8 Peters, 436; 8 L. Ed., 1001. United States vs. Clarke's Heirs, 16 Peters, 231; 10 L. Ed., 946.
[196] United States vs. Auguisola, 1 Wallace, 352; 17 L. Ed., 613.
[197] United States vs. Chaves, 159 U. S., 452; 40 L. Ed., 215.
[198] Ainsa vs. United States, 161 U. S., 208; 40 L. Ed., 673.
[199] United States vs. Repentigny, 5 Wallace, 211; 18 L. Ed., 627.
[200] Soulard vs. United States, 4 Peters, 511; 7 L. Ed., 938. Smith vs. United States, 10 Peters, 326; 9 L. Ed., 442.

Independence and Sovereignty

While individual rights and private property of inhabitants of transferred territory will be respected, the United States may require reasonable means for the determination of such rights, for instance the validity of titles, and may declare abandoned all claims not presented within a certain time.[201] Although a grant, or concession, made by an officer authorized by law to make it, is considered *prima facie* evidence of the officer's power for the purpose,[202] it is still incumbent upon an applicant for the confirmation of a grant to show the existence, regularity and archive records of the grant and his connection with it, and the evidence must be of sufficient probative force to create a just inference of the validity of his claim,[203] nor is it the duty of a nation to right the wrongs which may have been committed upon individuals prior to the cession unless, perhaps, where there was no opportunity to seek redress before the transfer.[204] Aliens can be divested of title only by legal proceedings, even where the constitution of a state provides that they shall not hold lands except by title directly from the government, especially where the constitution also declares that aliens shall have reasonable time to dispose of the lands in a manner provided by law, and this rule was applied to Mexicans who had remained in Texas, and owned property there, following that state's declaration of independence which by itself could not deprive them of their property.[205] An injunction

[201] Barker vs. Harvey, 181 U. S., 481; 45 L. Ed., 963.
[202] Delassus vs. United States, 9 Peters, 134; 9 L. Ed., 71. United States vs. Arredendo, 9 Peters, 691; 10 L. Ed., 93.
[203] United States vs. Ortiz, 176 U. S., 422; 44 L. Ed., 529.
[204] Cessna vs. United States, 169 U. S., 165; 42 L. Ed., 702.
[205] Airhart vs. Massieu, 98 U. S., 491; 25 L. Ed., 213. Jones vs. McMasters, 20 Howard, 8; 15 L. Ed., 805.

may be invoked to protect possession of owners of lands acquired prior to a treaty of cession.[206]

A corporation has the same rights to hold property following a change of sovereignty as a natural person.[207]

[206] Callsen vs. Hope, 75 Federal Reporter, 758.
[207] Society for the Propagation of the Gospel in Foreign Parts vs. Town of New Haven, *et al.*, 8 Wheaton, 464; 5 L. Ed., 662.

CHAPTER THREE

JURISDICTION OF STATES

§ 15. *Territorial limits of state jurisdiction.*—"All legislation is *prima facie* territorial." As a general rule, and bearing in mind certain exceptions, jurisdiction of states ceases at their boundary line.[1] Boundaries of states consist of arbitrary lines, drawn from one point to another, or of natural features, as rivers, hills or mountains.[2] Since questions of boundaries and problems of jurisdiction of internationally sovereign states must be determined by agreements among these states and are therefore entrusted to the political department of the government, whose decisions the courts must follow,[3] the judiciary seldom is called upon to lay down rules relating to boundaries between such states. In boundary controversies between states of the Union, American courts have, however, applied the rules of international law and thus we possess judicial decisions at least with regard to certain kinds of boundary questions, mostly rivers, forming the boundary between states.

According to Grotius, a river is not to be considered merely as water, "but as water confined in such and such banks, and running in such and such channel. Hence, there is water having a bank and a bed, over which the

---

[1] American Banana Co. vs. United Fruit Co., 231 U. S., 347; 53 L. Ed., 826.
[2] Hall, W. E., A. Treatise on International Law, The Clarendon Press, London & New York (1917), p. 124.
[3] Foster vs. Neilson, 2 Peters, 253; 7 L. Ed., 415.

water flows, called its channel, meaning, by the word 'channel,' the place where the river flows, including the whole breadth of the river." [4] The middle of the main channel of the stream is the true dividing line between independent states, and each state has jurisdiction on its side of the line, where the boundary between them is formed by a navigable river,[5] and in international law the terms "middle of the stream" and "mid-channel" are synonymous.[6] This is the doctrine of the "Thalweg," according to which, where territories are separated by a navigable river, the center of the deepest channel—the Thalweg—is considered the boundary.[7] But where a state makes to another a grant of territory on one side of a river, the river remains within its territory, jurisdiction of the grantee state extends to the river only, and the low water mark is its boundary.[8] A sudden and rapid change of a channel, termed in law avulsion, does not change the boundary line, and in case of such a change the boundary remains in the center of the old channel, although no water may be flowing through it.[9] So in case of changes by accretion, although the area of the owner's possession may vary, the stream still remains the boundary line, and where by virtue of a treaty the middle of a river was made the boundary line between states, and the jurisdiction of one of these states attached as a result to an island in the river, a subsequent turn in the course of the river did not deprive the latter of owner-

[4] Alabama vs. Georgia, 23 Howard, 505; 16 L. Ed., 556.
[5] Iowa vs. Illinois, 147 U. S., 1; 37 L. Ed., 55. Keokuk Hamilton Bridge Co. vs. Illinois, 175 U. S., 626; 43 L. Ed., 1185.
[6] Iowa vs. Illinois, *supra*.
[7] Louisiana vs. Mississippi, 202 U. S., 1; 50 L. Ed., 913.
[8] Handly vs. Anthony, 5 Wheaton, 374; 5 L. Ed., 113.
[9] Jones vs. Soulard, 24 Howard, 41; 16 L. Ed., 604.

ship once so acquired.[10] Obviously, to change boundaries every time certain rivers change their course would result in confusion and uncertainty.

When a river is navigable in fact, it is so regarded in law.[11] This means that a river is navigable when it may be used for commercial transportation, though not necessarily at all times;[12] but the possibility of floating any skiff or canoe does not make a river navigable.[13] That certain rivers are navigable or not are matters of general knowledge and therefore facts of which courts will take judicial notice.[14] A navigable river is a highway common to both nations where it forms the boundary; therefore, where a vessel makes use of such a boundary river to reach territory of the state whose flag it flies, it cannot be subjected to penalties imposed by one of the countries upon vessels entering its territory.[15]

The American Great Lakes possess all the essential characteristics of a sea and the term "high seas" is applicable to them; therefore a defendant, charged with an assault on board a steamer in the Detroit River, was properly tried before the Federal Circuit Court for the Sixth Circuit of the Eastern District of Michigan, that court having jurisdiction within the meaning of a statute enacted for the punishment of certain offences committed "upon the high seas, or in any arm of the sea, or in any

---

[10] Missouri vs. Nebraska, 196 U. S., 23; 49 L. Ed., 372. Nebraska vs. Iowa, 143 U. S., 359; 36 L. Ed., 186. Missouri vs. Kentucky, 11 Wall., 395; 20 L. Ed., 116.
[11] The Daniel Ball, 10 Wall., 557; 19 L. Ed., 999.
[12] The Montello, 20 Wall., 430; 22 L. Ed., 391.
[13] United States vs. Rio Grande Dam & Irrigation Co., 174 U. S., 690; 43 L. Ed., 1136.
[14] United States vs. Rio Grande Dam & Irrigation Co., *supra*.
[15] The Apollon, 9 Wheaton, 362; 6 L. Ed., 111.

river, haven, creek, basin or bay, within the admiralty jurisdiction of the United States, and out of the jurisdiction of any particular state, on board any vessel belonging in whole or part to the United States, or any citizen thereof, . . ." and authorizing trial "in the district where the offender is found or into which he is first brought." [16]

In Great Britain admiralty jurisdiction was confined to tidewater because there were no navigable streams beyond the ebb and flow of the tide, but this rule was manifestly inapplicable to conditions in the United States; hence the rule in this country is that the admiralty and maritime jurisdiction of the Federal Government is not limited to tidewaters, but extends to all bodies of water in fact used for carrying on commerce between different states, or with a foreign nation.[17] In an action brought for goods destroyed by fire in transit from Buffalo to Detroit, under a congressional enactment limiting the liability of shipowners, but containing the provision that the act shall not apply "to any vessel of any description whatsoever used in rivers or inland navigation," it was held that policy and justice alike require application of the limitation of liability to navigation of the Great Lakes as to that of the ocean.[18] But admiralty jurisdiction does not extend to rivers that are merely tributaries to any of the Great Lakes and do not connect any of these.[19] Lands covered by tide waters, and the fresh waters of the Great Lakes within

[16] United States vs. Rodgers, 150 U. S., 249; 37 L. Ed., 1071.
[17] The Propeller Genesee, 12 Howard, 443; 13 L. Ed., 1058.
[18] Moore vs. American Transportation Co., 24 Howard, 1; 16 L. Ed., 674.
[19] United States vs. Rogers, 46 Fed. Rep., 1.

Jurisdiction of States

the limits of the several states, are subject to the right of Congress to regulate navigation for purposes of commerce, but the ownership is that of the respective states.[20] Of course, Congress may by express provision exclude navigation upon the Great Lakes from the terms of a statute establishing regulations for navigation upon the high seas.[21]

It is one of the most familiar rules of international law that the limit of jurisdiction of a state over tidewaters is one marine league from the coast, and that such waters are considered a part of the territory of the sovereign,[22] and bays, sounds and straits, and other arms of the sea, which do not exceed two marine leagues in width at the mouth are within this limit and subject to such jurisdiction.[23] A statute of California fixed the boundaries of the state along the Pacific Ocean at a distance of three English miles from the shore, a marine league. Another statute provided that, where the death of a person is caused by the wrongful act of another, the heirs or personal representatives of the deceased may maintain an action for damages against the person causing the death, and it was held that this statute gives a right of action for wrongful death occurring on the high seas two miles from the shore.[24]

Recent treaties between the United States and a num-

[20] The Illinois Central Co. vs. People of the State of Illinois, 146 U. S., 387; 36 L. Ed., 1018. Shively vs. Bowlby, 152 U. S., 1; 38 L. Ed., 331.
[21] The New York, 175 U. S., 187; 44 L. Ed., 126.
[22] Commonwealth vs. Manchester, 139 U. S., 240; 35 L. Ed., 159. The Ann, Federal Cases, No. 397.
[23] Mahler vs. Norwich & N. Y. Transp. Co., 35 N. Y., 352; Cunard Steamship Co. vs. Mellon, 262 U. S., 100; 67 L. Ed., 894.
[24] *In re* Humboldt Lumber Mfs. Ass., 60 Fed. Rep., 428.

ber of maritime countries have in effect extended the authority of the United States beyond the conventional three-mile limit for the purpose of preventing smuggling of liquor into the United States. In so far as this projection of power depends upon treaty provisions, the problem is not for discussion in this connection. There is authority for the contention, however, that for purposes of preventing violation of its laws a country may act beyond its territorial and three-mile limits, and this position has been taken by the United States Supreme Court on general principles and at a time and in a matter where treaty provisions could not be invoked.[25] The decisions of the courts have not been quite consistent in this respect, and at least in one case, arising under customs regulations, the Supreme Court held invalid the seizure of a foreign vessel beyond territorial waters.[26] The executive department of the government at one time, in protesting against certain Mexican actions, declared an attack on an American vessel to be an international offence because it took place more than three miles from the Mexican coast.[27] The later tendency of the courts has been, however, to sustain seizures beyond territorial limits upon principles of international law.[28] It would seem that governments cannot be deprived of the right to take precautionary measures against con-

[25] Church vs. Hubbart, 2 Cranch, 187; 2 L. Ed., 249. The Apollon, 9 Wheaton, 362; 6 L. Ed., 111. Hudson & Smith vs. Guestier, 6 Cranch, 281, 3 L. Ed., 249.

[26] Rose vs. Himely, 4 Cranch, 242; 2 L. Ed., 608. See also Hudson & Smith vs. Guestier, *supra*.

[27] Woolsey, Lester H., Foreign Relations of the United States (1912), pp. 1289-1297.

[28] Dickinson, Edwin D., The American Journal of International Law, January, 1926, Rum Ship Seizures under the Recent Treaties.

Jurisdiction of States

spiracies entered into on the high seas for the purpose of violating their laws,[29] and where ships flying a foreign flag are concerned, their governments, even in the absence of treaties, probably would not make a complaint even if the territorial limits had been exceeded.[30]

The problem of jurisdiction of courts in case of seizures beyond the three-mile limit has given rise to discussion; but courts cannot decline to assume jurisdiction where it is conferred by clear statutory terms not violative of any constitutional provision.[31] Furthermore, it has been pointed out that the problem of the extent of authority for the seizure of foreign vessels is more properly a question for the political department to determine,[32] and the courts will of course follow such decisions.[33]

§ 16. *Jurisdiction over vessels.*—There being no territorial sovereign on the high seas, a ship at sea is deemed a part of the territory of the nation whose flag it properly flies; the territorial sovereign exercises jurisdiction over her to the same extent as when she is in any domestic port.[34] This principle partakes of the nature of personal

[29] Latham vs. United States, 2 Fed. (2nd), 208.
[30] Westlake, John, International Law, Cambridge University Press (1904), p. 172.
[31] Dickinson, Edwin D., The American Journal of International Law, *supra*.
[32] The Grace and The Ruby, 283 Fed., 475.
[33] The Kodiak, 53 Fed., 126.
[34] Wilson vs. McNamee, 102 U. S., 572; 26 L. Ed., 234. It has been pointed out, however, that the statement that a vessel is deemed to be a part of the territory of the nation whose flag she flies, must be understood as having a figurative, or, at any rate, a qualified meaning. Therefore, a child born on an American merchant vessel of Chinese parents, domiciled in the United States, but citizens of China, is not a citizen of the United States, and the child so born cannot invoke section 1 of article 14 of the Constitution of the United States which provides that "all persons born and naturalized in the United States, and subject to the jurisdiction thereof, are citizens of the United States." It would

sovereignty and has little, if any, application in foreign territorial waters where jurisdiction over her and those on board depends upon the tacit or express consent of the local sovereign.[35] Thus the federal courts did not have jurisdiction of the crime of murder committed on an American ship in a Chinese river which was within the jurisdiction of another sovereign, and this would have been so even if the application of the statute had not been limited to "high seas" only.[36] An indictment for murder is sufficient if as to locality it charges that the offence was committed on board an American vessel on the high seas, within the jurisdiction of the court and within the admiralty jurisdiction of the United States.[37] But to constitute the crime of murder on the high seas, the mortal stroke must be given, and the death occur, on the high seas;[38] therefore, a citizen of another state, or of a foreign country, may be convicted of unjustifiable homicide of a person who dies within the jurisdiction of the state he is brought into as a result of injuries inflicted upon him by the accused on board a foreign merchant vessel upon the high seas.[39] The principle that a vessel on the high seas is deemed, for jurisdictional purposes, to be a part of the territory of her sovereign, does not mean that a "ship has a right to draw round her a line of jurisdiction within which no other is at liberty to intrude";

seem that the rule of international law, relating to jurisdiction over vessels, really is one of expediency. But for the rule there would be uncertainty, for instance, as to jurisdiction over crimes committed on the high seas. See Lam Mow vs. Nagle, 24 F. (2d), 316.

[35] Cunard Steamship Co. vs. Mellon, 262 U. S., 100; 67 L. Ed., 894.
[36] United States vs. Wiltberger, 5 Wheaton, 76; 5 L. Ed., 37.
[37] St. Clair vs. United States, 154 U. S., 134; 38 L. Ed., 936. Anderson vs. United States, 170 U. S., 481; 42 L. Ed., 1116.
[38] United States vs. McGill, 4 Dallas, 426; 1 L. Ed., 894.
[39] Commonwealth vs. MacLoon, 101 Mass., 1.

she has a right to "use so much of the ocean she occupies, and as is essential to her movements," but beyond this she has no exclusive rights.[40]

§ 17. *Legal effects of territorial supremacy.*—In investigating the concept of sovereignty as expounded by the judiciary we have seen that the jurisdiction of each state within its own territory is exclusive and absolute and that any restriction, imposed upon it from external sources and without the state's consent, would be in derogation of sovereignty.[41] Briefly, the territorial sovereign is supreme within his jurisdiction. It may not be amiss to point out in this connection, however, that the very nature of international law, as it is now almost universally understood, presupposes national supremacy. International law is the law of states and for states, and did it operate directly upon individuals, it would partake of the nature of public law and cease to be international law.[42] What, more than anything else, makes the Federal Union a sovereign state is the very fact that federal laws operate directly upon individuals.[43] But as has been said in a case already referred to several times, now one of the classics of American jurisprudence, "a nation would justly be considered as violating its faith, although that faith might not be expressly plighted, which should suddenly and without previous notice, exercise its territorial powers in a manner not consonant to the usages and received obligations of the civilized world." [44]

[40] The Marianna Flora, 11 Wheaton, 1; 6 L. Ed., 405.
[41] *Supra,* Chapter I, sec. 8. See also Chapter I, sections 4 and 5.
[42] Holland, Thomas Erskine, The Elements of Jurisprudence, Oxford University Press (1910), p. 125.
[43] Corwin, Edward S., National Supremacy, Henry Holt & Co. (1913), New York City.
[44] The Exchange vs. McFaddon, 7 Cranch, 116; 3 L. Ed., 287.

Judicial Interpretation of International Law

It now remains to present some of the effects of national supremacy.

It is of course elementary that all persons residing within a certain territory do so subject to the laws of the territorial sovereign. Citizens of one state who commit offenses within the boundary lines of another state may be prosecuted and punished according to the laws of the latter.[45] The legislative power of every state extends also to all property within its borders, and property situated within the boundaries of one state can be affected by the laws of another state only in so far as comity permits.[46] The converse of this proposition is equally well established and elementary. The municipal laws of a state do not operate beyond its own territory, and no matter how general the language of a statute may be, courts will not construe its provisions to give them extraterritorial effect except as the object may properly be to control the state's citizens residing beyond its boundaries.[47] The courts of one country do not execute the penal laws of another country;[48] penal laws are those imposing a punishment for offenses against the state, and a court will determine for itself whether a law is penal or not.[49] Therefore, too, injured parties could not require the United States to make compensation for property taken on Mexican soil by Indians, or to make restitution thereof, although this property was brought into the United States by Indians having tribal relations

---

[45] McDonald vs. State, 80 Wis., 407; 50 N. W., 185.
[46] Pullman's Palace Car Co. vs. Pennsylvania, 141 U. S., 18; 35 L. Ed., 613. The Antelope, 10 Wheaton, 66; 6 L. Ed., 268.
[47] The Apollon, 9 Wheaton, 362; 6 L. Ed., 111.
[48] The Antelope, *supra*.
[49] Huntington vs. Attrill, 146 U. S., 657; 36 L. Ed., 1123.

Jurisdiction of States

with the Federal Government.[50] Because of this principle, when an American citizen violates the laws of another country, he must submit to such procedure and such punishment as the laws of that country prescribe unless treaty agreements provide otherwise.[51] It is to be remembered, too, that laws enacted by Congress to carry out provisions of treaties granting extraterritorial rights are not unconstitutional even if they do not require an indictment by a grand jury, or secure to the alleged offender jury trial.[52] Statutes providing for property succession of nonresident foreigners confer a right to be enjoyed within the state and are not objectionable as having an extraterritorial operation.[53]

Without entering upon a discussion of the whole question of transitory actions, and the tribunals before which such actions can be brought, it may be pointed out that the Supreme Court has declared that "torts originating within the waters of a foreign power may be the subject of a suit in a domestic court."[54] Admiralty courts of the United States have the discretion to assume jurisdiction over a collision on the high seas between two foreign vessels and where the controversy arises under the law of nations should do so; but such jurisdiction may be declined where it appears that justice can be as well rendered by referring the controversy to the ships'

[50] Corralitos Stock Co. vs. United States and Apache Indians, 33 Ct. Cl., 342; 178 U. S., 280; 44 L. Ed., 1069.
[51] Neely vs. Henkel, 180 U. S., 109; 45 L. Ed., 448.
[52] *In re* Ross, 140 U. S., 453; 35 L. Ed., 581. *Infra,* sec. 19, Extraterritorial jurisdiction.
[53] State vs. Smith, 70 Cal., 153; 12 Pac., 121. Blythe vs. Hinckley, 127 Cal., 153; 59 Pac., 787.
[54] Panama Railroad Co. vs. Napier Shipping Co., 166 U. S., 280; 41 L. Ed., 1004.

domestic tribunal.[55] Where the court assumes jurisdiction, general maritime law should be applied,[56] and maritime law cannot be abrogated as a matter of authority by local decisions of a state court.[57] Where a vessel is libeled for wages, admiralty courts as a matter of comity will administer the law of the country whose flag the vessel flies, the seamen having subjected themselves to this law by accepting service on such vessel.[58]

Respect for tribunals of other jurisdictions and their sovereignty, as well as the necessity of preventing recurrence of litigation between the same parties and in regard to the same subject matter, requires that full faith and credit be given to foreign judgments. It is therefore the general rule that a superior court of general jurisdiction, acting within the scope of its powers, is presumed to have jurisdiction to give the judgment it has rendered until the contrary is shown, and this presumption applies to the parties as well as the subject matter.[59] The courts of every country are exclusive judges of their own jurisdiction so far as it depends upon their country's municipal laws.[60] It has been said that where a court, in a condemnation case, has assumed jurisdiction, and it appears that this was done contrary to the law of nations, its decision will be disregarded;[61] but later it was held that "if jurisdiction be at all permitted . . . the court exercising it must necessarily decide, and that ultimately, or subject only to review of a superior

[55] The Belgenland, 114 U. S., 355; 29 L. Ed., 152.
[56] The Noddleburn, 28 Fed. Rep., 855.
[57] Workman vs. New York City, *et al.*, 179 U. S., 552; 45 L. Ed., 314.
[58] The Belvidere, 90 Fed. Rep., 106.
[59] Galpin vs. Page, 18 Wallace, 350; 21 L. Ed., 959.
[60] Rose vs. Himely, 4 Cranch, 241; 2 L. Ed., 608.
[61] Rose vs. Himely, *supra*.

Jurisdiction of States

tribunal of its own state, whether, in the particular case, she had jurisdiction, if any objection be made to it."[62] Where defendant appeared in a foreign court by counsel, and later attacked a judgment rendered on the ground that it was given in his absence and without his knowledge, but did not allege the attorneys' appearance was unauthorized, the judgment, in the absence of fraud, will be held conclusive.[63] Nevertheless, where a foreign judgment results from application of principles inconsistent with the public policy of the jurisdiction where action is brought upon it, enforcement cannot be had.[64] Also, the Supreme Court has applied to foreign judgments the principle of reciprocity, ruling that a French judgment is no more than *prima facie* evidence of the justice of the plaintiff's case and not conclusive upon the merits, since that is the rule applied to foreign judgments in France.[65] The decision was not only by a divided court, however, but furnishes cause for surprise for the reason that earlier in its history the court took the position that it will enforce the law of nations unless Congress shows by positive legislation that it desires otherwise. It is true that the latter decision did not involve a foreign judgment, but it did raise the question of reciprocity, and the Supreme Court refused to invoke a rule supposedly applied by Spain unless legislation to that effect was adopted by Congress.[66]

Stability of social institutions requires that marriages valid according to the laws of the country where they are

---

[62] Hudson & Smith vs. Guestier, 6 Cranch, 281; 3 L. Ed., 249.
[63] Ritchie vs. Mullen, 159 U. S., 235; 40 L. Ed., 133.
[64] Hohner vs. Gratz, 50 Fed. Rep., 369.
[65] Hilton vs. Guyot, 159 U. S., 113; 40 L. Ed., 95.
[66] The Nereide, 9 Cranch, 388; 3 L. Ed., 769.

Judicial Interpretation of International Law

celebrated be recognized as binding in other countries, and that is the general rule.[67] But if parties go on the high seas, where, strictly speaking, no territorial law can be said to exist, and are married there by the captain in deliberate avoidance of the laws of the state wherein they are domiciled, and immediately after the ceremony return to that state and continue to reside there, the laws of the domicile apply to the marriage.[68]

Passage of troops through the territory of a foreign sovereign is rare in modern times and is not favored by international law, and can legally take place only with the consent of the territorial sovereign.[69] It furnishes one of the cases in which a sovereign waives a portion of his territorial jurisdiction; the results of such waiver have been thus stated:

> In such case, without any express declaration waiving jurisdiction over the army to which this right of passage has been granted, the sovereign who should attempt to exercise it would certainly be considered as violating his faith. By exercising it, the purpose for which the free passage was granted would be defeated, and a portion of the military force of a foreign independent nation would be diverted from those national objects and duties to which it was applicable, and would be withdrawn from the control of the sovereign whose power and whose safety might greatly depend on retaining the exclusive command and disposition of this force. The grant of a free passage, therefore, implies a waiver of all jurisdiction over the troops during their passage, and permits the foreign general to use that discipline, and to inflict those punishments which the government of his army may require.[70]

[67] Earl, *et al.* vs. Godley, 42 Minn., 36; 44 N. W., 254.
[68] Norman vs. Norman (Cal.), 54 Pac., 143.
[69] Davis, George B., Elements of International Law, Harper & Bros., New York and London (1908), p. 85.
[70] The Exchange vs. McFaddon, *et al.*, 7 Cranch, 116; 3 L. Ed., 287.

Jurisdiction of States

Seizure of an American merchant vessel in foreign territorial waters by naval forces of the United States, for infringement of American law, has been declared an offence against the territorial sovereign, but one which cannot be taken cognizance of by the court and is only susceptible of adjustment between the respective governments.[71] Where seamen desert from foreign ships of war in American harbors they cannot be surrendered by United States authorities in the absence of a treaty to this effect.[72]

The exclusive nature of territorial jurisdiction finds further illustration in the rule emphatically laid down by courts of the United States to the effect that under international law merchant vessels of one country visiting the ports of another subject themselves to the laws governing the ports they visit.[73] It is true that experience has given rise to a rule of comity by virtue of which local authorities abstain from interfering with internal discipline of foreign vessels, but this rule does not extend to crimes disturbing the peace and tranquillity of the port,[74] and even the implied consent of the government to leave matters of internal discipline to the ship's authorities may be withdrawn.[75]

One country, however, cannot allow its territory to be used as a field of operations for the violation of the laws of another country. "A right secured by the law of nations to a nation, or its people, is one the United States as the representatives of this nation are bound to pro-

[71] Ship Richmond, 9 Cranch, 102; 3 L. Ed., 670.
[72] Tucker vs. Alexandroff, 183 U. S., 424; 46 L. Ed., 264.
[73] United States vs. Diekelman, 92 U. S., 520; 23 L. Ed., 742.
[74] Wildenhus' Case, 120 U. S., 1; 30 L. Ed., 565.
[75] Strathearn S. S. Co., Limited vs. Dillon, 252 U. S., 348; 64 L. Ed., 607.

tect." Therefore, counterfeiting of foreign currency is properly punished by federal laws in performance of the Government's international duty.[76]

§ 18. *Exemptions from territorial jurisdiction.*—One of the consequences of the legal equality of states may be observed in exemptions from territorial jurisdiction which have been established with regard to sovereigns. The person of a sovereign is exempt from arrest, detention or suit in foreign territory, and it may be added that under modern conditions the term *sovereign* undoubtedly would include all chiefs of state, whether monarchs or presidents. The exemption is based upon mutual consent, and the reasons therefor have been stated in the following language:

Why has the whole civilized world concurred in this construction? The answer cannot be mistaken. A foreign sovereign is not understood as intending to subject himself to a jurisdiction incompatible with his dignity and the dignity of his nation, and it is to avoid this subjection that the license has been obtained. The character to whom it is given, and the object for which it is granted, equally require that it should be construed to impart full security to the person who has obtained it. This security, however, need not be expressed; it is implied from the circumstances of the case. Should one sovereign enter the territory of another, without the consent of that other, express or implied, it would present a question which does not appear to be perfectly settled, a decision of which is not necessary to any conclusion to which the court may come in the cause under consideration. If he did not thereby expose himself to the territorial jurisdiction of the sovereign, whose dominions he had entered, it would seem to be because all sovereigns impliedly engage not to avail themselves of a power over their equal, which a romantic confidence in their magnanimity has placed in their hands.[77]

[76] United States vs. Arjona, 120 U. S., 479; 30 L. Ed., 728.
[77] The Exchange vs. McFaddon, et al., 7 Cranch, 116; 3 L. Ed., 287.

Jurisdiction of States

While a foreign sovereign, or government, is not subject to the courts of another country,[78] this immunity may be waived, and is considered to have been waived, when the sovereign enters litigation with a general appearance,[79] and this waiver is only emphasized when he has acted, during the litigation, in a manner consistent with a general appearance even if later, during the course of the controversy, a change of attitude has been attempted.[80] But the bringing of an action by a foreign sovereign in the courts of the United States is not a waiver of immunity and an affirmative judgment cannot be rendered against it, but it is subject to any set-off or counterclaim which may be pleaded as a defense to its claim in whole or in part.[81] Also, the appearance of a sovereign in a foreign court is made subject to the substantive law and procedure governing that court.[82] But a statute making final the decree of a Circuit Court of Appeals "in all cases where the jurisdiction is dependent entirely upon the opposite parties to the suit being aliens and citizens of the United States or citizens of different states" did not operate to exclude a foreign sovereign power from its right of appeal to the United States Supreme Court, for there is a distinction between foreign states and foreign citizens and Congress did not intend to prevent a foreign sovereign from exhausting all pos-

[78] See Chapter Two, section 11, Kinds of governments and their powers.
[79] The Sao Vincente, 260 U. S., 151; 67 L. Ed., 179. See also Beers vs. Arkansas, 20 Howard, 527; 15 L. Ed., 991.
[80] The Sao Vincente, 295 Fed. Rep., 829.
[81] French Republic vs. Inland Navigation Co., 263 Fed. Rep., 410. See also United States vs. Eckford, 6 Wallace, 484; 18 L. Ed., 920. A government which becomes a party in a trading company deprives itself, however, of its sovereign character and assumes that of a private citizen. Roumania vs. Guaranty Trust Co., 250 Fed. Rep., 341.
[82] The Jane Palmer, 270 Fed. Rep., 609.

sible remedies once he chooses to appear in the courts of the United States.[83]

The doctrine of immunity of sovereigns from suit applies to all proceedings against public property. Therefore, a damage action could not be maintained in an American state court against a Canadian railway which was government property and operated by the government;[84] and an attachment of a sovereign's property cannot be sustained, for that is one mode of compelling appearance.[85] A foreign government may appear in an admiralty court for the purpose of claiming a libeled vessel and raising the question of want of jurisdiction because of its control of the vessel, but the question should primarily be determined through diplomatic channels, so that the State Department, if it recognizes the claim, may make the necessary representations to the court by the Attorney General, or some other proper law officer acting under his direction.[86] Indeed, where a suggestion that a libeled vessel is owned by a foreign government is made by the ambassador of that country directly to the court, and not through the official chan-

[83] Colombia vs. Cauca Co., 190 U. S., 524; 47 L. Ed., 1159.

[84] Mason vs. Intercolonial Railway of Canada & Trustees, 197 Mass. 349. Whether or not the ship of a foreign government used and operated by it as a merchant vessel is, when within the waters of the United States, immune from arrest in admiralty, was declared to be an "important and new" problem and the proper solution "not plain but debatable" as late as June 6, 1921. Re Hussein Lufti Bey, 256 U. S., 619; 65 L. Ed., 1122. Since then it has been held, however, that the rule of immunity for public vessels, announced in The Exchange vs. McFaddon, does not exclude merchant ships held and used by a government. The court said: "We know of no international usage which regards the maintenance and advancement of the economic welfare of a people as any less a public purpose than the maintenance of a naval force." Berizzi Brothers Co. vs. Steamship Pesaro, 271 U. S., 562; 70 L. Ed., 1088.

[85] Nathan vs. Virginia, 1 Dallas, 77; 1 L. Ed., 44.

[86] Ex Parte Muir, 254 U. S., 522; 65 L. Ed., 383.

Jurisdiction of States

nels of the American Government, it cannot be entertained.[87] Where it properly appears that a foreign government has sanctioned the requisition of a vessel, the sanction of that government is conclusive upon the courts of this country as to the legality of such requisition.[88] A vessel is not protected against seizure, however, when at the time of the libel she was under charter to a foreign government, but not in its possession.[89]

Foreign ambassadors and ministers, and other representatives of their sovereigns and governments, duly accredited and recognized in their diplomatic capacity, are equally immune from arrest, detention, suit or process of any kind.[90] Indeed, this immunity is not a personal privilege of diplomatic representatives, but one of their country and government, and may therefore be waived only with the consent of the sovereign;[91] failure to plead it in a lower court is not a waiver and it may be raised in the appellate court when the case is taken there by a writ of error.[92] But while the immunity of a diplomatic representative may not be waived, it can be forfeited to the extent that a minister, or other accredited official of a foreign country, becomes an aggressor, in which case the person attacked has the right to defend himself as he may against any other assailant.[93]

Under the laws of the United States every person who

[87] The Pesaro, 255 U. S., 46; 65 L. Ed., 592. Societa Commerciale Italiana di Navigazioni vs. Maru Nav. Co., 280 Fed. Rep., 334.
[88] Gans S. S. Line vs. Isles Steamship Co., 257 U. S., 662; 66 L. Ed., 423.
[89] The Beaverton, 273 Fed. Rep., 539.
[90] United States vs. Benner, *et al.*, Fed. Cases No. 14,568.
[91] United States vs. Benner, *supra*.
[92] Davis vs. Packard, 7 Peters, 276; 8 L. Ed., 684. Stowell Consular Cases, 753.
[93] United States vs. Ortega, Federal Cases, 15,971. United States vs. Liddle, Federal Cases, 15,598.

"violates any safe conduct or passport duly obtained and issued under authority of the United States," or who "assaults, strikes, wounds, imprisons, or in any other manner offers violence to the person of a public minister, in violation of the law of nations, shall be imprisoned for not more than three years, and fined at the discretion of the court"; and another provision declares any judicial process whereby "the person of any public minister of any foreign prince or state authorized and received as such by the President, or any domestic or any domestic servant of any such minister, is arrested or imprisoned, or his goods or chattels are distrained, seized or attached" is void.[94]

This legislation by Congress is proper pursuant to the constitutional provision giving that body power "to define and punish . . . offences against the Law of Nations," [95] and is obligatory upon the state courts whose duty it is to quash proceedings against any one having diplomatic privileges.[96] But an indictment for an infraction of the law of nations, by an assault upon a foreign minister, is a public prosecution and therefore is not a case "affecting ambassadors, other public ministers and consuls." [97] Upon such indictment, proof that the person attacked is recognized by the Executive of the United States is conclusive as to his character, and the fact that the defendant did not have knowledge of this character is not a defense to the charge.[98] Where a person claiming a diplomatic character is refused free entry of goods

[94] Revised Statutes, sections 4062 and 4063.
[95] Constitution of the United States, Art. I., sec. 8, subd. 10.
[96] Ex parte Cabrera, Federal Cases, 2,278.
[97] United States vs. Ortega, 11 Wheaton, 467; 6 L. Ed., 521.
[98] United States vs. Ortega, Federal Cases, No. 15, 971.

Jurisdiction of States

usually accorded such persons, and where his own government had requested his resignation prior to the indictment, although it was given thereafter, the claim of exemption cannot be sustained.[99]

The immunities of a minister apply also to his house,[100] for international law identifies the property of a foreign minister with his person;[101] but while in the case of an assault upon the person of a minister lack of knowledge of his public character is no defense,[102] it has been said that, when the house of a minister is attacked, to constitute an offence against a foreign minister the defendant must have known that the home was a minister's domicile; otherwise the offence is merely one against the municipal laws of the state.[103] It was a breach of diplomatic privileges to enter the house of a diplomatic official and seize there a runaway slave.[104]

Diplomatic privileges attach to officials even after the conclusion of their duties and while they are awaiting accommodations to return to their country.[105]

Secretaries of legations enjoy the same immunities as their chiefs,[106] and it is safe to say that diplomatic privileges attach to all duly accredited officials of legations and embassies recognized by the Department of State. A foreign minister passing through this country on his way to his station is exempt from service of process in a

[99] Ex Parte Hitz, 111 U. S., 766; 28 L. Ed., 592.
[100] Respublica vs. De Longchamps, 1 Dallas, 111; 1 L. Ed., 59.
[101] United States vs. Hand, Federal Cases, No. 15,297.
[102] United States vs. Ortega, Federal Cases, No. 15,971.
[103] United States vs. Hand, *supra*.
[104] United States vs. Jeffers, Federal Cases, No. 15,471.
[105] Dupont vs. Pichon, 4 Dallas, 321; 1 L. Ed., 851.
[106] Respublica vs. DeLongchamps, *supra*. Ex parte Cabrera, Federal Cases, No. 2,278.

Judicial Interpretation of International Law

civil suit.[107] It has been said that servants of a minister are not liable for misdemeanors.[108]

Consuls are supposed to be clothed with authority for commercial purposes and are not diplomatic officials;[109] therefore, they are subject to local law in the same manner and to the same extent as other foreign residents.[110] A trading consul is liable in the same way as a domestic merchant,[111] and criminal laws and criminal procedure apply to consuls as they do to all other residents within the local sovereign's jurisdiction.[112] Whatever exemptions consuls enjoy, can be conferred upon them only by treaty.[113] But when a foreign consul enters into obligations on behalf of his government, he is not personally liable,[114] and foreign consuls have the right to institute proceedings where the rights of property of their fellow citizens are involved, and indeed it is their duty to watch over the interests of their citizens.[115] Of course, a sovereign may entrust a consul with diplomatic functions, but in that case these are simply added to his existing duties and must be recognized by the government of the country within which the official is to exercise his additional functions.[116]

[107] Wilson vs. Blanco, 4 N. Y., Supp., 714.
[108] United States vs. LaFontaine, Federal Cases, No. 15,580.
[109] The Anne, 3 Wheaton, 435; 4 L. Ed., 428.
[110] Cappell vs. Hall, 7 Wall., 542; 19 L. Ed., 244. *In re* Baiz, 135 U. S., 403; 34 L. Ed., 222. U. S. vs. Ravara, 2 Dallas, 297; 1 L. Ed., 222.
[111] Cappell vs. Hall, *supra*.
[112] United States vs. Trumbull, 48 Fed. Rep., 94.
[113] *In re* Dillon, Federal Cases, No. 3,914. United States vs. Trumbull, *supra*. See also American Treaty Provisions relating to consular Privileges and Immunities, by Irvin Stewart, American Journal of International Law, January, 1926.
[114] Jones vs. LeTombe, 3 Dallas, 384; 1 L. Ed., 647.
[115] The Bello Corrunes, 6 Wheaton, 152; 5 L. Ed., 229.
[116] The Anne, *supra*.

Jurisdiction of States

We have ascertained that private vessels entering a foreign port are subject to the jurisdiction of the territorial sovereign.[117] The rule as to ships of war, entering the port of a friendly power open to their reception, is different, even in the absence of express consent or a treaty, and such vessels are considered as exempt from local jurisdiction.[118] A war vessel being built in a foreign shipyard is from the beginning of its construction the property of the contracting government and becomes a ship from the moment it is launched.[119] If, however, a foreign public vessel brings into port a prize obtained as a result of violation of the laws of the local sovereign, the prize will be restored to the original owner,[120] and United States courts have jurisdiction for that purpose.[121]

As we have already seen, foreign troops entering or passing through territory with consent of the local sovereign are exempt from territorial jurisdiction.[122]

Closely akin to, though not identical with, the question of exemption from territorial jurisdiction is the problem of right of asylum in embassies and legations and on public and merchant vessels. In the very nature of the case, asylum presupposes the use of a building, or vessel, as a refuge from pursuit, and if we look at the matter from this point of view, no adjudicated American cases have been found setting forth and applying the rules of international law as to the right of asylum. The

---

[117] *Supra*, section 17, Legal effects of territorial supremacy.
[118] The Exchange vs. McFaddon, *et al.*, 7 Cranch, 116; 3 L. Ed., 287.
[119] Tucker vs. Alexandroff, 183 U. S., 424; 46 L. Ed., 264.
[120] The Gran Para, 7 Wheaton, 471; 5 L. Ed., 501. Talbot vs. Janson, 3 Dallas, 133; 1 L. Ed., 540.
[121] The Alberta vs. Moran, 9 Cranch, 359; 3 L. Ed., 758.
[122] *Supra*, sec. 17, Legal effects of territorial supremacy. Tucker vs. Alexandroff, 183 U. S., 424; 46 L. Ed., 264.

case of a dismissal of a constable for invading the premises of a secretary of a legation and seizing a fugitive slave does not aid in clarifying the question whether an asylum could have been granted and insisted upon by the diplomatic official;[123] where a crime is committed on board a merchant vessel and the local authorities assert the right to arrest and try the offender, the question is one of jurisdiction and not of asylum;[124] and a case of a ship detained by military authorities for failure to comply with regulations governing goods on board is obviously not one of asylum.[125]

The fact, of course, is that the right of asylum is of a nature not likely to arise in a judicial proceeding in the United States, and that one seeking information on this problem must examine the practice of states in this respect. In any event the question is one of importance only with regard to political refugees, since asylum to ordinary criminals certainly will not be granted. It is to be noted that the American Government has not looked with favor upon the practice of extraterritorial asylum.[126]

§ 19. *Extraterritorial jurisdiction.*—Extraterritoriality has been defined as "that condition by which a state, usually by virtue of a treaty, extends its jurisdiction beyond its own boundaries into the territory of another state and exercises the same over its nationals who, for the time being, may be sojourning within the territory of the other state."[127] It is probably more accurate to

---

[123] United States vs. Jeffers, Federal Cases, No. 15,471.
[124] Wildenhus' Case, 120 U. S. 1, 30 L. Ed., 565.
[125] United States vs. Diekelman, 92 U. S., 520; 23 L. Ed., 742.
[126] Snow, Freeman, Cases on International Law, The Boston Book Co. (1893), p. 142.
[127] *In re* Young John Allen's Will, Lobingier's Extraterritorial Cases, p. 92, Manila, Bureau of Printing (1920).

say that in modern times extraterritorial jurisdiction depends on treaty stipulations and the laws of the nations concerned.[128] Unless the right is conceded by clear agreement, no state can exercise judicial powers within the territory of another state.[129] The object of treaties conceding extraterritorial rights has been to obtain for the citizens of certain countries the benefits of their own criminal laws and procedure and yet to provide for their punishment for violation of any law of their own country;[130] but this does not mean that the jurisdiction of extraterritorial courts is, or has been, necessarily purely criminal. The law applied in these courts is usually that of the forum, i.e., that of the defendant's nationality,[131] and the jurisdiction of such tribunals includes the power to make effective whatever punishment the court has determined upon, to fix the place of its expiation outside of the extraterritorial jurisdiction, to control a prisoner while *en route* there, and to prevent all interference with this control.[132]

Congress having made applicable to Americans in China laws of the United States, the white slave traffic act, for instance, has been held operative in that jurisdiction;[133] but since by the Constitution a government is ordained "for the United States of America" and not for countries outside of its limits, constitutional guar-

[128] Dainese vs. Hale, 91 U. S., 13; 23 L. Ed., 190. *In re* Aubrey, 26 Federal Reporter, 848.
[129] *In re* Ross, 140 U. S., 453; 35 L. Ed., 581. United States vs. Smiley, *et al.*, Federal Cases, No. 16,317.
[130] Bibble vs. United States, Lobingier's Extraterritorial Cases, p. 120.
[131] Shekury vs. Brooks, Lobingier's Extraterritorial Cases, p. 225.
[132] United States vs. Kilgore, Lobingier's Extraterritorial Cases, p. 395.
[133] United States vs. Thompson, Lobingier's Extraterritorial Cases, p. 261.

Judicial Interpretation of International Law

anties, such as trial by jury, upon indictment or presentment by a grand jury, are not secured to American citizens residing abroad, and whatever rights or privileges they obtain, both as to substantive law and procedure, depend entirely upon the agreement between the two countries and upon legislation adopted pursuant to these agreements.[134]

Extraterritorial courts are courts of record and their judgments may be enforced in the United States at any time within the period fixed by the statute of limitations.[135] The court in China, founded and organized under a treaty with that country, has been declared to be "a separate, distinct and complete jurisdiction, similar to that of one of the unorganized territories of the United States."[136] An American citizen may acquire what has been termed an extraterritorial domicile in China, and in administering his estate the court will apply the law in force in China, as extended by Congress to American citizens residing in that country, and not the law of the state from which the decedent migrated to the Far East.[137]

The rule that one country does not enforce the penal laws of another country[138] is so firmly adhered to that United States courts have declined to entertain all suits of foreign states except those of a strictly civil nature, and therefore have even refused to enforce judgments for

[134] *In re* Ross, 140 U. S., 453; 35 L. Ed., 581.
[135] Newman vs. Basch, 152 N. Y., 456; Lobingier's Extraterritorial Cases, p. 469.
[136] Cunningham vs. Rogers, 1 Lobingier's Extraterritorial Cases, p. 109.
[137] *In re* Young John Allen's Will, Lobingier's Extraterritorial Cases, p. 92.
[138] See sec. 17, *supra*. Legal effects of territorial supremacy.

Jurisdiction of States

pecuniary penalties for violation of revenue laws, or other municipal laws.[139] Conviction of an infamous crime in one state does not prevent an individual from testifying in the courts of another state. "A sentence attacking the honor, rights or property of a criminal, cannot extend beyond the limits of the sovereign who pronounces it."[140] All this does not mean, however, that a state may not try and punish offences against its laws by its citizens because they have been committed outside of its territorial limits. The Texas Penal Code provides that "persons out of the state may commit and be liable to indictment and conviction for committing any of the offences enumerated in this chapter, which do not necessarily require a personal presence in this state, the object of this chapter being to reach and punish all persons offending against its provisions whether within or without the state." The Texas courts, in giving effect to this provision, declared that "although the penal laws of every country are in their nature local, yet an offence may be committed in one sovereignty in violation of the laws of another, and if the offender be afterwards found in the latter state, he may be punished according to the laws thereof, and the fact that he owes allegiance to another sovereignty is no bar to the indictment."[141] Under the statutes of Massachusetts a person may be convicted of subornation of perjury through the agency of another guilty party employed without the limits of the state.[142]

[139] Wisconsin vs. Pelican Insurance Co., 127 U. S., 289; 32 L. Ed., 239.
[140] Commonwealth vs. Green, 17 Mass., 514.
[141] Hanks vs. The State, 13 Texas Court of Appeals, 289.
[142] Commonwealth vs. Smith, 11 Allen, 243. In a recent case it was held by the United States Supreme Court that where prisoners had

Jurisdiction on the high seas, being beyond the territorial limits of states, may properly be considered in this connection. It is of a very limited nature. In times of peace the freedom of the seas is unquestioned. The sea is the "common highway of all; and no one can vindicate to himself a superior or exclusive prerogative there. Every ship sails there with the unquestionable right of pursuing her own lawful business without interruption; but, whatever may be that business, she is bound to pursue it in such manner as not to violate the rights of others." In times of peace public vessels of one nation cannot exercise the right of visitation and search of vessels of other nations, this being a strictly belligerent right.[143] The problem of maintaining law and order on ships on the high seas has been solved by the rule that a ship at sea is considered to be a part of the territory of the nation whose flag it properly flies.[144] The question of jurisdiction of maritime torts has been settled by a decision to the effect that in cases of collision on the high seas between vessels flying different flags the matter is a proper subject of inquiry in any court of admiralty which first obtains jurisdiction, and that in such cases United States courts should assume jurisdiction unless special reasons to the contrary appear.[145]

Piracy, which is ordinarily defined as robbery on the high seas, is an offence within the jurisdiction of all nations; it is an international crime "against all and

been guilty of acts outside the United States, but the results of which took effect in the United States, the federal laws thus violated applied. See opinion of Mr. Chief Justice Taff in Ford v. United States, 273 U. S., 593; 71 L. Ed., 793.

[143] The Marianna Flora, 11 Wheaton, 1; 6 L. Ed., 405.
[144] See section 16, Jurisdiction over vessels, *supra*.
[145] The Belgenland, 144 U. S., 355; 29 L. Ed., 152.

Jurisdiction of States

punished by all."[146] At one time there was a certain amount of confusion between the crime of piracy as attempted to be defined by municipal law and as defined by international law, but the situation has been simplified by a federal enactment to the effect that "Whoever, on the high seas, commits the crime of piracy as defined by the law of nations, and is afterwards brought into or found in the United States, shall be imprisoned for life."[147] Congress has the right to enact legislation for the punishment of pirates regardless of their nationality,[148] and a definition of piracy by reference to the law of nations meets the constitutional requirements.[149]

During the World War the question of right to arm merchantmen obtained a degree of importance.[150] International law does not prohibit the arming of neutral vessels for defensive purposes,[151] and during the Eighteenth Century the practice was general as a matter of protection against pirates.[152]

§ 20. *Extradition.*—Extradition has been succinctly defined as "the surrender of one state to another of an individual who is found within the territory of the former, and is accused of having committed a crime within the territory of the latter."[153] The problem of regula-

[146] U. S. vs. Pirates, 5 Wheaton, 184; 5 L. Ed., 64.
[147] Federal Criminal Code, sec. 290.
[148] United States vs. Palmer, 3 Wheaton, 610; 4 L. Ed., 47.
[149] United States vs. Smith, 5 Wheaton, 153; 5 L. Ed., 57. As to whether or not the crime of piracy has become obsolete, see article by E. D. Dickinson, Harvard Law Review, January, 1925; see further *supra,* sec. 4, Chapter I, Federal Legislation and International Law.
[150] Garner, J. W., Recent Developments in International Law, University of Calcutta (1925), p. 345.
[151] Hooper vs. U. S., 22 Ct. Cl., 408.
[152] Cushing vs. U. S., 22 Ct. Cl., 1.
[153] Lawrence, T. J., The Principles of International Law, Macmillan & Co., London & New York (1895), par. 132.

Judicial Interpretation of International Law

tion of surrender of accused persons to foreign governments is so obviously a phase of international intercourse that it is now difficult to realize that the exclusive power of the federal government in this respect has ever been doubted.[154] It now seems firmly settled that state laws providing for surrender of foreign fugitives from justice cannot be constitutionally adopted and enforced,[155] and that even in the absence of treaties, or acts of Congress, extradition of such individuals is a matter for the Federal Government. [156] Extradition of criminals is not, however, a duty imposed by international law, although it has been practiced often enough upon the principles of comity apart from treaties,[157] largely by states with legal systems under which personal liberty is not so carefully protected as in the United States and Great Britain.[158]

It has been declared even in the United States that there may be a surrender of a fugitive by a nation in the exercise of its discretion to do so and that the existence of a treaty providing for extradition for certain crimes does not deprive either nation from surrendering criminals in cases not coming within the terms of the treaty; but it is to be noted that in the case in question the delivery was made by authorities of a foreign country (Hawaii) for trial in a state of the Union, and that had it been a question of extradition from the United States, the fugitive undoubtedly, in the end, could have been surrendered by

[154] Holmes vs. Jannison, 14 Peters, 540; 10 L. Ed., 579.
[155] People vs. Curtis, 50 N. Y., 321.
[156] United States vs. Rauscher, 119 U. S., 407; 30 L. Ed., 425.
[157] United States vs. Rauscher, *supra*.
[158] Davis, George B., The Elements of International Law, Harper & Bros., New York and London (1908), p. 168.

virtue of treaty provisions or not at all. It was said, also, that the surrender of a fugitive as a matter of comity by a foreign nation for a crime not within the the terms of an extradition treaty does not violate any right secured to him by the agreement; but this necessarily means that no right was violated which American courts were bound legally to protect and that it was for the foreign country to determine whether it would give up an individual although not bound to do so by treaty, and that of the action of another state in this regard an accused person could not complain in an American court.[159] At any rate it is now the settled rule in the United States that extradition of fugitives from justice can be granted only by virtue of treaty provisions,[160] and it has long been the practice of the Federal Government not to ask for extradition in the absence of a treaty.[161]

From this principle it follows, both as a matter of logic and good faith between governments, that a fugitive extradited under a treaty can be placed on trial only for that offence for which he was extradited,[162] and if he is not tried for such offence, or is tried and acquitted, he cannot be arrested upon another charge without being given a reasonable time to leave the country.[163] Indeed, certain treaties provide expressly for an opportunity to leave the country of refuge after trial and acquittal, or in case of failure to prosecute for the offence for which extradition was had.[164] Where, however, the original

[159] Ex parte Fess, 102 Cal., 347.
[160] United States vs. Rauscher, *supra*. Tucker vs. Alexandroff, 183 U. S., 424; 46 L. Ed., 264.
[161] United States vs. Watts, 14 Fed. Rep. 130.
[162] United States vs. Rauscher, *supra*.
[163] United States vs. Rauscher, *supra*.
[164] Cosgrove vs. Winney, 174 U. S., 64; 43 L. Ed., 897.

complaint is withdrawn, or the prisoner discharged by the committing magistrate, he may be arrested a second time upon a new complaint charging the same offence.[165] The limitation that persons shall be tried only for the offence upon which the demand for extradition was grounded applies not only to arrest for crime, but to a subsequent arrest in a civil action as well, for otherwise extradition proceedings could be made vehicles for the collection of debts in certain classes of litigation.[165]

As a general rule, extradition can be had only for an act or acts that are a crime in both countries; but this rule, as well as other rules applicable to extradition proceedings, will be construed to give effect to the intentions of the contracting parties and to carry out the legitimate purposes of agreements providing for extradition of criminals.[167] Thus, when considering the laws in force in the United States, the courts will bear in mind that in the sphere of criminal legislation the power of the Federal Government is limited, and, therefore, a statute of the state is "a law of this country" as distinguished, for instance, from "a law of Great Britain."[168] To ascertain the objects of an extradition treaty, the essence of the offence will be considered and not merely its classification in a foreign code, or differing nomenclature.[169] So whether a given offence is extraditable or not will be determined by the law of the two countries at the time extradition is applied for, and not necessarily by the

[165] Collins vs. Loisel, 262 U. S., 426; 67 L. Ed., 1062.
[166] *In re* Reinitz, 39 Fed. Rep., 204.
[167] Wright vs. Henkel, 190 U. S., 40; 47 L. Ed., 948.
[168] *In re* Wright, 123 Fed. Rep., 463.
[169] *In re* Adutt, 55 Fed. Rep., 376.

Jurisdiction of States

common-law meaning of such terms, as, for instance, "murder" or "arson."[170]

The term "persons" will not be construed to except from extradition American citizens who are accused of having committed a crime in another country,[171] and when a proper request is presented and the necessary *prima facie* showing made, the United States will deliver such individuals to the country where the alleged crime occurred.[172] Where a country punishes its own citizens for offences perpetrated abroad, and does not surrender them for extradition, the executive may denounce the treaty, but the failure of one contracting party to observe reciprocity, even in violation of the treaty, does not abrogate it, and if the treaty has not been denounced, the courts will not interfere to prevent surrender of an American citizen for trial by the courts of the proper jurisdiction. Under such circumstances the treaty is voidable, not void.[173]

A country obtaining jurisdiction over territory subsequently to the commission of a crime is not entitled to the surrender of a fugitive for an offence "committed within the jurisdiction of either party"; such jurisdiction must exist at the time the act complained of occurred.[174] If a fugitive is removed from the country of refuge irregularly, for instance by kidnapping, although an extradition treaty with the country in question is in force, United States courts can give him no relief, since no right under the constitution, or laws, or treaties of the United

[170] Cohn vs. Jones, 100 Fed. Rep., 639.
[171] Charlton vs. Kelly, 229 U. S., 447; 57 L. Ed., 1274.
[172] Neely vs. Henkel, 180 U. S., 109; 45 L. Ed., 448.
[173] Charlton vs. Kelly, *supra*.
[174] *In re* Taylor, 118 Fed. Rep., 196.

Judicial Interpretation of International Law

States, has been violated, and extradition treaties are not a guarantee of an asylum, but simply provide for a denial of that asylum in certain cases and prescribe the procedure necessary to effect this purpose.[175] Political offenders are usually exempted from the operation of extradition treaties, and it is the duty of a committing magistrate to determine whether the crime charged is political or not. Thus, homicides committed during a state of siege and to maintain the authority of an existing government are political.[176]

An extradition proceeding resembles a hearing before a magistrate for the purpose of determining whether or not a person charged should be held to answer an indictment, and the evidence required must be such as would justify holding him for trial had the crime been committed in the United States.[177]

[175] Ker vs. Illinois, 119 U. S., 436; 30 L. Ed., 421. No doubt, however, the country where the kidnapping took place would have a grievance for the violation of its territory and could make such methods an object of a diplomatic protest.

[176] *In re* Ezeta, 62 Fed. Rep., 972.

[177] Benson vs. McMahon, 127 U. S., 457; 32 L. Ed., 234.

CHAPTER FOUR

CITIZENSHIP AND ALIENAGE

§ 21. *Citizenship and its sources.*—It has been pointed out that the term nationality is broader in scope than citizenship and that it may comprehend cases of persons who are not citizens and yet may claim to be nationals.[1] This is undoubtedly true, but cases of noncitizens, who may become entitled to the protection of a state by reason of domicil, belligerency, or for other reasons, are usually of a nature requiring the intercession of the political department and seldom, if ever, come before the courts. Primarily, too, questions of citizenship are determined by municipal law,[2] and from the point of view of international law become important only when the right of protection is involved, or when there arises the question of obligation of individuals toward a state within whose jurisdiction they do not reside.[3] Furthermore, the courts as a rule use the term citizenship. For those reasons this expression has been preferred here to the title "nationality" ordinarily properly enough employed in works on international law.

In discussing citizenship the Supreme Court of the United States has said:

Before its adoption, the Constitution of the United States did not in terms prescribe who should be citizens of the United

---

[1] Moore, John Bassett, A Digest of International Law, Vol. III, page 273.
[2] Stanberry, Attorney General, 1867, 12 Opinions, 319.
[3] Hall, William Edward, A Treatise on International Law, p. 233, The Clarendon Press, Seventh edition (1917).

States or of the several states, yet there were necessarily such citizens without such provision. There cannot be a nation without a people. The very idea of a political community, such as a nation is, implies an association of persons for the promotion of their general welfare. Each one of the persons associated becomes a member of the nation formed by the association. He owes it allegiance and is entitled to its protection. Allegiance and protection are, in this connection, reciprocal obligations. The one is compensation for the other; allegiance for protection and protection for allegiance.

For convenience it has been found necessary to give a name to this membership. The object is to designate by a title the person and the relation he bears to the nation. For this purpose the words "subject," "inhabitant" and "citizen" have been used, and the choice between them is sometimes made to depend upon the form of government. Citizen is now more commonly employed, however, and as it has been considered better suited to the description of one living under a republican government, it was adopted by nearly all of the states upon their separation from Great Britain, and was afterwards adopted in the Articles of Confederation and in the Constitution of the United States. When used in this sense it is understood as conveying the idea of membership of a nation, and nothing more.[4]

"Citizens," it has been declared in another leading case, "are members of the political community to which they belong. They are the people who compose the community, and who, in their associated capacity, have established or submitted themselves to the dominion of a government for the promotion of their general welfare and the protection of their individual as well as their collective rights."[5] More briefly, citizenship "carries the idea of connection or identification with the state,

[4] Minor vs. Happersett, 21 Wall., 162; 22 L. Ed., 627. The court is speaking here of the Fourteenth Amendment.
[5] United States vs. Cruikshank, 92 U. S., 542; 23 L. Ed., 588. Boyd vs. Nebraska, 143 U. S., 483; 36 L. Ed., 103.

and a participation in its function," and "it applies to a person possessing social and political rights, and sustaining social, political and moral obligations."[6] An even more satisfactory definition is one tersely stating that "a citizen may be defined to be one who owes allegiance to the state and has the right of reciprocal protection from it."[7] Under the American form of government, an individual may be a citizen of the United States and not be a citizen of any state,[8] a condition frequently important enough as a matter of municipal law, but one which seldom, if ever, can have any importance in international law, for a citizen of the United States, if entitled to international protection at all, is entitled to it because of his national citizenship and whether or not he has lost, or never acquired, any state citizenship—of any constituent American state—is wholly immaterial. In any event, "as a government, the United States is invested with all the attributes of sovereignty. As it has the character of nationality, it has the powers of nationality, especially those which concern its relation and intercourse with other countries."[9] In the absence of proof showing that a citizen has denationalized himself or ceased to be a citizen of the country of which he has been shown to be a citizen, the original citizenship is presumed to have continued.[10]

Every nation may determine for itself, by its own constitution and laws, what classes of persons are entitled to its citizenship.[11] By constitutional provision "all per-

[6] Harding vs. Standard Oil Co., et al., 182 Fed. Rep., 421.
[7] In re Rousos, 119 N. Y. S., 34.
[8] Prentiss vs. Brennan, 19 Fed. Cas., No. 11,385.
[9] Mackenzie vs. Hare, 239 U. S., 299; 60 L. Ed., 297.
[10] Hauenstein vs. Lynham, 100 U. S., 483, 25 L. Ed., 628.
[11] United States vs. Wong Kim Ark, 169 U. S., 649; 42 L. Ed., 890.

sons born or naturalized in the United States and subject to the jurisdiction thereof, are citizens of the United States and of the state wherein they reside,"[12] the constitution thus expressly recognizing two sources of citizenship—birth and naturalization.[13] This provision however, is no more than declaratory of the common-law rule to the effect that every child born in England, even of alien parents, was a natural-born subject, unless the child of a diplomatic representative not subject to local jurisdiction, or of an alien enemy in hostile occupation of the place where the child was born.[14] Under this provision all persons born in the United States are citizens thereof even when their parents are not eligible to citizenship by virtue of statutory prohibition, for Congress may not restrict the effect of birth, declared by the Constitution to confer complete citizenship. The only exceptions to this rule are, of course, children of diplomatic representatives.[15]

Even countries where the doctrine of citizenship by birth prevails provide often enough by statute that children of their citizens, residing abroad, acquire the citizenship of their parents.[16] This, of course, is at least a partial application of the doctrine of *jus sanguinis* and to that extent an abandonment of the doctrine of *jus soli*. Where, however, the right of expatriation is not denied, such statutory provisions are largely for the purpose of protecting the citizenship of children of parents who

---

[12] Constitution of the United States, Amendment XIV, Section 1.
[13] Elk vs. Wilkins, 112 U. S., 94; 28 L. Ed., 643.
[14] United States vs. Wong Kim Ark, *supra*.
[15] United States vs. Wong Kim Ark, *supra*.
[16] Ware vs. Wisner, 50 Fed. Rep., 310.

have gone abroad and are remaining there without any idea of changing their allegiance. From that point of view these statutes are rather in the nature of an exception to the general rule. In such instances, in cases of states that do not recognize the right of expatriation, examples of what has become known as dual citizenship may arise. But then we are confronted with a clash of two rival systems of municipal law and not with a situation to which any recognized rule of international law can be applied. If uniformity in this regard is to be arrived at, it can be reached only by agreements between states.

It is well to point out, however, that certain of the new states of Europe are fully aware of the inconveniences of dual citizenship. Thus the Czechoslovak Constitution provides that "a citizen or subject of a foreign state cannot at the same time be a citizen of the Czechoslovak Republic." [17]

In the United States the Federal Constitution grants to Congress the power to establish a uniform rule of naturalization,[18] and this power is exclusive.[19] Naturalization is the act of adopting a foreigner and clothing him with the privileges and rights of a native citizen,[20] and under the Constitution of the United States a naturalized citizen stands on an equal footing with the native citizen with the exception of eligibility to the Presidency.[21] Congress may adopt, and has adopted, general laws under which individuals may be naturalized,

[17] McBain and Rogers, The New Constitutions of Europe, Doubleday, Page & Co. (1923), p. 313.
[18] Constitution of the United States, Article I, sec. 8, par. 4.
[19] Boyd vs. State of Nebraska, 143 U. S., 483; 36 L. Ed., 103.
[20] Boyd vs. State of Nebraska, *supra*.
[21] Luria vs. United States, 231 U. S., 9; 58 L. Ed., 101.

Judicial Interpretation of International Law

but it has at times also provided for collective naturalization and has the power to do so.[22] Naturalization may be effected by treaty,[23] and treaties may, and sometimes do, extend the right, to inhabitants of conquered or ceded territory, to elect whether they shall retain allegiance to the abdicating government, or become citizens of the state acquiring sovereignty over the territory in question.[24]

In the case of a successful revolution, resulting in establishing a new independent state, the inhabitants of the territory involved as a rule have the right to elect whether or not they shall become citizens of the nation; but whether or not this right has been exercised and what the choice has been, may depend upon a variety of circumstances,[25] and is to a large extent a question of fact.[26] Those not withdrawing from the territory involved, and who continue to pursue the ordinary affairs of life therein, undoubtedly, by their actions, throw in their lot with the new order of things as citizens of the newly organized state. In the United States the rule was early established that the Declaration of Independence invested with the privileges of citizenship all those persons who resided in the country at the time and adhered to the interests of the colonies.[27]

In the United States naturalization is a judicial pro-

[22] Boyd vs. State of Nebraska, *supra.*
[23] Boyd vs. State of Nebraska, *supra.* Coutzen vs. United States, 179 U. S., 191; 45 L. Ed., 148. The American Insurance Co. vs. Canter, 1 Pet., 511; 77 L. Ed., 242.
[24] United States vs. De Repentigny, 5 Wall., 211; 18 L. Ed., 627.
[25] Inglis vs. Trustees, 3 Peters, 99; 7 L. Ed., 617.
[26] M'Ilvaine vs. Coxe's Lessee, 4 Cranch, 209; 2 L. Ed., 207. Shanks *et al.* vs. Dupont *et al.*, 3 Pet., 242; 7 L. Ed., 666.
[27] Inglis vs. Trustees, *supra.* M'Ilvaine vs. Coxe's Lessee, *supra.*

ceeding, entrusted to the courts, and an applicant for naturalization institutes a proceeding in a court of justice for the judicial determination of an asserted right.[28] It has been tersely declared that "the proceedings are strictly judicial."[29] The various departments of the government will not go behind a judicial decision of a court of law as evidenced by a certificate of naturalization,[30] but of course such a certificate may be assailed directly, in a proper proceeding, and set aside and annulled on the ground of fraud or on the ground that it was illegally procured.[31] Naturalization being a strictly judicial act, the action of the court must be entered of record, and in the absence of proof of loss or destruction of a record, the record is the only proper proof of naturalization and it cannot be proved by parol,[32] nor, if issued by a court of competent jurisdiction, can it be attacked collaterally.[33] Citizenship dates from the time the order of court is made,[34] and the finding has no retroactive effect.[35] In cases of corporations, for jurisdictional purposes the courts have adopted the rule that it is conclusively presumed that all stockholders are citizens of the state under whose laws the corporation has been created,[36] and while it may do business in all places allowed by its charter and permitted by local law, the charter remains the law of its existence and conduct and whatever disabilities are imposed thereby upon its con-

[28] *In re* Bodek, 63 Fed. Rep., 813.
[29] Green vs. Salas, 31 Fed. Rep., 106.
[30] *In re* Bodek, *supra*.
[31] Luria vs. United States, *supra*.
[32] Green vs. Salas, *supra*.
[33] Ackerman *et al.* vs. Haenck *et al.*, 147 Ill., 514; 35 N. E., 381.
[34] State vs. Boyd, 31 Neb., 682; 48 N. W., 739.
[35] *Ex parte* Kyle, 67 Fed. Rep., 306.
[36] Miller vs. Dows, 94 U. S., 445; 24 L. Ed., 207.

duct at home continue to be a condition of its activities abroad.[37]

It is a rule of international law that "aliens residing in a country, with the intention of making it a permanent place of abode, acquire, in one sense, a domicil there; and, while they are permitted by the nation to retain such a residence and domicil, are subject to its laws, and may invoke its protection against other nations,"[38] and individuals residing in a country other than their own in certain respects possess the same rights, and are obligated to perform the same duties as the citizens of that country, and no restrictions upon them are presumed by reason of their domicil of choice, or commercial domicil.[39]

Claims have occasionally been made that the term "citizen" or "subject" includes persons who by permanent domicil are entitled to the protection of the government within whose jurisdiction they have a domicil;[40] but this claim has little, if any, support in principle and certainly no support in judicial authority. Domicil, in and by itself, neither confers nor forfeits citizenship,[41] although it may be considered as evidence of implied renunciation of citizenship.[42] Domicil, in its ordinary acceptation, has been defined as "the place where a person lives and has his home."[43] Obviously, while such domicil entitles the person enjoying it to certain protection by the terri-

[37] Canada Southern R. R. Co. vs. Gebhard, 109 U. S., 527; 27 L. Ed., 1020.
[38] Fong Yue Ting vs. U. S., 149 U. S., 698; 37 L. Ed., 905.
[39] Law Ow Bew vs. U. S., 144 U. S., 47; 36 L. Ed., 340.
[40] Borchard, Edwin M., The Diplomatic Protection of Citizens Abroad, The Banks Publishing Co., New York (1916), p. 557.
[41] Borchard, Edwin M., The Diplomatic Protection of Citizens Abroad, *supra*, p. 558, and cases therein cited.
[42] See section 22 on Expatriation.
[43] Mitchell vs. United States, 21 Wall., 350; 22 L. Ed., 584.

torial sovereign, while living within his territory, no such bonds exist between such person and such sovereign that would entitle the person in question to protection outside of his domicil, in the absence of treaties conferring such right, or other special circumstances."[44]

A cautionary remark to this effect may be unnecessary, but it is perhaps well to say that a detailed discussion of the naturalization laws of the United States, and judicial decisions based thereon, has not been entered upon here, for the reason that these are wholly a matter of municipal legislation, and for an understanding of these the student and lawyer must consult the various statutes and decisions, as well as treatises especially devoted to the subject.

§ 22. *Expatriation.*—Expatriation is the voluntary renunciation or abandonment of citizenship and allegiance.[45] In the first case arising in this country, involving the question of expatriation, in the terminology of the natural rights school of the eighteenth century it was declared that "all members of a civil community are bound to each other by compact" and "that one of the parties to this compact cannot dissolve it by his own act."[46] Up until the adoption of the act of July 27, 1868,[47] the clear weight of authority was to the effect that a citizen could not denationalize himself without the consent of his government, Mr. Justice Story declaring the general

[44] Borchard, Edwin M., The Diplomatic Protection of Citizens Abroad, *supra*, discussion of Koszta Case, p. 570. See also *In re* Neagle, 135 U. S., 1; 34 L. Ed., 55.
[45] Borchard, Edwin M., The Diplomatic Protection of Citizens Abroad, *supra*, p. 674.
[46] Williams' Case, Fed. Cas. No. 17, 708.
[47] 15 U. S. Stats., 223; U. S. Rev. Stats., 1999.

doctrine to be that no person can by any act of his own, without the consent of his government, put off his allegiance, and become an alien.[48] Apart from the compact theory, the influence of which is evident in some of these decisions, the common law rule was also to the effect that expatriation could be accomplished only with the permission of the government.[49]

The act of July 27, 1868, already referred to, declares that the right of expatriation is a natural and inherent right of all people, and while this language is little more than a declaration of national policy, it has been said that if a consent of the nation is essential to valid expatriation this act is evidence thereof.[50] In any event it is now the settled doctrine of the United States that the right of expatriation is a fundamental one.[51]

The most obvious and indisputable method of expatriation is naturalization in any foreign state, or the taking of an oath of allegiance to any foreign state, and persons having performed either of these acts are deemed to have expatriated themselves by express statutory provision.[52] It is probable that nothing short of naturalization elsewhere, or oath of allegiance to another sovereign, can accomplish the expatriation of a native-born citizen, although protracted residence abroad without an intent to return to the United States may result in withdrawal

[48] Shanks vs. Dupont, 3 Pet., 246; 7 L. Ed., 666; Inglis vs. Sailor's Snug Harbor, 3 Pet., 101; 7 L. Ed., 617. Talbot vs. Janson, 3 Dallas, 133; 1 L. Ed., 540.
[49] Mackenzie vs. Hare, 239 U. S., 299; 60 L. Ed., 297.
[50] Mackenzie vs. Hare *et al.*, 165 Cal., 776; 134 Pac., 713.
[51] Green's Son vs. Salas, 31 Fed. Rep., 106. Browne vs. Dexter, 66 Cal., 39; 4 Pac., 913.
[52] Borchard, Edwin M., The Diplomatic Protection of Citizens Abroad, *supra*, p. 690.

of diplomatic protection by executive authorities.[53] Until recently marriage of an American-born woman was held to forfeit her citizenship under laws then in force,[54] but that rule has been changed by the provisions of the much discussed Cable Act, providing that "a woman citizen of the United States shall not cease to be a citizen of the United States by reason of her marriage after the passage of this act, unless she makes a formal renunciation of her citizenship before a court having jurisdiction over naturalization of aliens."[55]

In the case of naturalized citizens citizenship may be quite easily lost by comparatively short residence abroad. It is now provided by statute that "if any alien who shall have secured a certificate of citizenship under this act shall, within five years after the issuance of such certificate, return to the country of his nativity, or go to any other foreign country, and take permanent residence therein, it shall be considered prima facie evidence of a lack of intention on the part of such alien to become a permanent citizen of the United States at the time of filing his application for citizenship, and, in the absence of proper countervailing evidence it shall be sufficient in the proper proceeding to authorize the cancellation of his certificate of citizenship as fraudulent. . . ."[56] It will be noted that the presumption of lack of intention to become an American citizen arises, under this statute, only in cases of aliens leaving the country, to take residence elsewhere, within five years after the issuance of

[53] 34 Stat. L., pt. 1, p. 1228.
[54] Mackenzie vs. Hare, 239 U. S., 299; 60 L. Ed., 297.
[55] 42 Stat. L., pt. 1, p. 1021.
[56] Naturalization Laws and Regulations, sec. 15, Government Printing Office (1924).

a certificate of naturalization; that to avoid the certificate a judicial proceeding is necessary, and that the presumption may be rebutted by "countervailing evidence."

For the purpose of determining who is, or is not, entitled to protection by diplomatic officials of the United States, the Department of State has issued a set of elaborate instructions describing the methods of overcoming the presumption of expatriation.[57]

It remains now to point out some of the cases discussing acts that may or may not effect expatriation.

Entrance into the military service of another government, if not accompanied by an unconditional oath of allegiance, does not constitute expatriation.[58] Voting in Canada, where oath of allegiance to Great Britain had been declined, was held insufficient as evidence of expatriation.[59] Involuntary service in the military forces of another government does not raise a presumption of intention to renounce citizenship.[60] Where a native-born citizen acquired a residence abroad and married there, the fact would not be considered as evidence of expatriation, though, during a part of the time, war intervened between the country of his domicil and the United States and he did not take part in it.[61] The father of a child born in the United States cannot, by any of his acts, deprive the child of his citizenship.[62]

As a rule expatriation cannot be effected without a *bona fide* change of domicil, nor can it be asserted for

[57] Borchard, Edwin M., *supra,* p. 703.
[58] Santissima Trinidad, 7 Wheaton, 283; 5 L. Ed., 434.
[59] Ware vs. Wisner, 50 Fed. Rep., 310.
[60] State vs. Adams, 45 Iowa, 99; 24 American Reports, 760.
[61] United States vs. Gillies, Fed. Cas., No. 15,206.
[62] State vs. Jackson, 79 Vt., 504; 65 Am. Rep., 657; 8 L. R. A., N. S., 1245.

Citizenship and Alienage

the purpose of escaping the consequences of fraud, or to justify a violation of the laws of the country.[63]

Expatriation, or loss of citizenship in any other way, of itself does not work forfeiture of right to hold and own property.[64] But even an American citizen, who has not gone to the extent of divesting himself of his allegiance, may by his acts forfeit the right to the protection of the United States.[65]

§ 23. *Aliens, their rights and privileges.*—An alien is "one born out of the jurisdiction of the United States, and who has not been naturalized under their constitution and laws."[66] Aliens have been classified as resident and non-resident, the former being those who reside in a country to which they are foreigners,[67] while the latter are those residing outside the country or state.[68] An alien friend is one whose country is at peace with the United States,[69] and an alien enemy is one owing allegiance to an adverse belligerent nation.[70] Alienage, once established, is presumed to continue until the contrary is shown by competent evidence.[71]

The legal status of a foreigner is of course determined by the municipal laws of the country of residence.[72] Under modern conditions, however, the tendency has

[63] Roger vs. Whitham, 56 Wash., 190; 105 Pac., 628.
[64] The Santissima Trinidad, *supra*.
[65] The Charming Betsy, 2 Cranch, 64; 2 L. Ed., 208.
[66] Low Wah Suey vs. Backus, 225 U. S., 460; 56 L. Ed., 1165. Buffington vs. Grosvenor, 46 Kan., 730; 27 Pac., 137.
[67] *In re* Wehlitz, 16 Wis., 443; 84 Am. Dec., 700.
[68] *In re* Gill's Estate, 79 Iowa, 296; 44 N. W., 553.
[69] 2 Corpus Juris, 1043.
[70] Dorsey vs. Brigham, et al., 177 Ill., 250.
[71] Hauenstein vs. Lynham, 100 U. S., 483; 25 L. Ed., 628; Kadlec vs Pavik, 9 N. D. 278, 83 N. W. 5.
[72] Heirn vs. Bridault, 37 Miss., 209.

been to extend to foreigners all rights and privileges enjoyed by citizens, except those, of course, of a political nature, or those which, for reasons of what has become known as the police power, the state believes should be exercised by citizens only.[73] In any event, "an alien is not now regarded as 'the outside barbarian' he is considered in China, and the struggle in all commercial countries, for some centuries, has been to enlarge his privileges and powers as to all matters of property and trade."[74] In the United States the Fourteenth Amendment to the Constitution, providing that no state shall "deprive any person of life, liberty or property without due process of law; nor deny to any person within its jurisdiction the equal protection of the laws," is applicable not only to citizens, but protects aliens as well.[75] Indeed, by an express statutory provision it is declared that "all persons within the jurisdiction of the United States shall have the same right in every state and territory to make and enforce contracts, to sue, be parties, give evidence, and to the full and equal benefit of all laws and proceedings for the security of persons and property as is enjoyed by white citizens, and shall be subject to like punishments, pains, penalties, taxes, licenses and exactions of every kind, and to no other."[76] While this section was formulated primarily to protect the negro, it is broad enough to apply to aliens, and is significant even if nothing more than a declaration of policy.

The courts have declined to uphold discriminatory legislation against foreigners where the legislature trans-

---
[73] 2 Corpus Juris, 1046.
[74] Taylor *et al* vs. Carpenter, Fed. Cas. No. 13,785.
[75] Yick Wo vs. Hopkins, 118 U. S., 356; 30 L. Ed., 220.
[76] Revised Statutes, sec. 1977.

Citizenship and Alienage

gressed the bounds of legitimate classification. Thus a Pennsylvania law, imposing on every employer of foreign-born unnaturalized male persons over 21 years of age a tax of three cents a day for each day that each of such persons might be employed, and authorizing the deduction of that sum from the wages of such employees, was held to deprive these aliens of equal protection of the law and to be therefore in violation of the Fourteenth Amendment to the Constitution of the United States. The court did not hesitate to brand the act as being intended to hinder the employment of foreign-born unnaturalized male persons over 21 years of age.[77] Under an act authorizing boards of supervisors to maintain hospitals and poorhouses, and to appoint physicians to attend the indigent sick, an alien was not disqualified for such position by virtue of another law that no alien shall hold office, the position in question not being an office within the meaning of the Political Code.[78] A statute authorizing issuance of peddlers' licenses only to citizens was held unconstitutional as discriminatory between citizens and aliens.[79] An English citizen could maintain a libel action against a New York newspaper and alienage was no bar to the action.[80]

Foreign corporations are within the protection of the laws of the country when such protection is not inconsistent with public policy, or with local laws.[81] In an early case it was held that the American Revolution did

[77] Fraser vs. McConway & Torley Co., 82 Fed. Rep., 257.
[78] People ex rel. Attorney General vs. Wheeler, 136 Cal., 652; 69 Pac., 435.
[79] State vs. Montgomery, 94 Maine, 192; 47 Atl. Rep., 165. Discrimination against aliens by municipal ordinances is discussed by Charles Kneier, Georgetown Law Journal, February, 1928.
[80] Crashley vs. Press Pub. Co., 179 N. Y., 27; 71 N. E., 258.
[81] The Bank of Augusta vs. Earle, 3 Pet., 519; 10 L. Ed., 274.

not affect the rights of private individuals, or of corporations, to hold property in the United States.[82] Nevertheless, it should be remembered that a corporation is not a citizen within the meaning of the constitutional provision that the citizens of each state shall be entitled to all the privileges and immunities of citizens of the several states,[83] and that foreign corporations cannot do business in another state as a matter of right,[84] but can do so only upon the terms prescribed by the state, if permitted to enter at all.[85]

§ 24. *Aliens, their duties.*—It has been held axiomatic that "protection and allegiance" are reciprocal[86] and the principle has led to the formulation, by the courts, of the doctrine of temporary allegiance described in the following language:

By allegiance is meant the obligation of fidelity and obedience which the individual owes to the government under which he lives, or to his sovereign in return for the protection he receives. It may be an absolute or permanent obligation, or it may be a qualified and temporary one. The citizen or subject owes an absolute and permanent allegiance to his government or sovereign, or at least until, by some open and distinct act, he renounces it and becomes a citizen or subject of another government or another sovereign. The alien, whilst domiciled in the country, owes a local and temporary allegiance, which continues during the period of his residence.

This obligation of temporary allegiance by an alien resident in a foreign country is everywhere recognized by publicists

---

[82] The Society for the Propagation of the Gospel in Foreign Parts vs. The Town of New Haven, 8 Wheaton, 464; 5 L. Ed., 462.

[83] Paul vs. Virginia, 8 Wall., 168; 19 L. Ed., 357.

[84] The Horn Silver Mining Co. vs. New York, 143 U. S., 305; 36 L. Ed., 164.

[85] Cooper Mfg. Co. vs. Ferguson, 113 U. S., 727; 28 L. Ed., 1137.

[86] Luke vs. Calhoun Co., 52 Ala., 115.

and statesmen. In the case of Thrasher, a citizen of the United States resident in Cuba, who complained of injuries suffered from the government of that island, Mr. Webster, then Secretary of State, made, in 1851, a report to the President in answer to a resolution of the House of Representatives, in which he said: "Every foreigner born residing in a country owes to that country allegiance and obedience to its laws so long as he remains in it, as duty upon him by the mere fact of his residence, that temporary protection which he enjoys, and is as much bound to obey its laws as native subjects or citizens. This is the universal understanding in all civilized states and nowhere a more established doctrine than in this country." And again: "Independently of a residence with intention to continue such residence; independently of any domicilation: independently of the taking of any oath of allegiance, or of renouncing any former allegiance, it is well known that, by the public law, an alien or a stranger born, for so long a time as he continues within the dominions of a foreign government, owes obedience to the laws of that government, and may be punished for treason or other crimes as a native born subject might be, unless his case is varied by some treaty stipulation!" 6 Web. Works, 526.[87]

§ 25. *Aliens, their disabilities.*—It is axiomatic, and hardly requires extended citation of authorities, that in the absence of special legislation granting political rights, aliens are excluded from the exercise of the right of suffrage, or holding office, under a government within whose jurisdiction they reside, but to which they do not owe unqualified allegiance. It has been said that as to all independent popular governments "it is an acknowledged principle, which lies at the very foundation, and the enforcement of which needs neither the aid of statutory or constitutional enactments or restriction, that the gov-

[87] Carlisle vs. United States, 16 Wall., 147; 21 L. Ed., 426. See also United States vs. Diekelman, 92 U. S., 520; 23 L. Ed., 742.

ernment is instituted by the citizens for their liberty and protection, and that it is to be administered, and its powers and functions exercised, by them and through their agency." [88] Thus, in Iowa an alien is ineligible to the office of sheriff, although naturalization prior to his induction to office removed the disability.[89]

While the modern tendency has been to grant aliens substantially the same civil and property rights as to citizens, and to exclude them from the exercise of political rights and privileges,[90] for reasons of public policy the laws do impose upon them certain limitations in their activities and do deny them some rights enjoyed by citizens. In the United States this discrimination has been frequently sustained by applying the doctrine of police power and for what have been deemed reasons of public welfare. Thus it has been held a valid exercise of the police power to refuse liquor licenses to aliens, while granting them, upon a showing of good moral character, to citizens.[91] As a rule aliens are disqualified for jury service, but generally speaking, an objection on this ground will not be entertained if interposed after the juror has been sworn or affirmed, if the complaining party had an opportunity of challenge.[92] A state may bar aliens from holding stock in corporations organized under its laws, or impose upon them such conditions as it considers proper.[93] Admission to the bar is entirely

[88] State *ex. rel.* Oft vs. Smith, 14 Wis., 497. State ex. rel. Schuet vs. Murray, 28 Wis., 96; 9 Am. Rep., 489.

[89] State *ex. rel.* Perine *et al.* vs. Van Beek *et al.*, 87 Iowa, 569; 54 N. W., 525.

[90] Fenwick, Charles G., International Law, The Century Co., New York and London (1924), p. 178.

[91] Trageser vs. Gray, 20 Atl., 905.

[92] Kohl vs. Lehlback, 160 U. S., 293; 40 L. Ed., 432.

[93] State vs. Travelers' Ins. Co., 40 Atl. Rep., 465.

Citizenship and Alienage

within the province of state regulation and aliens may be barred from the practice of law on the ground of alienage only.[94] An alien who has voluntarily enlisted in the army of the United States, cannot claim his discharge on account of being a non-citizen,[95] and an alien who had made his declaration of intention to become a citizen of the United States and had voted under the laws and constitution of the state was a citizen of the state—though not of the United States—and could be drafted into the militia of the United States.[96]

Under the common law aliens were capable of acquiring, holding and transmitting personal property in the same manner as citizens, the reason for this being that "personal estate is of a transitory and movable nature; and besides, this indulgence is necessary to strangers for the advancement of trade."[97] The rule as to real property was different, however, at least to the extent that an alien could not take lands by operation of law, i.e., by descent, since the alien had no inheritable blood,[98] but he could take by an act of the parties, i.e., by purchase, and maintain the lands against every one except the crown or the state.[99] In this respect, too, the rigor of the common law rule has been relaxed in many states, largely for the purpose of aiding in the development of these commonwealths;[100] but of course the statutes of the various states are by no means uniform, and in each

---

[94] *In re* Takuji Yamashita, 30 Wash., 234; 70 Pac., 482.
[95] United States vs. Cottingham, 40 Am. Dec., 710.
[96] *In re* Wehlitz, 16 Wis., 443; 84 Am. Dec., 700.
[97] 1 Blackstone's Commentaries, 372.
[98] Fairfax's Devisee vs. Hunter's Lessee, 7 Cranch, 603; 3 L. Ed., 453. Governeur's Heirs vs. Robertson *et al.*, 11 Wheaton, 332; 6 L. Ed., 488.
[99] 2 Corpus Juris, 1051, and cases cited.
[100] *In re* Gill's Estate, 79 Iowa, 296; 44 N. W., 553.

case the student or lawyer must consult the state laws and the decisions based thereon.[101] Whenever this can be done without doing violence to the wording of the statute, courts will construe such laws as conferring power to hold real estate upon the aliens as a class.[102] Rights of aliens to hold and transmit property may be regulated by treaties, and a state law in conflict with a treaty in force must yield to the provisions of the latter,[103] but these provisions affect only citizens of the contracting states.[104]

Aliens may maintain actions before courts of competent jurisdiction and enforce their rights before judicial tribunals,[105] but this is rather a matter of comity than of right.[106] The practice of permitting aliens to enforce their rights, unless its exercise would result in an injustice to the state, is so universal now that the distinction between right and comity really is a purely theoretical one. The tendency of the decisions is well illustrated by the ruling that a Colorado statute, giving a right of action for wrongful death, first, to the husband or wife of the deceased, or, second, to his child or children, or, third, to his father and mother, or the survivor of them, includes among its beneficiaries non-resident aliens having the prescribed relationship to the deceased, and in the language of the decision, quoting a Georgia opinion,

[101] Easton vs. Huott, 95 Iowa, 473; 64 N. W., 408. Abrams vs. State, 45 Wash., 327; 88 Pac., 327. Sullivan vs. Burnett, 105 U. S., 334; 26 L. Ed., 1124.

[102] Hall vs. Hall, 81 N. Y., 130.

[103] *In re* Stixrud's Estate, 58 Wash., 339; 109 Pac., 343. See also chapter on Treaties, *infra*.

[104] Wunderle *et al.* vs. Wunderle, 144 Ill., 40; 33 N. E., 195.

[105] Taylor vs. Carpenter, *supra*.

[106] Disconto Gesellschaft vs. Umbreit, 208 U. S., 570; 52 L. Ed., 625.

Citizenship and Alienage

that "whenever a Georgia mother can recover, any other mother can do so under like circumstances." [107]

It is well settled that a government has the power to exclude foreigners from the country whenever, in its opinion, public interests require such action,[108] and this power includes the right to expel or deport non-citizens. "This right is based on the fact that, the foreigner not making a part of the nation, his individual reception into the territory is matter of pure permission, of simple tolerance, and creates no obligation." [109] The power is inherent in sovereignty and in the United States is vested in the National Government, which may exercise it through treaties entered into by the Executive and confirmed by the Senate, or through statutes enacted by Congress in accordance with the Constitution, conferring upon it the power to regulate commerce with foreign nations, including the entrance of ships, the importation of goods and the bringing of persons into the United States.[110] Supervision of admission of aliens to the United States may be entrusted by Congress to an appropriate department of the government, and the decisions of executive or administrative officials, acting within the scope of the authority conferred upon them by Congress, constitute due process of law.[111]

[107] Ferrara vs. Auric Mining Co., 43 Colo., 496; 95 Pac., 952.
[108] Chae Chan Ping vs. United States, 130 U. S., 581; 32 L. Ed., 1068.
[109] Fong Yue Ting vs. United States, 149 U. S., 698; 37 L. Ed., 905.
[110] Nishimura Ekiu vs. United States, 142 U. S., 651; 35 L. Ed., 1146.
[111] Nishimura Ekiu vs. United States, *supra*.

CHAPTER FIVE

TREATIES

§ 26. *Treaties and the treaty-making power in the United States.*—A treaty is primarily a compact between two independent nations,[1] or, as another definition more briefly would have it, it is a contract between nations,[2] while others, perhaps, more comprehensive, declare that a treaty is a compact "between states or organized communities or their representatives,"[3] or "a compact formed between two nations or communities having the right of self-government."[4]

From the point of view of international law the treaty-making power of independent states is unlimited, except, of course, that states cannot properly enter into any agreements in any way infringing upon the rights of other sovereign states.[5] In the United States, however, the Constitution declares treaties to be the supreme law of the land, and the nature of the Federal Government is such that viewed from the constitutional standpoint

[1] Edye vs. Robertson, 112 U. S., 580; 28 L. Ed., 792.
[2] The Diamond Rings, 183 U. S., 176; 46 L. Ed., 138.
[3] United States vs. Hunter, 21 Fed. Rep., 615.
[4] Worcester vs. Georgia, 6 Peters, 515; 6 L. Ed., 483.
[5] Fenwick, Charles G., International Law, The Century Co., New York and London (1924), p. 330. The author points out that treaties to commit an international crime, such as the partition of Poland, if violated by the contracting parties, would not arouse a demand on the part of third parties to keep "faith," and he takes the position that agreements of two states to violate international law would undoubtedly be repudiated by third states. There can be no doubt as to the correctness of this position.

[156]

the treaty-making power cannot be considered unlimited even when it is conceded that a treaty is not a legislative act and "does not generally effect, of itself, the object to be accomplished, especially so far as its operation is infraterritorial; but is carried into execution by the sovereign power of the respective parties to the instrument." [6] The problem has been discussed often enough from all possible points of view, but for the sake of completeness as well as because of the growing importance of the subject, a restatement of the essential principles may be of some use.

Article VI, Clause 2, of the Federal Constitution, is quite sweeping in its language, and, standing alone, would also make the treaty-making power unlimited. All students of American government are familiar with it, but that we may develop the problem in an orderly way it is desirable again to set it forth: "This Constitution, and the laws of the United States which shall be made in pursuance thereof, and all treaties made, or which shall be made in pursuance thereof, and all treaties made, or which shall be made, under the authority of the United States, shall be the supreme law of the land; and the judges in every state shall be bound thereby, anything in the Constitution or laws of any state to the contrary notwithstanding." This clause, however, does not stand alone, and both as a matter of principle and following a large number of decisions, the Constitution must be considered in its entirety, with a view to the nature of the instrument, as well as to its other provisions.

The provisions particularly to be borne in mind are

[6] Foster vs. Neilson, 2 Pet., 257; 7 L. Ed., 415. The United States vs. Arredondo *et al.*, 6 Pet., 691; 8 L. Ed., 547.

Judicial Interpretation of International Law

Article I, Section 8, par. 18 of the Constitution and Amendment Ten to this document. Under the first of these the national government has only such powers as are bestowed by the Constitution, including power to make "all laws necessary and proper" for carrying into execution enumerated powers, and those conferred in terms upon the other departments of the national government. Under the Tenth Amendment the powers not delegated to the "United States by the Constitution nor prohibited by it to the states are reserved to the states respectively, or to the people."

Considering these clauses, and the relation of one to another, the meaning is obvious and the intention clear: all powers not expressly or by necessary implication granted to the United States are reserved to the individual states. But the power to make treaties is conferred upon the Federal Government and it follows that everything is given that ordinarily and properly goes with such power.

The treaty-making power cannot be unlimited, for otherwise it could be used to destroy those very things which the Constitution was framed to protect. "It need hardly be said that a treaty cannot change the Constitution or be held valid if it be in violation of that instrument. This results from the nature and fundamental principles of our Government."[7] The United States being a person in international law, necessarily any treaty is binding upon this international law person, if properly entered into and approved by the Senate. But within what limitations is a treaty the supreme law of the land? Does a treaty always bind all persons subject

[7] Cherokee Tobacco vs. United States, 11 Wall., 616; 20 L. Ed., 227.

[158]

Treaties

to the jurisdiction of the United States, and does it always determine the status of things and factors within this jurisdiction? These are questions that may become of practical importance from the point of view of the citizen. Again, may the treaty-making power undertake to do things that cannot be accomplished by ordinary legislation?

It is tempting to come to the conclusion, and certain authors have done so, that the treaty-making power is coextensive with that of Congress, viz., that a treaty cannot do what an act of Congress cannot accomplish. This theory would seem to be demolished by the ruling of the Supreme Court of the United States, in an opinion by Mr. Justice Holmes, in which it is declared: "Acts of Congress are supreme law of the land when made in pursuance of the Constitution, while treaties are declared to be so when made under the authority of the United States. We do not mean to imply that there are no qualifications to the treaty-making power; but they must be ascertained in a different way. . . . When the Constitution-makers formulated the Constitution, they called into life a being the development of which could not be foreseen. Cases must be considered in the light of our whole national experience." [8]

A little reflection will show that there is a considerable sphere of interests and questions that may be regulated by treaties, but not by an act of Congress. It is clear, and judicially established, that the United States may, by treaties, provide for the mutual rights of citizens of either country, party to a treaty, in the other.[9] Yet it

[8] Missouri vs. Holland, 252 U. S., 416; 64 L. Ed., 641.
[9] Hauenstein vs. Lynham, 100 U. S., 483; 25 L. Ed., 628.

Judicial Interpretation of International Law

cannot be contended for a moment that, generally speaking, Congress could pass an act, apart from any treaty, wholly as a matter of federal legislation, regulating the rights of aliens in any State, or all States, and distinguishing these rights from those of the citizens.[10] An act of Congress which sought to regulate the killing of migrating birds within the States, by itself and not in pursuance of any treaty, was held unconstitutional,[11] but when an act, having the same object, was enacted to enforce a treaty, the regulation was upheld.[12]

It has been observed: "It is not now an open question that the removal of alien disability to inherit and dispose of real property is a proper subject of treaty regulation and within the treaty-making power, and that treaty stipulations to this effect override any inconsistent state legislation. This principle has been asserted not less clearly by the state than by the federal courts."[13]

Quite early in the history of the republic it was decided that titles of aliens to property, and their right to sell and devise the same, may be protected and regulated by treaty.[14] A treaty with France, entered into in 1778, enabled French subjects to hold lands in the United States and was enforced by the courts.[15] Under a treaty between the United States and Switzerland, where a Swiss citizen left real estate in Virginia, his heirs, also citizens of Switzerland, had the absolute right to sell the

[10] Holmes vs. Jannison, 14 Peters, 540; 10 L. Ed., 579. Santos Case, 7 Fed. Cas., No. 4016.
[11] United States vs. Shaurer, 214 Fed., 154. United States vs. McCullagh, 221 Fed., 288.
[12] Missouri vs. Holland, *supra*.
[13] Crandall, S. B., Treaties, Their Making and Enforcement, 2d Ed., Washington, 1916.
[14] Fairfax's Devisee vs. Hunter's Lessee, 7 Cranch, 603; 3 L. Ed., 602.
[15] Chirac vs. Chirac, 2 Wheaton, 259, 4 L. Ed., 257.

Treaties

property, and to withdraw the proceeds from the country within such time as the laws of Virginia permitted, and there being no statute of limitations applicable to the case, there could be no default arising from the lapse of time.[16] Where a treaty with Prussia provided that on the death of any person holding real estate within the territory of the one party, if such real estate would by the law of the land descend to the subject of the other, were he not disqualified by alienage, such citizen shall be allowed a reasonable time to sell the property and withdraw the proceeds, real estate in Iowa devised to a citizen of Prussia descended on the death of such citizen to his heirs, who were also Prussian citizens.[17]

These, however, are considerations of an affirmative nature. When discussing limitations of the treaty-making power, the question is, What cannot be done? To what extent this power is limited has been frequently discussed without being definitely defined, no treaty having ever been declared void by the courts.[18] The Supreme Court said in a very early case: "If the court possesses a power to declare treaties void, I shall never exercise it but in a very clear case indeed." [19]

Nevertheless, as a matter of principle, and on the basis of some of the opinions, certain fairly safe conclusions may be arrived at.

It has been stated that the treaty-making power would not authorize a cession of any portion of the territory of a state without the consent of that state.[20] In an earlier

---
[16] Hauenstein vs. Lynham, 100 U. S., 483; 25 L. Ed., 628.
[17] Doehrel vs. Hilmer *et al.* (Iowa), 71 N. W., 204.
[18] 38 Cyc., 966.
[19] Ware vs. Hylton, 3 Dall., 199; 1 L. Ed., 568.
[20] De Geofroy vs. Riggs, 133 U. S., 258; 33 L. Ed., 642.

case it was declared: "It is a sound principle of national law, and applies to the treaty-making power of this government . . . that all questions of disputed boundaries may be settled by the parties to the treaty: And to the exercise of these high functions of the government within its constitutional powers, neither the rights of a state, not those of an individual, can be interposed."[21] But when does rectification of a boundary cease and cession of territory commence? This problem has arisen in other countries and fairly recently was acute in one of the new republics of central Europe.

In the Insular Cases it was held that under the Constitution only Congress has power to incorporate new territory with the United States, and that as a result the treaty-making power cannot do so. It is because of this distinction that the islands in question are not considered a part of the United States.[22] It is also on this theory that the Supreme Court has held that the bill of rights is in force only in the United States itself and does not apply to territory belonging to it.[23] Territory of the United States, and territory belonging to the United States, are two different things.

Vested rights cannot be destroyed by treaties. Where a plaintiff was disputing the right of the State of Louisiana under a treaty of 1853 with France to impose a succession tax upon property anterior to the treaty, the court said: "If the property vested in him at the time, it could vest only in the manner and upon conditions authorized by the laws of the state, and certainly a treaty, subsequently (i.e., to the vesting of the property)

[21] Latimer vs. Poteet, 14 Peters, 4; 10 L. Ed., 328.
[22] Downes vs. Bidwell, 182 U. S., 244; 45 L. Ed. 1088.
[23] Hawaii vs. Mankichi, 190 U. S, 197; 47 L. Ed.,1016.

made by the United States with France could not divest rights of property already vested in the state, even if the words of the treaty had imported such intention." [24] Of course, this decision did not hold the treaty invalid, but simply inapplicable to a given situation.

There is a line of cases employing language which can serve as a fair guide both to lawyers, as well as to American negotiators with foreign governments. In an early case the United States Supreme Court said that it must be assumed that the power to make treaties should extend to all those objects which in the intercourse of nations had usually been regarded as proper subjects of negotiation and treaty, if not inconsistent with the nature of the American Government and the relation between the States and the United States.[25]

In a later case it is declared: "That the treaty-making power in the United States extends to all proper subjects of negotiations between the United States and the governments of other nations is clear. . . . The treaty power, as expressed in the Constitution, is in terms unlimited except by those restraints which are found in that instrument against the action of the Government or its Departments, and that arising from the nature of the Government itself and that of the States. It would not be contended that it extends so far as to authorize what the Constitution forbids, or a change in the character of the Government or in that of any of the States, or a cession of any portion of the territory of the latter without its consent. But with these exceptions it is not perceived that there is any limit to the questions which can be

[24] Prevost vs. Greneaux, 19 Howard, 1; 15 L. Ed., 572.
[25] Holmes vs. Jennison, *supra*.

adjusted touching any matter which is properly the subject of negotiations with a foreign country."[26]

In one of the leading state cases the situation is put very tersely: "The only questions to be considered with regard to the subject matter of the treaty are: (1) Whether it is a proper subject of treaty according to international law or the usage and practice of civilized nations; and (2) whether it is prohibited by any of the limitations contained in the Constitution."[27]

If, then, the question should be asked, Can the treaty-making power be employed in reference to matters not legitimately a subject for international agreement? the answer must be in the negative, not only by reason of the decisions quoted, but also as a matter of principle and sound rules of constitutional interpretation. Certainly the framers of the Federal Constitution did not intend to confer this power for any other purpose but the one of making possible treaties within the legitimate sphere of international agreements. In other words, "the treaty-making power must be confined to its proper function and exercised in good faith."[28]

All the cases hereinbefore referred to could be upheld by applying this comprehensive, elastic and at the same time clear rule. The Missouri Migratory Bird Case beyond doubt came within the rule.[29] Preservation of bird life was and is a matter of concern not only to the state of Missouri and the United States, but Canada as well, and the matter was therefore susceptible of international agreement.

[26] De Geofroy vs. Riggs, *supra*.
[27] People vs. Gerke, 5 Cal., 381.
[28] Willoughby, Constitutional Law of the United States, page 504.
[29] Missouri vs. Holland, *supra*.

Treaties

As discussed up to this point, the question, in all probability, is destined to remain of an academic nature, since it is not to be expected that officials entrusted with treaty negotiations would consider embodying in a treaty provisions not legitimately a subject matter of international agreement, and it is certain that the Senate would refuse its consent to any such agreement. In 1899 the Department of State declined a proposal of the British Government to negotiate a treaty to prevent discriminatory legislation by the several States of the United States, subjecting foreign fire insurance companies to higher taxes than domestic companies, on the ground that the people would hardly permit encroachments upon the exercise of powers of local legislation and that, therefore, to negotiate such a treaty would in all probability be futile.[30]

But other important considerations remain to be noticed.

There is a class of treaties, probably the majority, that is self-executing, and if a treaty affects solely the judicial department it belongs to this class. It is not necessary in this connection to cite authorities to the proposition that courts will give effect to the provisions of a treaty in deciding cases properly before them. It is equally obvious that if the executive department has the power completely to carry out the provisions of a treaty it is self-executing. "Our Constitution declares a treaty to be the law of the land. It is, consequently, to be regarded in courts of justice as equivalent to an act of the legislature, whenever it operates of itself without the aid of any

---

[30] Moore, J. B., International Law Digest, Government Printing Office, Washington (1906), par. 735.

legislative provision." [31] But what is the situation when legislative action is necessary to carry out treaty provisions?

The moral obligation is, of course, beyond dispute. "If a treaty require the payment of money to carry it into effect, and the money can only be raised or appropriated by an act of the legislature, the existence of the treaty renders it morally obligatory on Congress to pass the requisite law; and its refusal to do so would amount to a breach of public faith and afford just cause for war." [32] It has been stated that the proposition "that Congress is under no obligation to make the stipulated appropriation, has not been seriously advanced by the House since 1868, although individual advocates of this view have not been wanting.[33]

Nevertheless, it is well to bear in mind that while the moral obligation exists, "a treaty is the supreme law of the land in respect of such matters only as the treaty-making power, without the aid of Congress, can carry into effect. Where a treaty stipulates the payment of money for which an appropriation is required, it is not operative in the sense of the Constitution. Every foreign government may be required to know that so far as the treaty stipulates to pay money the legislative sanction is required.[34]

An example of the need of money to carry a treaty into

[31] Foster vs. Neilson, *supra*. See also *infra*, sec. 25, Enforcement of Treaties.
[32] Duer, Outlines of Constitutional Jurisprudence of the United States, p. 138.
[33] Crandall, S. B., Treaties, Their Making and Enforcement, *supra*, p. 177.
[34] Turner vs. American Baptist Missionary Union, 5 McLean, 347.

Treaties

effect is the purchase of Alaska by the United States from Russia. Money bills under the Constitution must originate in the House of Representatives. At one time it was quite doubtful that the House would vote the money to complete the purchase, and had it refused finally so to do, in effect there would have been no treaty, and certainly no purchase.

If a treaty, standing alone and without the consent of Congress, cannot require the United States Government to expend money, it is equally clear that a treaty cannot compel any affirmative action by a State, and, indeed, it has never been held, either by the Supreme Court of the United States, or any other court, that such an affirmative action could successfully be required.[35] Certainly no State Government could be required, by treaty, to assume any obligation against its will. This idea was forcefully expressed by Senator John Sharp Williams, at the time a member of the House, in an address before the American Academy of Political and Social Science: "That the treaty can give an alien equal rights with the citizen, even within a State, concerning a subject-matter that the Federal Government would otherwise not control, I do not doubt, but that it can give him superior privileges to a citizen I deny. If by treaty with Japan, for example, California can be forced to admit Japanese, or by treaty with China it can be forced to admit Chinese, to the same schools with white children, then by treaty with Haiti or Santo Domingo negroes from those islands could be admitted to the same schools with white

[35] Putney, A. H., United States Constitutional History and Law, Illinois Book Exchange (1908), pages 157-158.

Judicial Interpretation of International Law

children in Mississippi, let us say, where native-born negroes, citizens of the United States, cannot attend white schools." [36]

On the whole there is little doubt that in practice the question of the treaty-making power of the United States should present no special difficulties. And the good sense of American negotiators will surely save the courts the necessity of ever declaring any treaty invalid as having transgressed even the broad powers granted by the Constitution.

Negotiation and conclusion of treaties is, of course, one of the prerogatives of the executive branch of the Government,[37] and in the exercise of this power the Executive may even conclude another treaty providing for a retrial of awards already made by a commission by virtue of the provisions of a prior treaty.[38] In concluding treaties, even where this is done for the protection or satisfaction of private rights, the United States acts in its sovereign capacity and not as an agent and mere representative of those who have lodged the appeal for protection, and rights determined as a result of treaty provisions become solemn international obligations to be discharged by the state found to be liable.[39] Governments enter into treaties through duly authorized agents, plenipotentiaries, or commissioners, but before a treaty can become effective ratifications must be exchanged.[40] In the United States treaties must be submitted for approval to

---

[36] Congressional Record, June 3, 1908.
[37] Frelinghuysen vs. Key, 110 U. S., 64; 28 L. Ed., 71.
[38] Frelinghuysen vs. Key, *supra*.
[39] Great Western Insurance Company vs. United States, 112 U. S., 193; 28 L. Ed., 687.
[40] *Ex parte* Ortiz, 100 Fed. Rep., 955.

Treaties

the Senate and approved by a two-thirds vote by that body before exchange of ratifications can take place.[41] Until such exchange is accomplished, the treaty is inchoate and may be defeated by the action of either contracting party.[42] As for the function of the Senate, it should be added that in a concurring opinion it has been declared that its power "is limited to a ratification of such terms as have already been agreed upon between the President, acting for the United States, and the commissioners of the other contracting power. The Senate has no right to ratify the treaty and introduce new terms into it, which shall be obligatory upon the other power, although it may refuse its ratification, or make such ratification conditional upon the adoption of amendments to the treaty.[43] A written declaration, however, attached to the treaty at the time of its ratification, explaining ambiguous language in the instrument, or adding new and distinct stipulations, becomes in fact a part of the treaty, and is as binding as if the provisions had been inserted in the body of the treaty.[44]

§ 27. *Enforcement and interpretation of treaties.*—A treaty being an agreement between two independent states, and, short of war, there being no international machinery for the enforcement of such agreements, its observance by a nation, and enforcement by its public agencies, depends primarily upon the honor and interest of international persons that are parties to it.[45] Where

[41] United States Constitution, Art. 2, par. 2, sec. 2.
[42] Armstrong et al. vs. Bidwell, 124 Fed. Rep., 690.
[43] The Diamond Rings, 183 U. S., 176; 46 L. Ed., 138. See also New York Indians vs. United States, 170 U. S., 1; 42 L. Ed., 927.
[44] Doe vs. Braden, 16 Howard, 635; 14 L. Ed., 1090.
[45] Edye vs. Robertson, 112 U. S., 580; 28 L. Ed., 798; La Ninfa, 75 Fed. Rep., 513.

an infraction or a violation of a treaty occurs, the government concerned, in an appropriate case on its own behalf, or, where its citizens have suffered, acting for them, but still itself as a party, may seek redress by diplomatic negotiations, representations, and reclamations,[46] and if such remonstrances have failed, a violation of a treaty may afford legal justification for war.[47] These are questions, however, for the political department of the government, and courts, deriving their powers from municipal law, as a rule cannot take cognizance of treaty infractions; they are not a supervisory agency for the purpose of enforcing treaties which the United States as a sovereign nation may choose to disregard.[48] So through what internal arrangements a sovereign carries out his treaty obligations is wholly his concern; other contracting states are properly interested in their observance, but not the machinery employed to effectuate this object.[49] Treaties, however, frequently do confer and regulate private rights, enforceable by judicial action,[50] and since the Federal Constitution makes treaties the supreme law of the land, their provisions in this respect are taken cognizance of as are other laws obligatory upon the courts.[51]

A treaty may be self-executing, and susceptible of being enforced by judicial tribunals without any sup-

[46] Edye vs. Robertson, *supra*. Botiller vs. Dominguez, 130 U. S., 238; 32 L. Ed., 926. Whitney vs. Robertson, 124 U. S., 190; 31 L. Ed., 386.
[47] Edye vs. Robertson, *supra*. *In re* Ah Lung, 18 Fed. Rep., 28.
[48] Chae Chan Ping vs. U. S., 130 U. S., 581; 32 L. Ed., 1068. Minnesota Canal, etc., Co. vs. Pratt, 101 Minn., 197; Whitney vs. Robertson, *supra*.
[49] Taylor *et al.* vs. Morton, 23 Fed. Cas., No. 13,799.
[50] Edye vs. Robertson, *supra*.
[51] Edye vs. Robertson, *supra*. See also sec. 26, Treaties and the treaty-making power in the United States, *supra*.

Treaties

not for the judiciary.[60] A court would not pass upon the question whether or not a prize capture was made by a duly commissioned captor, this being a matter for the government and captor, and one of which a claimant could not take advantage.[61]

When does a treaty take effect? The question is of course important because treaties may, and frequently do, determine the rights and power of the contracting governments, or their citizens. The general rule is that as respects the rights of the governments entering into a treaty it is considered effective from the date of its signature and that exchange of ratifications has a retroactive effect, confirming the treaty from the date thereof.[62] Any act between the signing of a treaty and its ratification, violating the provisions of the agreement, would certainly violate its spirit and indeed amount to a fraud upon the other party.[63] Where, however, a treaty operates on individual rights the rule is different, and the instrument does not affect the rights of private interests established between the date and exchange of ratifications. The reason for this is that "in this country a treaty is something more than a contract, for the Federal Constitution declares it to be the law of the land. If so, before it can become a law, the Senate, in whom rests the authority to ratify it, must agree to it. But the Senate is not required to adopt or reject it as a whole, but may modify or amend it, as was done with the treaty under consideration. As the individual citizen, on whose

[60] Doe et al. vs. Braden, 16 Howard, 635; 14 L. Ed., 1090.
[61] The Amiable Isabella, 6 Wheaton, 412; 5 L. Ed., 191.
[62] Haver vs. Yaker, 9 Wall., 321; 19 L. Ed., 571. Davis vs. The Police Jury of Concordia, 9 Howard, 280; 13 L. Ed., 138.
[63] The United States vs. D'Auterive et al., 10 Howard, 607; 13 L. Ed., 560. See also De Lima vs. Bidwell, 182 U. S., 222; 45 L. Ed., 1041.

Judicial Interpretation of International Law

rights of property it operates, has no means of knowing anything of it while before the Senate, it would be wrong in principle to hold him bound by it, as the law of the land, until it was ratified and proclaimed. And to construe the law so as to make the ratification of the treaty relate back to its signing, thereby devesting a title already vested, would be manifestly unjust, and cannot be sanctioned." [64]

Treaties being agreements in the nature of contracts, they are, as a general rule, governed by those canons of construction and interpretation applicable to agreements in writing between individuals, the primary object being to give effect to the intent of the contracting parties. For this purpose all parts of a treaty will always be considered with a view to give reasonable operation to the whole document.[65] "By the stipulations of a treaty are to be understood its language and apparent intention manifested in the instrument, with a reference to the contracting parties, the subject matter, and persons on whom it is to operate." [66]

An illustration of the application of principles of contractual construction to treaties is afforded by an adoption of the rule, frequently invoked with respect to agreements between individuals, that the enumeration of certain powers with respect to a particular subject matter is tantamount to an exclusion of all other powers with reference to the same subject matter; in other words,

[64] Haver vs. Yaker, *supra*. Davis vs. The Police Jury of Concordia, *supra*. *Ex parte* Ortiz, 100 Fed. Rep., 955.
[65] Sullivan vs. Kidd, 254 U. S., 433; 65 L. Ed., 344.
[66] United States vs. Arredondo, 6 Pet., 691; 8 L. Ed., 547. United States vs. Texas, 162 U. S., 1; 40 L. Ed., 867.

Treaties

treaties, too, are interpreted in the light of the rule, *Expressio unius est exclusio alterius*.[67]

Good faith being the very foundation of all international order, it will not be presumed that any state intends to provide, by a treaty, the means of perpetrating a fraud upon another state, and for this reason a treaty will always be construed as a whole in order to be applied to *bona fide* transactions.[68] In construing treaties, courts will interpret their language in its ordinary meaning and without resort to any artificial or special sense, unless this is clearly demanded by the provisions in question,[69] and if a treaty is so drawn as to permit two constructions, one restrictive of rights claimed under it and the other liberal, favoring an assertion of such rights, a liberal interpretation will be adopted.[70] In arriving at a conclusion as to the intent of the parties, if at the time of the exchange of ratifications an explanatory declaration is attached to the instrument, such declaration will be considered as if it were in the body of the instrument.[71] While the construction of a treaty regulating private rights is a judicial function, the interpretation placed upon a treaty adopted and followed by the political departments, where this has been expressed, will be given much weight by the judiciary;[72] but where, following the ratification of a treaty, the Senate resolved, by a resolution of less than two-thirds of a quorum, that it was not

[67] Tucker vs. Alexandroff, 183 U. S., 424; 46 L. Ed., 264.
[68] The Amistad, 15 Pet., 518; 10 L. Ed., 826.
[69] Geofroy vs. Riggs, 133 U. S., 258; 33 L. Ed., 642.
[70] Hauenstein vs. Lynham, 100 U. S., 483; 25 L. Ed., 628.
[71] Doe, *ex dem.* Clark *et al.* vs. Braden, 16 Howard, 635; 14 L. Ed., 1090.
[72] Sullivan vs. Kidd, *supra*.

intended to incorporate the inhabitants of the Philippines into citizenship of the United States, nor permanently to annex these islands, the resolution was without legal significance and the meaning of the treaty of peace with Spain could not be controlled by this expression of the Senate's views.[73] It is the practice of states to make treaties in the languages of the countries participating and to declare each version to be "original," and where this occurs neither controls nor is to be preferred to the other, for each expresses the meaning of the parties respectively, in their own language as, in the opinion of each, expressing the intention of both.[74]

It has become a very frequent, if not universal, practice of states, especially with regard to commercial intercourse and regulation of private rights, to insert into treaties what is known as the "most favored nation" clause, the object of which usually is to provide for an equality of treatment by one state of other states.[75] By virtue of this clause a state obtains the same concessions and privileges which have been granted by either party to another state, or states, provided these concessions are of a similar nature to those stipulated for by the treaty.[76] The nature of the clause is such that, if its spirit and provisions are violated by legislation, the courts cannot take cognizance of such infraction,[77] so that the scope of these treaties, solely as a matter of international law, has never been settled by the United States Supreme

[73] The Diamond Rings, 183 U. S., 176; 46 L. Ed., 138.
[74] United States vs. Arredondo, 6 Pet., 691; 8 L. Ed., 547.
[75] Fenwick, Charles G., International Law, The Century Co., New York and London (1924), p. 335.
[76] Davis, George C., The Elements of International Law, Harper and Bros., New York and London (1908), p. 248.
[77] Taylor vs. Morton, Fed. Cas. No. 13,799.

Treaties

Court.[78] Nevertheless, in some of their phases, as a matter of interpretation of acts of Congress, especially in tariff matters, the court has discussed in several cases the effect and operation of this provision. Thus it has been said that a treaty with Denmark, containing the "most favored nation" clause, did not require the United States to grant to the latter, without compensation, privileges accorded to the Hawaiian Islands in consideration of concessions considered valuable.[79] In a case following this ruling it was said that the clause relied upon "is a pledge of the contracting parties that there shall be no discriminating legislation against the importation of articles which are the growth, produce, or manufacture of their respective countries, in favor of articles of like character, imported from any other country. It has no greater extent. It was never designed to prevent special concessions, upon sufficient consideration, touching the importation of specific articles into the country of the other. It would require the clearest language to justify a conclusion that our Government intended to preclude itself from such engagements with other countries, which might in the future be of the highest importance to its interests."[80]

Laws under which an exporter was remitted an excise tax imposed on sugar sold in Russia, and also obtained a certificate of substantial market value, provided in effect for a bounty which authorized the Secretary of the Treasury to impose upon the sugar, when imported into the United States, an additional duty equal to the entire amount of the bounty, under an act of Congress passed

[78] Fenwick, Charles G., International Law, *supra*, p. 366, footnote 2.
[79] Bartram vs. Robertson, 122 U. S., 116; 30 L. Ed., 1118.
[80] Whitney vs. Robertson, 124 U. S., 190; 31 L. Ed., 386.

for the purpose of neutralizing advantages which certain countries grant their exporters by legislation of this nature in favor of their exporters.[81]

State pilotage laws, when applied to British vessels coming from foreign ports, did not conflict with the provisions of a treaty with Great Britain specifying that "no higher or other duties or charges shall be imposed in any ports of the United States on British vessels than those payable in the same ports by vessels of the United States," because of the exemption of coastwise steam vessels from pilotage under either federal or state legislation.[82]

§ 28. *Termination of treaties.*—Treaties are of various kinds, dealing with a large variety of subjects, and may

[81] Downs vs. United States, 187 U. S., 496; 47 L. Ed., 275.
[82] Olsen vs. Smith, 195 U. S., 332; 49 L. Ed., 224. The question of application of the most-favored-nation clause has arisen in a number of cases involving the administration of estates of decedents. A treaty with Argentina conferred upon the consular officers of that country the right "to intervene in the possession, administration, and judicial liquidation of the estate of the deceased, conformably with the laws of the country, for the benefit of the creditors," and it was claimed that a subsequent treaty with Italy, containing the most-favored-nation clause, gave an Italian consul the right to administer the estate of an Italian citizen dying intestate in one of the United States. The California courts denied the validity of this claim on the ground that this provision, if applicable, cannot be construed as intended to supersede the local law as to the administration of estates of deceased persons, and this view was upheld by the United States Supreme Court. Rocca vs. Thompson, 223 U. S. 317, 56 L. Ed. 453. The New York courts have adopted a much more liberal view and have held that the most-favored-nation clause of the Italian treaty carried with it the benefits of the Argentine treaty and conferred upon Italian consuls the right of administration of decedents' estates. *In re* Fattosini 38 Misc. 18, 67 N. Y. Supp. 1119; *In re* Lobrasciano, 38 Misc. 415, 77 N. Y. Supp. 1040; *In re* Scutella, 129 N. Y. Supp. 20. Massachusetts and Alabama courts have adopted the New York rule. *In re* Wyman, 191 Mass. 276, 77 N. E. 379; Carpigiani vs. Hall, 172 Ala. 287, 55 So. 248. For a recent application of the California rule see *In re* Clausen, 74 Cal. 420, 259 Pac. 1094.

Treaties

be terminated in various ways.[83] An extinction of a treaty by expiration of the time for which its life was fixed in the instrument itself is perhaps the simplest mode of treaty termination. When that occurs, the treaty simply lapses, as does any other agreement entered into only for a certain period. Another method of treaty termination presenting little, if any, difficulties, is in satisfying its objects, viz., in carrying out its provisions.[84] When, however, a treaty is of indefinite duration, the question whether or not it may be terminated, and if so, in what manner, not only arises, but may become one of considerable delicacy. There is no doubt that such a treaty may be annulled under certain circumstances.[85] It has been said that, as in the case of a contract, if the consideration fails, or important provisions are not complied with by one party to the compact, the treaty may be terminated. With apparent approval, the court quotes in this case certain observations made by eminent writers on international law under what circumstances treaty abrogation may occur:

When a state of things which was the basis of the treaty, and one of its tacit conditions, no longer exists. In most of the old treaties were inserted the *clausula rebus sic stantibus*, by which the treaty might be construed as abrogated when material circumstances on which it rested changed. To work this effect it is not necessary that the facts alleged to have changed should be material conditions. It is enough if they were strong inducements to the party asking abrogation.

The maxim "*Conventio omnis intelligitur rebus sic stantibus*" is held to apply to all cases in which the reason for a

---

[83] Terlinden vs. Ames, 184 U. S., 270; 46 L. Ed., 534.
[84] Hall, William Edward, A Treatise on International Law, Seventh Edition (The Clarendon Press), page 357.
[85] Hooper vs. United States, 22 Ct. Cl., 408.

treaty has failed, for there has been such change of circumstances as to make its performance impracticable except at an unreasonable sacrifice. Wharton's Com. Am. Law., par. 161.

Treaties, like other contracts, are violated when one party neglects or refuses to do that which moved the other party to engage in the transaction. When a treaty is violated by one party in one or more of its articles, the other can regard it as broken and demand redress, or can still require its observance. Woolsey, par. 112.[87]

A case can hardly be imagined where the courts would apply the maxim *rebus sic stantibus* and declare a treaty unenforceable on that ground. For this reason a discussion of the maxim is not within the scope of this treatise. It may be observed, however, that unless there is a clear failure of consideration, or an open violation of treaty provisions, whether a change has taken place, justifying denunciation of a treaty, may be a highly debatable question, and, therefore, whenever possible, the issue should not be left for determination by a party or parties involved, but should be considered a justiciable one.

A violation of a treaty by one party thereto makes the treaty voidable and not void, and the option to declare it terminated is in the hands of the sovereign power of the injured country.[88] A treaty is not revoked because it has become oppressive to one of the parties, and in any event its revocation or denunciation requires a public act of which courts must take notice.[89]

A treaty may of course be terminated by a subsequent agreement between the states concerned and any pro-

[86] Hooper vs. United States, *supra*.
[87] Hooper vs. United States, *supra*.
[88] Ware vs. Hylton, 3 Dallas, 199; 1 L. Ed., 197. *In re* Thomas, 23 Fed. Cas. 13,887. Chae Chan Ping vs. United States, 130 U. S., 581; 32 L. Ed., 1068. Charlton vs. Kelly, 228 U. S., 447; 57 L. Ed., 1274.
[89] Schulz vs. Raines and Co., 164 N. Y. S., 454.

Treaties

visions of an earlier treaty, inconsistent with a later one, are deemed abrogated.[90] Also, a termination of treaties may occur where one power absorbs another state,[91] but this is not necessarily so; a state may enter a federation and where its powers to execute treaties remain unimpaired, the fact of surrender of sovereignty in other respects does not in itself abrogate treaties it has entered into prior to its acquisition of a new international and constitutional status.[92]

In the United States, an act of Congress passed after a treaty had taken effect must be enforced by the courts and legislation enacted subsequent to a treaty controls, not the provisions of the treaty,[93] or, as the rule has been otherwise stated, "so far as a treaty made by the United States with any foreign nation can become the subject of judicial cognizance in the courts of this country it is subject to such Acts as Congress may pass for its enforcement, modification or repeal."[94] Owing to this rule, unavoidable by judicial tribunals, it is frequently said that treaties may be terminated by a later statute. Probably it is better to say that a treaty may be rendered unenforceable by the courts as a result of the provisions of a later statute, but to declare it terminated by reason of a subsequent statute is of doubtful accuracy. As we have seen, infraction of a treaty by a state party thereto

[90] *In re* Strobel's Estate, 39 N. Y. S., 169. Junkers vs. Chemical Foundation, 287 Fed. Rep., 597. See also *In re* Ross, 140 U. S., 453; 35 L. Ed., 581.
[91] Terlinden vs. Ames, 184 U. S., 270; 46 L. Ed., 534.
[92] Terlinden vs. Ames, *supra*. See Junkers vs. Chemical Foundation, *supra*.
[93] Alvarez y Sanchez vs. United States, 216 U. S., 167; 54 L. Ed., 432.
[94] Edye vs. Robertson, 112 U. S., 190; 28 L. Ed., 798. Chae Chan Ping vs. U. S., 130 U. S., 581; 32 L. Ed., 1068. Whitney vs. Robertson, 124 U. S., 190; 31 L. Ed., 386.

makes it voidable at the option of the injured party, and a statute enacted in violation of a treaty is an infraction thereof, but cannot be said to terminate it unless the other party to the compact chooses to regard it so. No contract can be legally terminated except in accordance with the provisions thereof, or for other valid reasons, or by mutual consent of the parties; an unilateral act of either party, without legal justification, does not bring it to an end. Courts cannot afford redress for violation of a treaty, but its international obligations continue [95] and failure to fulfil them may give occasion for reclamations of one party upon the other [96] and the aggrieved party may even attempt enforcement by war.[97] Therefore, to emphasize, a treaty may be rendered judicially unenforceable by subsequent Congressional legislation, but it is not thereby terminated as an international obligation.

Article VI of the Federal Constitution declares a treaty the supreme law of the land and places it on the same footing as an act of Congress. It follows, therefore, that where a valid treaty conflicts with a prior Congressional enactment, the courts will enforce the treaty provisions, but before a court will disregard a Federal statute in favor of a treaty, the two must be absolutely incompatible, for repeals by implication are not favored.[98]

A treaty would not be the supreme law of the land if it could be overridden by a state statute or even a state constitution. Therefore, state constitutions and state

[95] Whitney vs. Robertson, *supra*.
[96] Taylor vs. Morton, Fed. Cas. No. 13,799.
[97] Edye vs. Robertson, *supra*.
[98] Johnson vs. Browne, 205 U. S., 309; 51 L. Ed., 816. Hamilton vs. Erie R. Co., 114 N. E., 399; 219 N. Y., 343.

Treaties

laws must yield to treaty agreements properly entered into under the authority of the United States, if and when a conflict arises between the provisions of these instruments.[99]

It has been stated with considerable frequency, by many writers on international law, that war dissolves all treaties between the contracting parties.[100] Thus stated, however, the rule is no longer generally recognized, certainly not by courts in the United States. In an early case the United States Supreme Court declared:

> But we are not willing to admit the doctrine urged at the bar, that treaties become extinguished, *ipso facto*, by war between the two governments, unless they should be revived by an express or implied renewal on the return of peace. Whatever may be the latitude of doctrine laid down by elementary writers on the law of nations, dealing in general terms in relation to this subject, we are satisfied that the doctrine contended for is not universally true. There may be treaties of such a nature, as to their object and import, as that war will put an end to them; but where treaties contemplate a permanent arrangement of territorial and other national rights, or which, in their terms, are meant to provide for the event of an intervening war, it would be against every principle of just interpretation to hold them extinguished by the event of war. If such were the law, even the treaty of 1783, so far as it fixed our limits, and acknowledged our independence, would be gone, and we should have had again to struggle for both upon original revolutionary principles. Such a construction was never asserted, and would be so monstrous as to supersede all reasoning.
>
> We think, therefore, that treaties stipulating for permanent rights, and general arrangements, and professing to aim at

[99] Ware vs. Hylton, 3 Dallas, 199; 1 L. Ed., 568. Hauenstein vs. Lynham, 100 U. S., 483; 25 L. Ed., 628. Maryland Casualty Co. *et al.* vs. Chamos *et al.*, 263 S. W., 370.

[100] Fritz Schulz, Jr. Co. vs. Raines and Co., 164 N. Y. S., 454.

Judicial Interpretation of International Law

perpetuity, and to deal with the case of war as well as of peace, do not cease on the occurrence of war, but are, at most, only suspended while it lasts; and unless they are waived by the parties, or new and repugnant stipulations are made, they revive in their operation at the return of peace.[101]

In a much more recent decision the modern and prevailing doctrine has been stated in language meriting extensive quotation:

"The effect of war upon the existing treaties of belligerents is one of the unsettled problems of international law. The older writers sometimes said that treaties ended *ipso facto* when war came. 3 Phillimore, Int. L. 794. The writers of our own time reject these sweeping statements. 2 Oppenheim, Int. L. par. 99; Hall, Int. L. 398, 401; Fiore, Int. L. (Borchard's Transl.), par. 845. International law today does not preserve treaties or annul them, regardless of the effects produced. It deals with such problems pragmatically, preserving or annulling as the necessities of war exact. It establishes standards, but it does not fetter itself with rules. When it attempts to do more, it finds that there is neither unanimity of opinion nor uniformity of practice. 'The whole question remains as yet unsettled.' Oppenheim, *supra*. This does not mean, of course, that there are not some classes of treaties about which there is general agreement. Treaties of alliance fall. Treaties of boundaries or cessions, 'dispositive' or 'transitory' conventions, survive. Hall, Int. L. pp. 398, 401, *supra*; Westlake, Int. L. 34; Oppenheim, *supra*. So, of course, do treaties which regulate the conduct of hostilities. Hall, *Supra*; 5 Moore, Dig. Int. L. 372; Society for Propagation of the Gospel *vs.* Town of New Haven, 8 Wheaton 464, 5 L. Ed. 662.

"Intention in such circumstances is clear. These instances do not represent distinct and final principles. They are illus-

---

[101] The Society for the Propagation of the Gospel vs. The Town of New Haven, 8 Wheaton, 464; 5 L. Ed., 662.

Treaties

trations of the same principle. They are applications of a standard. When I ask what that principle or standard is, and endeavor to extract it from the long chapters in the books, I get this, and nothing more: That provisions compatible with a state of hostilities, unless expressly terminated, will be enforced, and those incompatible rejected.

"Treaties lose their efficacy in war only if their execution is incompatible with war. Bluntschli, Droit International Codifie, sec. 538."

That in substance was Kent's view, here, as often, in advance of the thought of his day:

"All those duties, of which the exercise is not necessarily suspended by the war, subsist in their full force. The obligation of keeping faith is so far from ceasing in time of war that its efficacy becomes increased, from the increased necessity of it. 1 Kent, Comm. p. 176.

"That, also more recently, is the conclusion embodied by the Institute of International Law in the rules voted at Christiania in 1912, which defined the effects of war on international conventions. In these rules, some classes of treaties are dealt with specially and apart. Treaties of alliance, those which establish a protectorate or a sphere of influence, and generally treaties of a political nature, are, it is said, dissolved. Dissolved, too, are treaties which have relation to the cause of war. But the general principle is declared that treaties which it is reasonably practicable to execute after the outbreak of hostilities must be observed then, as in the past. The belligerents are at liberty to disregard them only to the extent and for the time required by the necessities of war. Scott, Resolutions of the Institute of Int. Law, p. 172. *Cf.* Hall, Int. Law (7th Ed.) 399; 2 Westlake, Int. p. 35; 2 Oppenheim, Int. L. par. 99, 276.

"This, I think, is the principle which must guide the judicial department of the government when called upon to determine during the progress of a war whether a treaty shall be observed, in the absence of some declaration by the political departments of the government that it has been suspended or annulled. A treaty has a twofold aspect. In its primary operation it is a compact between independent states. In its secondary operation, it is a source of private rights for individuals within states. Head Money Cases, 112 U. S., 580, 598; 28 L. Ed., 798. Granting that the termination of the compact involves the termination of the rights, it does not follow, because there is a privilege to rescind, that the privilege has been exercised. The question is not what states may do after war has supervened, and this without breach of their duty as members of the society of nations. The question is what courts are to presume that they have done.

"President and Senate may denounce the treaty, and thus terminate its life. Congress may enact an inconsistent rule, which will control the action of the courts. Fong Yue Ting vs. U. S., 149 U. S., 698; 37 L. Ed., 905. The treaty of peace itself may set up new relations, and terminate earlier compacts, either tacitly or expressly. The proposed treaties with Germany and Austria give the victorious powers the privilege of choosing the treaties which are to be kept in force or abrogated. But until some one of these things is done, until some one of these events occur, while war is still flagrant, and the will of the political departments of the government unrevealed, the courts, as I view their function, play a humbler and more cautious part. It is not for them to denounce treaties generally *en bloc*. Their part it is, as one provision or another is involved in some actual controversy before them, to determine whether, alone or by force of connection with an inseparable scheme, the provision is inconsistent with the policy or safety of the nation in the emergency of war, and hence presumably intended to be limited to times of peace. The mere fact that other portions of the treaty are suspended or even abrogated, is not conclusive. The treaty does not fall in its entirety unless it has the character of an indivisible act.

"To determine whether it has this character, it is not enough to consider its name or label. No general formula suffices. We must consult in each case the nature and purpose of the specific articles involved." [102]

[102] Techt vs. Hughes et al., 229 N. Y., 222; 128 N. E., 185.

Treaties

Rights acquired by virtue of treaty provisions, for instance to hold lands in the United States, are not divested by the abrogation of the compact.[103]

[103] Carneal *et al.* vs. Banks, 10 Wheaton, 181; 6 L. Ed., 297. Chirac vs. Chirac, 2 Wheaton, 259; 4 L. Ed., 257.

CHAPTER SIX

REMEDIAL MEASURES FALLING SHORT OF WAR

§ 29. *Arbitration.*—The object of international arbitration is "the settlement of differences between states by judges of their own choice, and on the basis of respect for law."[1] The parties to the dispute form or designate the tribunal which is to pass upon their claims and contentions and frequently settle, by treaty or another appropriate instrument of submission, the rules or principles which are to govern the case.[2] In the very nature of things, therefore, questions of international arbitration do not reach the courts very often, and when they do, it is almost entirely in connection with problems of distribution of awards, their finality, the limits of the arbitrators' authority, etc.

The decision of an arbitral tribunal, acting within the scope of the powers conferred upon it, is conclusive and final and cannot be reviewed by any judicial tribunal,[3] nor can an award be defeated by a party to the arbitration proceeding where it is made by a majority of the commission and the latter, under the power given to it by the submission agreement, determined that a

[1] Art. 15, Convention for the Pacific Settlement of International Disputes, 1899.
[2] Hall, W. E., A Treatise on International Law, The Clarendon Press, London, 1917, p. 373. Fenwick, Charles G., International Law, The Century Co., New York and London (1924), p. 403.
[3] Comegys and Pettit vs. Vasse, 1 Pet., 193; 7 L. Ed., 191. Frevall vs. Bache, 14 Pet., 95; 10 L. Ed., 369; La Ninfa, 75 Fed., 513.

Remedial Measures Falling Short of War

majority vote should govern, and this is so although the commissioners of the defeated government resigned after the discussions were closed.[4]

Claims may be prosecuted before commissions by attorneys representing the parties in interest, and there is nothing immoral or illegal in a contract for professional services.[5]

As a rule, arbitral commissioners decide merely as to the validity of a claim and the amount to be paid in accordance with international law, but its ownership, where a transfer or assignment has been made, or is claimed to have been made, depends upon the local jurisprudence where the transaction is alleged to have been made.[6] Commissions do not possess the powers exercised by judicial tribunals, such as the means of compelling attendance of witnesses, and if there are conflicting claims as to the actual ownership of an award, it is better to leave their determination to the ordinary course of judicial proceedings.[7]

While the results of arbitral proceedings are conclusive as between nations parties thereto, the claimant's government may institute an investigation, if circumstances warrant such a step, to ascertain whether or not its influence had been used to obtain an allowance of a fraudulent claim, and this may be done by a new treaty or by appropriate legislation conferring the necessary powers upon the executive. Indeed, where there is cause

---

[4] Colombia vs. Cauca Co., 190 U. S., 524; 47 L. Ed., 1159.
[5] Wright vs. Tebbitts, 91 U. S., 252; 23 L. Ed., 320.
[6] Phelps vs. McDonald, 99 U. S., 298; 25 L. Ed., 473.
[7] Comegys vs. Vasse, *supra*. See also Clark vs. Clark, 17 Howard, 315; 15 L. Ed., 77, and Judson vs. Corcoran, 17 Howard, 612; 15 L. Ed., 231.

to suspect that the power of the nation has been used for improper purposes, it is a matter of national honor that a new inquiry be instituted as to the *bona fides* of the claim.[8]

§ 30. *Nonintercourse and embargo.*—Nonintercourse laws have been passed, in the early history of the United States, prohibiting trade and other relations with states offending against international law.[9] While nonintercourse acts are no doubt perfectly proper as a method of bringing an offending state to reason and observance of international law, their efficacy is more than doubtful, and the experiences of this country in its early history, with these acts, have not been of such a nature as to encourage their adoption except, perhaps, in wholly exceptional circumstances and in a limited way. In any event, their interpretation and enforcement by the courts depends entirely upon the provisions and wording of such legislation when resorted to.[10]

An embargo decrees, of course, nonintercourse, and is therefore frequently associated with the latter, but it is much narrower in scope. In the strict sense of the term, an embargo is no more than a detention of ships in port,[11] but it has also been defined as "a special form of reprisal, and consists in general in the sequestration of

[8] Frelinghuysen vs. Key, 110 U. S., 63; 28 L. Ed., 71. United States *ex rel.* Boynton vs. Blaine, 139 U. S., 306; 35 L. Ed., 183. La Abra Silver Mining Co. vs. United States, 175 U. S., 423; 44 L. Ed., 223.

[9] Wilson, George Grafton, Handbook of International Law, West Publishing Co., St. Paul (1910), p. 233.

[10] For construction of the nonintercourse statutes, see, for instance, The Patriot, Fed. Cas., No. 13,985. The New York, 3 Wheat., 59; 4 L. Ed., 333. The Samuel, 1 Wheaton, 9; 4 L. Ed., 23.

[11] Lawrence, T. J., The Principles of International Law, Macmillan and Co., London and New York (1895), p. 295. The William King, 2 Wheaton, 148; 4 L. Ed., 206.

Remedial Measures Falling Short of War

the public or private property of an offending state. It may sometimes be applied by a state to its own vessels."[12] Students of American history are familiar with the difficulties that accompanied attempts to enforce embargo acts prior to the War of 1812, and the disadvantages attending this method of enforcement of international law, by one power acting alone, have been shown to be so serious that return to that weapon, always double-edged, is not at all likely.[13] A general economic boycott, analogous to the measures contemplated by the Covenant of the League of Nations against members of the League resorting to war in disregard of other provisions of the Covenant,[14] would of course present a situation materially differing from an embargo imposed by a single state, and perhaps could hope for a measure of real success.

§ 31. *Retaliation and reprisals.—Display of force.*—Retaliation, which may be defined as an endeavor by one state to make another, or its citizens, suffer the same amount of evil which the latter has inflicted upon the former,[15] is an executive and not a judicial measure, and the Supreme Court has declined to adopt it except where constrained to do so as a result of legislation or executive acts binding upon the judiciary. In a discussion of the subject, Chief Justice Marshall declared:

. . . the court is decidedly of opinion that reciprocating to the subjects of a nation, or retaliating on them, its unjust

[12] Wilson, George Grafton, Handbook of International Law, West Publishing Co., St. Paul, Minn. (1910), p. 232.
[13] For a discussion of American Embargo Acts of 1807 and 1808, see The William King, *supra*.
[14] Covenant of the League of Nations, Article 16.
[15] Halleck, H. W., International Law, H. H. Bancroft and Co., San Francisco (1861), p. 296.

Judicial Interpretation of International Law

proceedings toward our citizens, is a political, not a legal measure. It is for the consideration of the government, not of its courts. The degree and kind of retaliation depend entirely on considerations foreign to this tribunal. It may be the policy of the nation to avenge its wrongs in a manner having no affinity to the injury sustained, or it may be its policy to recede from its full rights and not to avenge them at all. It is not for its courts to interfere with the proceedings of the nation and to thwart its views. It is not for us to depart from the beaten track prescribed for us, and to tread the devious and intricate path of politics. Even in the case of salvage, a case peculiarly within the discretion of the courts, because no fixed rule is prescribed by the law of nations, Congress has not left it to this department to say whether the rule of foreign nations shall be applied to them, but has by law applied that rule. If it be the will of the government to apply to Spain any rule respecting captures which Spain is supposed to apply to us, the government will manifest that will by passing an act for the purpose. Till such an act be passed, the court is bound by the law of nations which is a part of the law of the land.[16]

It has been held that in the absence of statute or treaty, the comity of the United States does not require that judgments of a foreign country be recognized as conclusive in this country, where such foreign country does not give like effect to American judgments.[17] Whatever may be thought of the soundness of this ruling, it

[16] The Nereide, 9 Cranch, 388, 3 L. Ed., 769. See also The Frances and Eliza, 8 Wheaton, 398; 5 L. Ed., 645, and The Pitt, 8 Wheaton, 371; 5 L. Ed., 639.

[17] Hilton vs. Guyot, 159 U. S., 113; 40 L. Ed., 95. In a very recent case the District Court of the United States for the Western District of Washington held that a German citizen, convicted in Prussia of a crime involving moral turpitude, but fully pardoned before entering the United States, was not subject to deportation from the United States, for after a pardon the individual concerned has the same right as other citizens so far as the laws of his country are concerned, and because it is probable that a like comity would be shown by Germany in case of American nationals found in that country. Hempel vs. Weedin, 23 (2d) Fed. Rep., 949.

should not be necessary to point out that this is not retaliation, but a question of reciprocity.

Vattel, quoted with approval in a judicial opinion, declares that "reprisals are used between nation and nation to do justice to themselves when they cannot otherwise obtain it." [18] In the words of an American authority, "reprisals are resorted to for the redress of injuries inflicted upon the state, in its collective capacity, or upon the right of individuals to whom it owes protection in return for their allegiance. They consist in the forcible taking of things belonging to the offending state, or of its subjects, and holding them until a satisfactory reparation is made for the injury." [19]

Reprisals are not easy to distinguish from acts of war and most certainly bring countries, once resorted to, to the very brink of war. A series of prolonged reprisals has been declared to constitute a limited war; limited in the sense that such war does not abrogate treaties, suspend private rights, or authorize indiscriminate seizures and condemnations.[20]

In order to enforce their demands, and to obtain redress for injuries, nations have at times resorted to a display of force, or have exercised it where threats did not bring about the desired change or satisfaction. Such questions, too, are political and cannot be passed upon and decided by the courts. Where they arise incidentally, in cases properly before judicial tribunals, the judiciary will follow the action of the executive and legislative departments, whatever these may be.[21]

[18] Cushing vs. United States, 22 Ct. Cl., 1.
[19] Halleck, H. W., International Law, *supra*, p. 297.
[20] Gray vs. United States, 21 Ct. Cl., 340.
[21] Perrin vs. United States, 4 Ct. Cl., 543.

LIST OF AUTHORITIES CITED

American Journal of International Law Supplement, 1919.
American Journal of International Law Supplement, 1920.

Blackstone, William, Sir, Commentaries on the Laws of England. Callaghan & Co., Chicago, 1899.
Borchard, Edwin M., The Diplomatic Protection of Citizens Abroad. The Banks Law Publishing Co., New York, 1916.
Burgess, John W., Political Science and Comparative Constitutional Law. Ginn & Co., 1913.

Congressional Record, June 3, 1908.
Constitution of the United States of America.
Convention for the Pacific Settlement of International Disputes, 1899, Art. 15.
Cornell Law Review, February, 1928; note by James D. Hurly: Recognition; Retroactive effect.
Corpus Juris.
Corwin, Edward S., National Supremacy. Henry Holt & Co., New York City, 1913.
Covenant of the League of Nations, Art. 16.
Crandall, S. B., Treaties, Their Making and Enforcement, 2d Ed., Washington, 1916.
Crane, R. T., The State in Constitutional and International Law, Johns Hopkins University Studies in Historical and Political Science.
Cyclopedia of Law and Procedure, Vol. XXIX.

Davis, George B., Elements of International Law. Harper & Bros., New York and London, 1918.
Dickinson, E. D., The Equality of States in International Law. Cambridge, Harvard University Press, 1920.
Dickinson, E. D., Harvard Law Review, January, 1925.
Dickinson, E. D., Recent Recognition Cases, The American Journal of International Law, April, 1925.

Judicial Interpretation of International Law

Dickinson, E. D., The American Journal of International Law, January, 1926, Rum Ship Seizures Under the Recent Treaties.

Dickinson, E. D., The Russian Reinsurance Company Case, The American Journal of International Law, October, 1925.

Duer, Outlines of Constitutional Jurisprudence of the United States.

Elliott, J., Debates on the Adoption of the Federal Constitution. J. B. Lippincott Co., 1891.

Farrand, Max, The Framing of the Constitution. Yale University Press, 1923.

Farrand, Max, Records of the Federal Convention. Yale University Press, 1911.

Federal Criminal Code, Sec. 290.

Fenwick, Charles G., International Law. The Century Co., New York and London, 1924.

Garner, J. W., Recent Developments in International Law. University of Calcutta, 1925.

Garner, J. W., Presidential Address before The American Political Science Association, December 29, 1924. The American Political Science Review, February, 1925.

Georgetown Law Journal, February, 1928; article by Charles Kneier.

Hall, W. E., A Treatise on International Law. The Clarendon Press, London, 1917.

Halleck, H. W., International Law. H. H. Bancroft & Co., 1861.

Holland, Thomas Erskine, The Elements of Jurisprudence. Oxford University Press, 1910.

Holdsworth, W. S., A History of English Law. Methuen & Co., Ltd., London, 1925.

Jenkins, Sir Leoline, Life of; see Stowell & Munro, International Cases. Houghton Mifflin Co., Boston, 1916.

Latané, John H., From Isolation to Leadership. Doubleday, Page & Co., 1918.

Lawrence, T. L., Some Disputed Questions in Modern International Law. Deighton, Bell & Co., Cambridge, 1884. Essay 1, Is There a True International Law?

Lawrence, T. J., The Principles of International Law. Macmillan & Co., London and New York, 1895.

List of Authorities Cited

Lawyers' Reports Annotated, Vol. XXII, p. 502.
Lee, Guy Carleton, Historical Jurisprudence. The Macmillan Co., New York, 1911.

Macy and Gannaway, Comparative Free Government. The Macmillan Co., 1919.
McBain and Rogers, The New Constitutions of Europe. Doubleday, Page & Co., 1923.
Madison, James, The Federalist. The Central Law Journal Co., 1917.
Madison, James, Journal. G. B. Putnam's Sons, 1908.
Merriam, C. E., History of the Theory of Sovereignty Since Rousseau. Columbia University Studies in History, Economics and Public Law.
Moore, John Bassett, International Law Digest. Government Printing Office, Washington, 1916.

Naturalization Laws and Regulations, Sec. 15. Government Printing Office, 1924.

Potter, Pitman R., International Law and National Law in the United States. American Journal of International Law, April, 1925.
Putney, A. H., United States Constitutional History and Law. Illinois Book Exchange, 1908.

Scott, James Brown, Cases on International Law. West Publishing Co., St. Paul, 1922.
Snow, Freeman, Cases on International Law. The Boston Book Co., 1893.
Stanberry, Attorney General, 1867, 12 Opinions, 319.
Stewart, Irvin, American Treaty Provisions, American Journal of International Law, January, 1926.
Stowell & Munro, International Cases. Houghton Mifflin Co., Boston, 1916.

Thorpe, F. N., The Essentials of American Constitutional Law. G. P. Putnam's Sons, New York, 1917.
Twiss, Travers, The Law of Nations. Longmans, Green, Longmans & Roberts, 1861.

U. S. Rev. Stats., 1899.

Judicial Interpretation of International Law

United States Statutes at Large.

Warren, Charles, The Supreme Court and the Sovereign States. Princeton University Press, 1924.

Westlake, J., International Law. Cambridge University Press, 1904.

Willoughby, W. W., Constitutional Law of the United States. Century Co.

Wilson, George Grafton, Handbook of International Law. West Publishing Co., St. Paul, 1910.

Woolsey, Theodore D., Introduction to the Study of International Law, Scribner, Armstrong & Co., New York, 1875.

Woolsey, Lester H., Foreign Relations of the United States, 1912.

TABLE OF CASES CITED

Abrams vs. State, 45 Wash., 327; 88 Pac., 327............... 154
Ackerman et al. vs. Haenck et al., 147 Ill., 514; 35 N. E., 381.. 141
Adula, The, 176 U. S., 361; 44 L. Ed., 505................... 25
Adutt, *In re*, 55 Fed. Rep., 376............................. 132
Agency of Canadian Car & Foundry Co. vs. American Can Co.,
   258 Fed. Rep., 363...................................... 87
Ah Lung, *In re*, 18 Fed. Rep., 28............................ 170
Ainsa vs. United States, 161 U. S., 208; 40 L. Ed., 673........ 98
Airhart vs. Massieu, 98 U. S., 491; 25 L. Ed., 213............ 99
Alabama vs. Georgia, 23 Howard, 505; 16 L. Ed., 556........ 102
Alberta, The, vs. Moran, 9 Cranch, 359; 3 L. Ed., 758......... 123
Alexander vs. Roulet, 13 Wallace, 386; 20 L. Ed., 564......... 94
Alvarez y Sanchez vs. United States, 216 U. S., 167; 54 L. Ed.,
   432 181
American Banana Co. vs. United Fruit Co., 213 U. S., 347; 53
   L. Ed., 826.. 75-101
American Insurance Co. vs. Canter, 1 Peters, 511; 7 L. Ed.,
   242 88-91-93-140
Amiable Isabella, The, 6 Wheaton, 412; 5 L. Ed., 191........ 173
Amistad, The, 15 Pet., 518; 10 L. Ed., 826.................. 175
Anderson vs. United States, 170 U. S., 481; 42 L. Ed., 1116.... 108
Ann, The, Fed. Cas., No. 397............................... 105
Anne, The, 3 Wheaton, 435; 4 L. Ed., 428................... 122
Antelope, The, 10 Wheaton, 66; 6 L. Ed., 268.......... 24-75-110
Apollon, The, 9 Wheaton, 362; 6 L. Ed., 111......... 103-106-110
Armstrong et al. vs. Bidwell, 124 Fed. Rep., 690.............. 169
Aubrey, *In re*, 26 Fed. Rep., 848........................... 125

Baiz, *In re*, 135 U. S., 403; 34 L. Ed., 222................... 122
Baldy vs. Hunter, 171 U. S., 388; 43 L. Ed., 208............ 61-67
Ball, Daniel, The, 10 Wall., 557; 19 L. Ed., 999.............. 103
Bank of Augusta, The, vs. Earle, 13 Pet., 519; 19 L. Ed., 274.. 149
Barker vs. Harvey, 181 U. S., 481; 45 L. Ed., 963........... 99
Bartram vs. Robertson, 122 U. S., 116; 30 L. Ed., 1118........ 177

Judicial Interpretation of International Law

Bartram vs. Robertson, 15 Fed. Rep., 212..................... 171
Beaverton, The, 273 Fed. Rep., 539........................ 119
Beers vs. Arkansas, 20 Howard, 527; 15 L. Ed., 991....... 33-117
Belgenland, The, 114 U. S., 355; 29 L. Ed., 152............112-128
Bello Corrunes, The, 6 Wheaton, 152; 5 L. Ed., 229......... 122
Belvidere, The, 90 Fed. Rep., 106.......................... 112
Benson vs. McMahon, 127 U. S., 457; 32 L. Ed., 234......... 134
Berizzi Bros. Co. vs. Pesaro, 271 U. S., 562; 70 L. Ed., 1088.. 118
Biddle vs. United States, Lobingier's Extraterritorial Cases.... 141
Blythe vs. Hinckley, 127 Cal., 153; 59 Pac., 787.............. 111
Bodek, *In re*, 63 Fed. Rep., 813............................. 141
Bodemueller vs. United States, 39 Fed. Rep., 437............ 80
Botiller vs. Dominguez, 130 U. S., 238; 32 L. Ed., 926......... 170
Bourne vs. Bourne, 204 N. Y. S., 866........................ 66
Boyd vs. Nebraska, 143 U. S., 483; 36 L. Ed., 103.... 136-139-140
Brown, Jonathan, vs. United States and Brulé Sioux, 32 Ct. Cl., 432 77
Browne vs. Dexter, 66 Cal., 39; 4 Pac., 913.................. 144
Brown vs. Maryland, 12 Wheaton, 419; 6 L. Ed., 678......... 18
Buffington vs. Grosvenor, 46 Kan., 730; 27 Pac., 137......... 147
Burthe vs. Denis, 133 U. S., 514; 33 L. Ed., 768............. 80

Cabrera, *Ex parte*, Fed. Cas., No. 2,278...................120-121
Callsen vs. Hope, 75 Fed. Rep., 758........................ 100
Caminetti vs. United States, 242 U. S. 470; 61 L. Ed., 442.... 8
Canada Southern R. R. Co. vs. Gebhard, 109 U. S., 527; 27 L. Ed., 1020 142
Cappell vs. Hall, 7 Wall., 542; 19 L. Ed., 244................. 122
Carlisle vs. United States, 16 Wall., 147; 21 L. Ed., 426........ 151
Carneal *et al.* vs. Banks, 10 Wheaton, 181; 6 L. Ed., 297...... 187
Carpigiani vs. Hall, 172 Ala., 287; 55 So., 248................ 178
Cessna vs. United States, 169 U. S., 185; 42 L. Ed., 702....... 99
Chae Chang Ping vs. United States, 130 U. S., 581; 32 L. Ed., 1068 11-31-155-170-180-181
Charlton vs. Kelly, 229 U. S., 447; 57 L. Ed., 1274........ 133-180
Charming Betsy, The, 2 Cranch, 64; 2 L. Ed., 208.......... 9-147
Cherokee Nation vs. Georgia, 5 Peters, 1-52; 8 L. Ed., 25... 29-33
Cherokee Nation vs. Southern Kansas R. R. Co., 33 Fed. Rep., 900 37
Cherokee Tobacco Co. vs. United States, 11 Wall., 616; 20 L. Ed., 227 158
Chew Heong vs. United States, 112 U. S., 536; 28 L. Ed., 770... 171

Table of Cases Cited

Chicago, Rock Island & Pac. Ry. Co. vs. McGlinn, 114 U. S., 542; 29 L. Ed., 270..................................... 97
Chinese Exclusion Cases (Chae Chang Ping vs. United States), 130 U. S., 581; 32 L. Ed., 1068........ 11-31-155-170-180-181
Chirac vs. Chirac, 2 Wheaton, 259; 4 L. Ed., 257......... 160-187
Chisholm vs. Georgia, 2 Dallas, 456; 2 L. Ed., 453........... 29
Church vs. Hubbart, 2 Cranch, 187; 2 L. Ed., 249........... 106
Clark vs. Clark, 17 Howard, 315; 15 L. Ed., 77.............. 189
Clausen, *In re*, 74 Cal., 420; 259 Pac. 1094.................. 178
Coffee vs. Groover, 123 U. S., 1; 31 L. Ed., 51.............. 74
Cohens vs. Virginia, 5 Wheaton, 264; 5 L. Ed., 257........... 32
Cohn vs. Jones, 100 Fed. Rep., 639......................... 133
Collins vs. Loisel, 262 U. S., 426; 67 L. Ed., 1062............ 132
Columbia vs. Cauca Co., 190 U. S., 524; 47 L. Ed., 1159....118-189
Comegyss vs. Vasse, 1 Peters, 193; 7 L. Ed., 191........81-188, 89
Commonwealth vs. Green, 17 Mass., 514.................... 127
Commonwealth vs. MacLoon, 101 Mass., 1.................. 108
Commonwealth vs. Manchester, 139 U. S., 240; 35 L. Ed., 159. 105
Commonwealth vs. Smith, 111 Allen, 243.................... 127
Commonwealth of Virginia vs. State of West Virginia, 220 U. S., 1; 55 L. Ed., 353.. 93
Com. vs. Rowe, 112 Ky. 482; 66 S. W., 29.................. 8
Conrad, The, 37 Ct. Cl., 459............................... 81
Cooper, *Ex parte*, 143 U. S., 472; 36 L. Ed., 232.............. 172
Cooper Mfg. Co. vs. Ferguson, 113 U. S., 727; 28 L. Ed., 1137 150
Corralitos Stock Co. vs. United States and Apache Indians, 33 Ct. Cl., 342; 178 U. S., 280; 44 L. Ed., 1069........... 111
Cosgrove vs. Winnly, 174 U. S., 64; 43 L. Ed., 897........... 131
County of St. Clair vs. Livingston, 23 Wallace, 46; 23 L. Ed., 59 90
Coutzen vs. United States, 179 U. S., 191; 45 L. Ed., 148...... 140
Crashley vs. Press Pub. Co., 179 N. Y., 27; 71 N. E., 258... 149
Cross vs. Harrison, 16 Howard, 190; 14 L. Ed., 899.........74-95
Cunard Steamship Co. vs. Mellon, 262 U. S., 100; 67 L. Ed., 894 105-108
Cunningham vs. Rogers, Lobingier's Extraterritorial Cases.... 126
Cushing vs. United States, 22 Ct. Cl., 1..................129-193

Dainese vs. Hale, 91 U. S., 13; 23 L. Ed., 190............... 125
Davis vs. Packard, 7 Peters, 276; 8 L. Ed., 684.............. 119
Davis vs. The Police Jury of Concordia, 9 Howard, 279; 13 L. Ed., 138 ....94-172, 173-174

[201]

Judicial Interpretation of International Law

De Geofroy vs. Riggs, 133 U. S., 258; 33 L. Ed., 642......161-164
Delassus vs. United States, 9 Peters, 134; 9 L. Ed., 71......... 99
De Lima vs. Bidwell, 182 U. S., 1; 45 L. Ed., 1041......95-173
Dewing vs. Perdicaries, 96 U. S., 193; 24 L. Ed., 654......... 62
Diamond Rings, The, 183 U. S., 176; 46 L. Ed., 138..95-156, 169-176
Dillon, *In re*, Fed. Cas., No. 3,914........................... 122
Disconto Gesellschaft vs. Umbreit, 208 U. S., 570; 52 L. Ed., 625 154
Divina Pastora, 4 Wheaton, 52; 4 L. Ed., 50................. 47-55
Doe *et al.* vs. Braden, 16 Howard, 635; 14 L. Ed., 1090,
169-172, 173-175
Doehrel vs. Hilmer *et al.* (Iowa), 71 N. W., 204............. 101
Dooley vs. United States, 182 U. S., 222; 45 L. Ed., 1074...... 96
Dooley vs. United States, 183 U. S., 151; 43 L. Ed., 128...... 96
Dorsey vs. Brigham *et al.*, 177 Ill., 250..................... 147
Downes vs. Bidwell, 182 U. S., 244; 45 L. Ed., 1088........95-162
Downs vs. United States, 187 U. S., 496; 47 L. Ed., 275...... 178
Dupont vs. Pichon, 4 Dallas, 321; 1 L. Ed., 851............. 121

Earl *et al.* vs. Gedley, 42 Minn., 36; 44 N. W., 254............ 114
Easton vs. Huett, 95 Iowa, 473; 64 N. W., 408............... 154
Edye vs. Robertson, 112 U. S., 190; 28 L. Ed., 792-798,
156-169, 170-181, 182
Elk vs. Wilkins, 112 U. S., 94; 28 L. Ed., 643.............. 138
Ely's Administrator vs. United States, 171 U. S., 220; 43 L. Ed., 142 92-94
Estrella, The, 4 Wheaton, 298; 4 L. Ed., 574................ 48
Exchange, The, vs. McFaddon et al., 7 Cranch, 116; 3 L. Ed., 287 ....38-74, 109-114, 116-123
Ezeta, *In re*, 62 Fed. Rep., 972............................. 134

Fairfax's Devisee vs. Hunter's Lessee, 7 Cranch, 603; 3 L. Ed., 453 153-160
Farmer's National Bank vs. Sutton Mfg. Co., 52 Fed. Rep., 191 2
Fattosini, *In re*, 38 Misc., 18; 67 N. Y. S., 1119.............. 178
Faulkner vs. Hart, 82 N. Y., 413........................... 2
Ferrara vs. Auric Mining Co., 43 Col., 496; 95 Pac., 952..... 155
Fess, *Ex parte*, 102 Cal., 347.............................. 131
Fleming vs. Page, 9 Howard, 603; 13 L. Ed., 276............ 73-95
Fong Yue Ting vs. United States, 149 U. S., 698; 37 L. Ed., 905 142-155

Table of Cases Cited

Ford vs. Surget, 97 U. S., 594; 24 L. Ed., 1018.............. 53
Ford vs. United States, 273 U. S., 593; 71 L. Ed., 793...... 128
Foster vs. Neilson, 2 Pet., 253; 7 L. Ed., 415,
                                     43-101, 157-166, 171-172
Frances and Eliza, The, 8 Wheaton, 398; 5 L. Ed., 645...... 192
Franklin vs. Twogood, 25 Iowa, 529....................... 3
Fraser vs. McConway & Torlay Co., 82 Fed. Rep., 257....... 149
Frelinghuysen vs. Key, 110 U. S., 63; 28 L. Ed., 71...... 168-190
French Republic vs. Inland Navigation Co., 263 Fed. Rep.,
  410 117
Frevall vs. Bache, 14 Pet., 95; 10 L. Ed., 369.............. 188

Galpin vs. Page, 18 Wallace, 350; 21 L. Ed., 959............ 112
Gans S. S. Line vs. Isles Steamship Co., 257 U. S., 662; 66 L.
  Ed., 423 119
Garcia vs. Lee, 12 Peters, 511; 10 L. Ed., 226...........143-171
Gatton vs. Chicago, R. I. & P. C. R. Co., 95 Iowa, 112; 28 L.
  R. A., 566 2
Gelston vs. Hoyt, 3 Wheaton, 324; 4 L. Ed., 381............41-45
Geofroy vs. Riggs, 133 U. S., 258; 33 L. Ed., 642...........95-175
Gill's Estate, *In re*, 79 Iowa, 296; 44 N. W., 553...........147-153
Gouverneur's Heirs vs. Robertson *et al.*, 11 Wheaton, 332; 6
  L. Ed., 488 153
Grace, The, and The Ruby, 283 Fed., 475................... 107
Gran Para, The, 7 Wheaton, 471; 5 L. Ed., 501............. 123
Gray vs. United States, 21 Ct. Cl., 340..................... 193
Great Western Insurance Company vs. United States, 122 U. S.,
  193; 28 L. Ed., 687 168
Green vs. Salas, 31 Fed. Rep., 106......................141-144
Grunert vs. Spaulding, 78 N. W. (Wis., 1899), 606............ 39

Hall vs. Hall, 61 N. Y., 130................................ 154
Hamilton vs. Erie R. R. Co., 114 N. E. 399; 219 N. Y., 343... 182
Hanauer vs. Woodruff, 15 Wallace, 439; 21 L. Ed., 224........ 62
Handly vs. Anthony, 5 Wheaton, 374; 5 L. Ed., 113.......... 102
Hanks vs. The State, 13 Texas Court of Appeals, 289......... 127
Harcourt vs. Gaillard, 12 Wheaton, 523; 6 L. Ed., 716.......92-94
Harding vs. Standard Oil Co. *et al.*, 182 Fed. Rep., 421....... 137
Harris vs. Powers, 129 Ga., 74; 58 S. E., 1038................ 20
Hauenstein vs. Lynham, 100 U. S., 483; 25 L. Ed., 628,
                                     137-147-159-161, 175
Haver vs. Yaker, 9 Wall., 321; 19 L. Ed., 571............173-174

Judicial Interpretation of International Law

Hawaii vs. Mankichi, 190 U. S., 197; 47 L. Ed., 1016......... 162
Heirn vs. Bridault, 37 Miss., 209.....................19-28-147
Hempel vs. Weedin, 23 (2d) Fed. Rep., 949................. 192
Henderson vs. Poindexter's Lessee, 12 Wheaton, 530; 6 L. Ed., 718 92
Hepburn vs. Elzey, 2 Cranch, 445; 2 L. Ed., 332........... 29
Hewitt vs. Speyer, 250 Fed. Rep., 367.....................75-84
Hilton vs. Guyot, 159 U. S., 113; 40 L. Ed., 95....9-25-26-113-192
Hitz, Ex parte, 111 U. S., 766; 28 L. Ed., 592................. 121
Hodgson vs. Dexter, 1 Cranch, 345; 2 L. Ed., 130.......... 84
Hohner vs. Gratz, 50 Fed. Rep., 369....................... 113
Holmes vs. Jannison, 14 Peters, 540; 10 L. Ed., 579....130-160-163
Hooper vs. United States, 22 Ct. Cl., 408..............129-178-180
Horn vs. Lockhart, 17 Wallace, 570; 21 L. Ed., 657......... 60
Horn Silver Mining Co., The, vs. New York, 143 U. S., 305; 36 L. Ed., 164 150
Hudson & Smith vs. Guestier, 6 Cranch, 281, 3 L. Ed., 249... 106
Humboldt Lumber Co. Mfg. Asso., 60 Fed. Rep., 428......... 105
Huntington vs. Attrill, 146 U. S., 657; 36 L. Ed., 1123....... 110

Illinois Central Co. vs. People of the State of Illinois, 146 U. S., 387; 36 L. Ed., 1018............................ 105
Indiana vs. Kentucky, 136 U. S., 479; 34 L. Ed., 329........88-91
Inglis vs. Sailor's Snug Harbor, 3 Pet., 101; 7 L. Ed., 617.... 144
Inglis vs. Trustees, 3 Peters, 99, 7 L. Ed., 617................. 140
Iowa vs. Illinois, 147 U. S., 137; 37 L. Ed., 55............... 102
Itata, The, 56 Fed. Rep., 505............................... 57

James & Co. vs. Second Russian Insurance Co., 239 N. Y., 248; 146 N. E., 369......................................66-67-69
Jane Palmer, The, 270 Fed. Rep., 609....................... 117
Johnson vs. Browne, 205 U. S., 309; 51 L. Ed., 816............ 182
Johnson vs. McIntosh, 8 Wheaton, 543; 5 L. Ed., 681.........88-89
Johnson Lighterage Co., The, No. 24; 231 Fed. Rep., 365...... 84
Jones vs. Letombe, 3 Dallas, 384, 1 L. Ed., 647.............. 122
Jones vs. McMasters, 20 Howard, 8; 15 L. Ed., 805........... 99
Jones vs. Meehan, 175 U. S., 1; 44 L. Ed., 49................. 171
Jones vs. Soulard, 24 Howard, 41; 16 L. Ed., 624............ 102
Jones vs. United States, 137 U. S., 202; 34 L. Ed., 691,
                                                    42-46-88-90-92
Judson vs. Corcoran, 17 Howard, 612; 15 L. Ed., 231.......81-189
Junkers vs. Chemical Foundation, 287 Fed. Rep., 597........ 181

Table of Cases Cited

Kadlec vs. Pavik, 9 N. D., 1278; 83 N. W., 5................ 147
Keene vs. McDonough, 8 Peters, 318; 8 L. Ed., 955.......... 74
Keith vs. Clark, 97 U. S., 454; 24 L. Ed., 1071...............31-86
Kennett vs. Chambers, 14 Howard, 38; 14 L. Ed., 316.....26-41-42
Keokuk Hamilton Bridge Co. vs. Illinois, 175 U. S., 626; 43 L. Ed., 1185 102
Ker vs. Illinois, 119 U. S., 436; 30 L. Ed., 421............... 134
Ker & Co. vs. Couden, 223 U. S., 268; 56 L. Ed., 432....... 90
Kestor, The, 110 Fed. Rep., 432............................ 15
Ketchum vs. Buckley, 99 U. S., 188; 25 L. Ed., 473.......... 88
Knox vs. Lee (Legal Tender Cases), 12 Wallace, 455; 20 L. Ed., 313 32
Kodiak, The, 53 Fed. Rep., 126............................ 107
Kohl vs. Lehlback, 160 U. S., 293; 40 L. Ed., 432............ 152
Kyle, *Ex parte*, 67 Fed. Rep., 306.......................... 141

La Abra Silver Mining Co. vs. United States, 175 U. S., 423; 44 L. Ed., 223.. 190
Lam Mow vs. Nagle, 24 Fed. Rep. (2d), 316............... 108
Lane County vs. Oregon, 7 Wallace, 76; 19 L. Ed., 101........ 32
La Ninfa, 75 Fed. Rep., 513............................169-188
Latham vs. United States, 2 Fed. Rep. (2d), 208............ 107
Latimer vs. Poteet, 14 Peters, 4; 10 L. Ed., 328............. 162
Law Ow Bew vs. United States, 144 U. S., 47; 36 L. Ed., 340.. 142
Lehigh Valley R. R. vs. State of Russia, 21 Fed. Rep. (2d), 396 46-63
Leitensdeffer vs. Webb, 20 Howard, 176; 15 L. Ed., 891...... 74
Lilla, The, 2 Spr., 177; Fed. Cas., No. 8,343................. 54
Lobrasciano, *In re*, 38 Misc., 415; 77 N. Y. S., 1040........... 178
Louisiana vs. Mississippi, 202 U. S., 1; 50 L. Ed., 913....... 102
Low Wah Suey vs. Backus, 225 U. S., 460; 65 L. Ed., 1165... 147
Luke vs. Calhoun Co., 52 Ala., 115........................ 150
Luria vs. United States, 231 U. S., 9; 58 L. Ed., 101......139-141
Lusitania, The, 231 Fed. Rep., 715........................ 10

Mackenzie vs. Hare, 239 U. S., 299; 60 L. Ed., 297.....137-144-145
Mackenzie vs. Hare *et al.*, 165 Cal., 776; 134 Pac., 713........ 144
Mahler vs. Norwich & N. Y. Transp. Co., 35 N. Y., 352...... 105
Marianna Flora, The, 11 Wheaton, 1; 6 L. Ed., 405........109-128
Martin vs. Hunter's Lessee, 1 Wheaton, 314; 4 L. Ed., 97.....171
Martin vs. Waddell, 16 Peter, 367; 10 L. Ed., 997............ 89

Judicial Interpretation of International Law

Maryland Casualty Co. *et al..* vs. Chamos *et al.*, 263 S. W., 370 183
Mason vs. Intercolonial Railway of Canada & Trustees, 197 Mass., 349 118
McDonald vs. State, 80 Wis., 407; 50 N. W., 185.............. 110
M'Ilvaine vs. Coxe's Lessee, 4 Cranch, 209; 2 L. Ed., 207, 40-91-140
Meade vs. United States, 9 Wall., 691; 19 L. Ed., 687........ 172
Miller vs. Dows, 94 U. S., 445; 24 L. Ed., 207............... 141
Minnesota Canal, etc., Co. vs. Pratt, 101 Minn., 197......... 170
Minor vs. Happersett, 21 Wall., 162; 22 L. Ed., 627.......... 136
Missouri vs. Holland, 252 U. S., 416; 64 L. Ed., 641....159-160-164
Missouri vs. Kentucky, 11 Wall., 395; 20 L. Ed., 116......... 103
Missouri vs. Nebraska, 196 U. S., 23; 49 L. Ed., 372......... 103
Mitchell vs. United States, 21 Wall., 350; 22 L. Ed., 584.... 142
Montello, The, 20 Wall., 430; 22 L. Ed., 391................. 103
Moore vs. American Transportation Co., 24 Howard, 1; 16 L. Ed., 674 104
More vs. Steinbach, 127 U. S., 70; 32 L. Ed., 51............88-94
Mormon Church vs. United States, 136 U. S., 1; 34 Ed., 481..88-91
Mortimer vs. New York Elevated R. R. Co., 6 N. Y. Supp., 898 88-89-90
Muir, *Ex parte*, 254 U. S., 522; 65 L. Ed., 383.............. 118
Mumford vs. Wardwell, 6 Wallace, 423; 18 L. Ed., 756....... 92

Nathan vs. Virginia, 1 Dallas, 77; 1 L. Ed., 44.............. 33
Neagle, *In re*, 135 U. S., 1; 34 L. Ed., 55.................. 143
Nebraska vs. Iowa, 143 U. S., 359; 36 L. Ed., 186............88-90
Neely vs. Henkel, 180 U. S., 109; 45 L. Ed., 448......73-111-133
Nereide, The, 9 Cranch, 388; 3 L. Ed., 769...............113-192
New Hampshire vs. Louisiana, 108 U. S., 76; 27 L. Ed., 656... 79
Newman vs. Beasch, 152 N. Y. S., 456; Lobingier's Extraterritorial Cases 126
New Orleans, City of, vs. Abbagnate, 62 Fed. Rep., 240....... 77
New Orleans vs. Steamship Co., 20 Wallace, 387; 22 L. Ed., 354 72
New Orleans vs. United States, 223 U. S., 268; 56 L. Ed., 432..88-90
New York, The, 3 Wheat., 59; 4 L. Ed., 333.................. 190
New York, The, 175 U. S., 187; 44 L. Ed., 126..............10-105
New York Indians vs. United States, 170 U. S., 1; 42 L. Ed., 927 169

Table of Cases Cited

Nishimura Ekiu vs. United States, 142 U. S., 651; 35 L. Ed., 1146 155
Noddleburn, The, 28 Fed. Rep., 855...................... 112
Norman vs. Norman (Cal.), 54 Pac., 143.................... 114
Nueva Anna, The, 6 Wheaton, 193; 5 L. Ed., 239............41-45

Oetjen vs. Central Leather Co., 246 U. S., 297; 62 L. Ed., 726..46-76
Olsen vs. Smith, 195 U. S., 332; 49 L. Ed., 224.............. 178
O'Reilly de Camara vs. Brooke, 209 U. S., 45; 52 L. Ed., 676... 94
Ortiz, *Ex parte*, 100 Fed. Rep., 955......................168-174

Panama Railroad Co. vs. Napier Shipping Co., 166 U. S., 280; 41 L. Ed., 1004.. 111
Paquette Habana, The, 175 U. S., 677; 44 L. Ed., 320........10-24
Patriot, The, Fed. Cas. No. 13,985......................... 190
Pattillo vs. Alexander, 96 Ga., 60; 29 L. R. A., 616............ 1
Paul vs. Virginia, 8 Wall., 168; 19 L. Ed., 357.............. 150
Penhallow et al., vs. Doane's Administrators, 3 Dallas, 54; 1 L. Ed., 507 39
Pennsylvania vs. Wheeling, etc., Bridge Co., 13 Howard, 518; 14 L. Ed., 518... 2
Penza, The, 277 Fed. Rep., 91.............................. 62
People *ex rel.* Attorney General vs. Wheeler, 136 Cal., 652; 69 Pac., 435 149
People vs. Curtis, 50 N. Y., 321............................ 130
People vs. Gerke, 5 Cal., 381............................... 164
People vs. McLeod, 1 Hill, 377; 37 Am. Dec., 328............. 23
Perrin vs. United States, 4 Ct. Cl., 543..................... 193
Pesaro, The, 255 U. S., 46; 65 L. Ed., 592................... 119
Peterhoff, The, 5 Wallace, 28; 18 L. Ed., 564................ 10
Phelps vs. McDonald, 99 U. S., 298; 25 L. Ed., 473.......... 189
Pitt, The, 8 Wheaton, 371; 5 L. Ed., 639................... 192
Poindexter vs. Greenhow, 114 U. S., 270; 29 L. Ed., 185...... 39
Pollard vs. Hogan, 3 Howard, 212; 11 L. Ed., 565............ 93
Preobrazhenski et al. vs. Cibrario et al., 192 N. Y. S., 275.... 63
Prentiss vs. Brennan, 19 Fed. Cas., No. 11,385............... 137
Prevost vs. Greneaux, 19 Howard, 1; 15 L. Ed., 572......... 163
Propeller Genesee, 12 Howard, 443; 13 L. Ed., 1058.......... 104
Prize Cases, The, 2 Black, 635; 17 L. Ed., 459............... 53
Pullman's Palace Car Co. vs. Pennsylvania, 141 U. S., 18; 35 L. Ed., 613... 110

Judicial Interpretation of International Law

Reinitz, *In re*, 39 Fed. Rep., 204............................ 132
Republic of Honduras vs. Soto, 112 N. Y., 310; 19 N. E., 845.. 33
Republic of Mexico vs. De Arangoiz, 12 N. Y. Super. Ct., 634.. 33
Respublica vs. DeLongchamps, 1 Dallas, 111; 1 L. Ed., 59...19-121
Rhode Island vs. Massachusetts, 4 Howard, 591; 11 L. Ed., 1116 88-91
Rhode Island vs. Massachusetts, 12 Peters, 657.............. 2
Ricaud vs. American Metal Co., 246 U. S., 304; 62 L. Ed., 733 46-75
Riddell vs. Fuhrman, 233 Mass., 69; 123 N. E., 237.......... 19
Ritchie vs. Mullen, 159 U. S., 235; 40 L. Ed., 133............. 113
Rocca vs. Thompson, 223 U. S., 317; 56 L. Ed., 453......... 178
Rocke vs. Washington, 19 Ind., 53; 81 Am. Dec., 376......... 31
Rogday, The, 278 Fed. Rep., 294........................... 62
Roger vs. Whitham, 56 Wash., 190; 105 Pac., 628............ 147
Rose vs. Himely, 4 Cranch, 239-241; 2 L. Ed., 608...45-54-106-112
Ross, *In re*, 140 U. S., 453; 35 L. Ed., 581.........111-125-126-181
Roumania vs. Guaranty Trust Co., 250 Fed. Rep., 341......64-111
Rousos, *In re*, 119 N. Y. S., 34............................ 137
Russian Government vs. Lehigh Valley R. R. Co., 293 Fed. Rep., 133; also 21 Fed. Rep. (2d), 396...................46-63
Russian Reinsurance Company vs. Stoddard, 240 N. Y. S., 149; 147 N. E., 703..66-70
Russian Socialist Federated Soviet Republic vs. Cibrario, 235 N. Y., 255; 139 N. E., 259............................ 65

Sao Vincente, The, 295 Fed. Rep., 829...................... 117
Sao Vincente, The, 260 U. S., 151; 67 L. Ed., 179............ 117
St. Clair vs. United States, 154 U. S., 134; 38 L. Ed., 936.... 108
Samuel, The, 1 Wheaton, 9; 4 L. Ed., 23.................... 190
Santissima Trinidad, The, 7 Wheaton, 283-337; 5 L. Ed., 280-434 55-146-147
Santos Case, 7 Fed. Cas., No. 4,016........................ 160
Sapphire, The, 11 Wallace, 164; 20 L. Ed., 127..............33-87
Schooner Endeavor, The, 37 Court of Claims, 242........... 14
Schooner Jane, The, 37 Court of Claims, 24.................. 14
Schooner Nancy, The (1892), 27 Court of Claims, 99......... 13
Schulz vs. Raines and Co., 164 N. Y. S., 454............180-183
Scotia, The, 14 Wallace, 170; 20 L. Ed., 822................10-25
Scutella, *In re*, 129 N. Y. S., 20............................ 178
Shanks vs. Dupont, 3 Pet., 242, 246; 7 L. Ed., 666.........140-144
Shekury vs. Brooks, Lobingier's Extraterritorial Cases........ 125
Ship Richmond, 9 Cranch, 102; 3 L. Ed., 670............... 115

Table of Cases Cited

Ship Rose, The, 36 Court of Claims, 290..................... 13
Shively vs. Bowlby, 152 U. S., 1; L. Ed., 331............... 88-105
Siren, The, 7 Wallace, 152; 19 L. Ed., 129.................. 84
Smith vs. Alabama, 124 U. S., 465; 31 L. Ed., 508........... 2
Smith vs. United States, 10 Peters, 326; 9 L. Ed., 442...... 98
Societa Commerciale Italiana di Navigazioni vs. Maru Nav. Co., 280 Fed. Rep., 334...................................... 119
Society for the Propagation of the Gospel vs. The Town of New Haven, 8 Wheaton, 464; 5 L. Ed., 662........100-160-184
Sokoloff vs. National City Bank, 239 N. Y., 158; 145 N. E., 917   68
Soulard vs. United States, 4 Peters, 511; 7 L. Ed., 938........ 98
Sprott vs. United States, 20 Wallace, 459; 22 L. Ed., 371..... 61
State vs. Adams, 45 Iowa, 99; 24 American Reports, 760.... 146
State vs. Boyd, 31 Neb., 682; 48 N. W., 739................. 141
State vs. Jackson, 79 Vt., 504; 65 Am. Rep., 657............ 146
State vs. Montgomery, 94 Maine, 192; 47 Atl. Rep., 165..... 149
State *ex rel.* Oft vs. Smith, 14 Wis., 497..................... 152
State *ex rel.* Perine et al., vs. Van Beek et al., 87 Iowa, 569; 54 N. W., 525... 152
State *ex rel.* Schuet vs. Murray, 28 Wis., 96; 9 Am. Rep., 489. 152
State vs. Smith, 70 Cal., 153; 12 Pac., 121.................. 111
State vs. Travelers' Ins. Co., 40 Atl. Rep., 465............. 152
Stearns vs. United States, 6 Wallace, 589; 18 L. Ed., 843..... 94
Stixrud's Estate, *In re*, 58 Wash., 339; 109 Pac., 343......... 154
Strathearn S. S. Co., Limited, vs. Dillon, 252 U. S., 348; 64 L. Ed., 607... 115
Strobel's Estate, *In re*, 39 N. Y. S., 169..................... 181
Strother vs. Lucas, 12 Peters, 410; 9 L. Ed., 1137.......... 97
Sullivan vs. Burnett, 103 U. S., 334; 26 L. Ed., 1124......... 154
Sullivan vs. Kidd, 254 U. S., 433; 65 L. Ed., 344..........174-175

Takuji Yamashita, *In re*, 30 Wash., 234; 70 Pac., 482........ 153
Talbot vs. Janson, 5 Dallas, 133; 1 L. Ed., 540...........123-144
Tartar Chemical Co. vs. United States, 116 Fed. Rep., 726..... 45
Taylor, *In re*, 118 Fed. Rep., 196........................... 133
Taylor et al., vs. Carpenter, Fed. Cas., No. 13,785...........148-150
Taylor vs. Morton, Fed. Cas., No. 13,799..............170-176-182
Techt vs. Hughes et al., 229 N. Y., 222; 128 N. E., 185...... 186
Terlinden vs. Ames, 184 U. S., 270; 46 Ed., 534........87-179-181
Texas, State of, vs. White et al., 7 Wall., 700, 19 L. Ed., 227.. 30
Thirty Hogsheads of Sugar vs. Boyle, 9 Cranch, 119; 3 L. Ed., 701 24-26
Thomas, *In re*, 23 Fed. Cas., 13,837....................... 180

Judicial Interpretation of International Law

Thorington vs. Smith, 8 Wallace, 1; 19 L. Ed., 363...........60-61
Three Friends, The, 166 U. S., 1; 41 L. Ed., 897.....48-49-50-51-57
Titus vs. United States, 20 Wallace, 475; 22 L. Ed., 400..... 88
Trageser vs. Gray, 20 Atl., 905........................... 152
Triquet vs. Bath, Burrage: Reports vol. III, p. 1478......... 1
Tucker vs. Alexandroff, 183 U. S., 424; 46 L. Ed., 264...115-123-175
Turner vs. American Baptist Missionary Union, 5 McLean, 347,
   24 Fed. Cas., No. 14,251...........................166-171

Underhill vs. Hernandez, 169 U. S., 250; 42 L. Ed., 456......75-78
Union Bank vs. Hill, 3 Caldw. (Tenn.), 325................ 38
United States vs. The Ambrose Light, 25 Fed. Rep., 408......55-57
United States vs. Arjona, 120 U. S., 479; 30 L. Ed., 728..18-77-116
United States vs. Arredondo et al., 6 Pet., 691; 8 L. Ed., 547,
                                                157-174-176
United States vs. Arredondo et al., 9 Peters, 691; 10 L. Ed., 93   99
United States vs. Auguisola, 1 Wallace, 352; 19 L. Ed., 613... 98
United States vs. Bell, 248 Fed. Rep., 992.................... 15
United States vs. Bevans, 3 Wheaton, 336; 4 L. Ed., 404.... 8
United States vs. Benner et al., Fed. Cas., No. 14,568......... 119
United States ex rel. Boynton vs. Blaine, 139 U. S., 306; 35 L.
   Ed., 183 190
United States vs. Carlisle, 16 Wallace, 147; 21 L. Ed., 426.... 83
United States vs. Chaves, 159 U. S., 452; 40 L. Ed., 215...... 98
United States vs. Clarke, 8 Peters, 436; 8 L. Ed., 1001........ 98
United States vs. Clarke's Heirs, 16 Peters, 231; 10 L. Ed.,
   946 98
United States vs. Cottingham, 40 Am. Dec., 710............ 153
United States vs. Cruikshank, 92 U. S., 542; 23 L. Ed., 588...78-136
United States vs. D'Auterive et al., 10 Howard, 609; 13 L.
   Ed., 560 93-173
United States vs. Diekelman, 92 U. S. 520; 23 L. Ed., 742,
                                                79-115-124-151
United States vs. Eckford, 6 Wallace, 484; 18 L. Ed., 920..... 117
United States vs. Gillies, Fed. Cas., No. 15,206............. 146
United States vs. Hand, Fed. Cas., No. 15,297............... 121
United States vs. Huckabee, 16 Wallace, 434; 22 L. Ed., 457.. 88
United States vs. Hunter, 21 Fed. Rep., 615................. 156
United States vs. Hutchings, 26 Fed. Cas., No. 15,429.......40-41
United States vs. Jeffers, Fed. Cas., No. 15,471............. 124
United States vs. Jeffers, Fed. Cas., No. 15,471............. 121
United States vs. Kilgore, Lobingier's Extraterritorial Cases... 125

Table of Cases Cited

United States vs. La Abra Silver Mining Co., 29 Ct. Cl., 432... 82
United States vs. LaFontaine, Fed. Cas., No. 15,580......... 122
United States vs. Lariviere, 93 U. S., 188; 23 L. Ed., 846.... 171
United States vs. Liddle, Fed. Cas., No. 15,598............... 119
United States vs. McCullagh, 221 Fed. Rep., 288............ 160
United States vs. McGill, 4 Dallas, 426; 1 L. Ed., 894....... 108
United States vs. McRae, L. R. 8 Eq. 69, Scott's Cases...... 88
United States vs. Montault, 12 Howard, 47; 13 L. Ed., 887... 93
United States vs. O'Keefe, 11 Wallace, 178; 20 L. Ed., 131.... 83
United States vs. Ortega, 11 Wheaton, 467; 6 L. Ed., 521..... 120
United States vs. Ortega, Fed. Cas., No. 15,971...........119-120
United States vs. Ortiz, 176 U. S., 422; 44 L. Ed., 529........ 99
United States vs. Palmer, 3 Wheaton, 610; 4 L. Ed., 471....47-129
United States vs. Percheman, 7 Peters, 51; 8 L. Ed., 604.... 97
United States vs. Pico, 23 Howard, 326; 16 L. Ed., 464......43-94
United States vs. Pirates, 5 Wheaton, 184; 5 L. Ed., 64.....17-129
United States vs. Prioleau, 2 Hem. & M., 559............... 88
United States vs. Rauscher, 119 U. S., 407; 30 L. Ed., 425..130-131
United States vs. Ravara, 2 Dallas, 297; 1 L. Ed., 222...... 122
United States vs. Repentigny, 5 Wallace, 211; 18 L. Ed., 627,
    92-98-140
United States vs. Reynes, 9 Howard, 127; 13 L. Ed., 74....... 172
United States vs. Rice, 4 Wheaton, 246; 4 L. Ed., 562...... 72
United States vs. Rio Grande Dam & Irrigation Co., 174 U. S.,
    690; 43 L. Ed., 1136.................................... 103
United States vs. Rodgers, 150 U. S., 249; 37 L. Ed., 1071.... 18
United States vs. Rodgers, 46 Fed. Rep., 1................. 104
United States vs. Schooner Peggy, 1 Cranch, 103; 2 L. Ed., 49 171
United States vs. Shaurer, 214 Fed. Rep., 154............... 160
United States vs. Siem, 299 Fed. Rep., 582.................. 16
United States vs. Smiley et al., Fed. Cas., No. 16,317......... 125
United States vs. Smith, 5 Wheaton, 153; 5 L. Ed., 57.....57-129
United States vs. Texas, 152 U. S., 1; 40 L. Ed., 867....... 174
United States vs. Thompson, 257 U. S., 432; 66 L. Ed., 299... 16
United States vs. Thompson, Lobingier's Extraterritorial Cases 125
United States vs. Trumbull, 48 Fed. Rep., 94............... 122
United States of America vs. Wagner, L. R., 2 Chancery
    Appeals, 582 33
United States vs. Watts, 14 Fed. Rep., 130.................. 131
United States vs. Weed, 5 Wallace, 62; 18 L. Ed., 531........ 57
United States vs. White, 27 Fed. Rep., 200 28
United States vs. Wiltberger, 5 Wheaton, 76; 6 L. Ed., 37.... 108

Judicial Interpretation of International Law

United States vs. Wong Kim Ark., 169 U. S., 649; 42 L. Ed.,
    890 137-138
United States vs. Yorba, 1 Wallace, 422; 17 L. Ed., 635..43-94-172

Vandeput, The, 37 Ct. Cl., 396........................... 81
Vilas vs. City of Manila, 220 U. S., 345; 55 L. Ed., 491....... 93

Ware vs. Hylton, 3 Dallas, 199; 1 L. Ed., 568.....8-26-161-180-183
Ware vs. Wisner, 50 Fed. Rep., 310.......................138-146
Watchful, The, 6 Wallace, 91; 18 L. Ed., 763................ 57
Watters, Horace Co. vs. Gerard, 189 N. Y. 302; 82 N. E., 143.. 20
Wehlitz, *In re*, 16 Wis., 443; 84 Am. Dec., 700..............147-153
Whitfield vs. United States, 92 U. S., 165; 23 L. Ed., 400...... 88
Whitney vs. Robertson, 124 U. S., 190; 31 L. Ed., 386,
    170-177-181-182
Wildenhus' Case, 120 U. S., 1; 30 L. Ed., 565..............115-124
William King, The, 2 Wheaton, 146; 4 L. Ed., 206.........190-191
Williams vs. Bruffy, 96 U. S., 176; 24 L. Ed., 716........53-60-67
Williams' Case, Fed. Cas. No. 17,708....................... 143
Williams vs. Suffolk Ins. Co., 13 Peters, 415; 10 L. Ed., 226.... 44
Wilson vs. Blanco, 4 N. Y. Supp., 714..................... 122
Wilson vs. McNamee, 123 U. S., 572; 26 L. Ed., 234.......... 107
Wisconsin vs. Pelican Insurance Co., 127 U. S., 289; 32 L. Ed.,
    239 127
Worcester vs. Georgia, 6 Peters, 515; 8 L. Ed., 483........... 156
Workman vs. New York City *et al.*, 179 U. S., 552, 45 L. Ed.,
    314 112
Wright, *In re*, 123 Fed. Rep., 463........................... 132
Wright vs. Henkel, 190 U. S., 40; 47 L. Ed., 948............. 132
Wright vs. Tebbitts, 91 U. S., 252; 23 L. Ed., 320............ 189
Wulfson vs. Russian Socialist Federated Soviet Republic, 234
    N. Y., 378; 138 N. E., 25..............................41-63
Wunderle *et al.* vs. Wunderle, 144 Ill., 40; 33 N. E., 195..... 154
Wyman, *In re*, 191 Mass., 276; 77 N. E., 379................ 178

Yick Wo vs. Hopkins, 118 U. S., 356; 30 L. Ed., 220.......... 148
Young vs. United States, 97 U. S., 39; 24 L. Ed., 992......... 83
Young, John Allen's Will, *In re*, Lobingier's Extraterritorial
    Cases, 92 124-126

INDEX

Abandonment of territory, 92
Accretion, acquisition of territory by, 90
Act of Congress. See *Congress*
Acts of sovereign not to come under foreign courts, 75 *sqq.*
Acts of Soviet, effect in U. S., 68
Acts of states in rebellion, legality of, 61
Acts of unrecognized governments, validity of, 67 *sqq.*
Agents, government, responsibility of, 84
Alaska, purchase by treaty, 167
Algeria, part of France, 45
Alien, definition, 147
Aliens, disabilities of, 151 *sqq.*
Aliens, duties of, 150
Aliens, jurisdiction of federal courts over, 23
Aliens, may sue, 154
Aliens, rights and privileges, 147, 152
Aliens, right to exclude, 155
Aliens, right to hold property, 160
Allegiance, definition, 150
Arbitration, 188 *sqq.*
Arbitration, fraudulent claims under, 189
Arbitration, object of international, 188
Arbitration. See also *Commissions, international*
Arbitration. See also *Tribunals, arbitral*
Armed merchant vessels, 129
Articles of Confederation, 4
Asylum, extradition treaty not guarantee of, 133
Asylum in embassies, legations and vessels, 123
Austinian conception of law, 36

Austro-Hungarian Empire, 92
Award of claims commission, decision final, 81
Award of International commission, participation in, 80

Bank of Tennessee, 85
Belligerency, cases in American Civil War, 51 *sqq.*
Belligerency, definition, 48
Belligerency, how determined, 54
Belligerency, nature of, 48 *sqq.*
Belligerency, recognition of, a political act, 48
Belligerency, recognition and rights, 50 *sqq.*
Belligerent rights, nature of, 53 *sqq.*
Belligerent rights to form government, 73
Belligerent right to search ships, 128
Belligerents, South American colonies as, 54
Belligerents. See also *Insurgents*
Birds, treaty on migratory, 160, 164
Blackstone, William, Sir, Commentaries, international law a part of common law, 1
Boundaries of states, 101 *sqq.*
Boundaries, settled politically, not judicially, 42
British creditors in Revolutionary War, 6
British government, right of U. S. citizens to prosecute claims against, 83
British subjects in American Court of Claims, 82
Buenos Ayres, controversy over title to Falkland Islands, 44
Burgess, John W., 16

[213]

Index

Cable Act, citizenship not lost by marriage, 145
California, date of conquest, 94
California, when became territory of U. S., 43
Caroline, The, case, 20
Carranza, Mexican government of, 75, 76
Castine, British import duties at, in 1814, 72
Cession of territory, laws remaining in force after, 93
Changes in international law, 25
Chase, Mr. Justice, 26
  definition of state, 30
China, American Laws there operative, 125 *sqq*.
Citizen, definition, 136
Citizens, relation to state in U. S., 79
Citizenship, 135 *sqq*.
Citizenship by birth, 138
Citizenship by naturalization, 139 *sqq*.
Citizenship compared to nationality, 135
Citizenship, definition by Supreme Court, 135
Citizenship determined by municipal law, 135
Citizenship, eligibility, 137
Citizenship, loss by naturalized citizens, 145
Citizenship, Senate resolution on Philippines, 176
Citizenship, sources, 135
Civil law, Louisiana, 1
Civil War, cases on belligerency, 51 *sqq*.
Civil war, definition, 51
Civil war, recognition of factions, 47
Colonies, sovereignty and independence of, 3 *sqq*.
Commission, claims, decision final, 81
Commission, international claims, participation in awards of, 80
Commissioners, arbitral. See *Tribunals, arbitral*
Comity, definition, 65

Common law, brought to America by colonists, 2
Common law, enforcement in Federal courts, 2
Common law, international law as part of, 1; 18 *sqq*.
Commonwealth under Cromwell, as de facto government, 58
Confederacy, Southern, as de facto government, 58 *sqq*.
Confederacy, Southern, as unrecognized government, 59 *sqq*.
Confederacy, Southern, concession made to in its military character, 53
Conference, Peace, after World War, 92
Congress, Act of, giving federal courts jurisdiction over certain aliens, 23
Congress, Act of, in violation of international law, 11
Congress, jurisdiction on high seas, 18
Congress of the Confederacy, 4
Congress, power in sphere of international law, 6, 7, 16, 76
Connecticut, sovereignty of, 3
Conquered territory, conqueror's acts therein valid, 72, 73
Conquest, acquisition of new territory by, 89
Constitution, Amendment 10, powers of U. S., 20, 158
  Amendment 11, 79
  Amendment 14, applying to aliens, 148
  Article one, section 8, piracy, 6, 7, 16
  Article one, section 8, paragraph 18, 158
  Article six, treaties supreme law of land, 182
  Article six, clause 2, on treaties, 157
Constitution, careful phraseology of, 5
Constitution, Congress' power over international law, 76
Constitution, framed in contemplation of continuance of common law, 2

[214]

Index

Constitution, giving power to make treaties, 7
Constitution, international law in, 3
Constitution, limitations on sovereignty of U. S. by, 39
Constitution, superiority of international law, 11
Constitutional theory of sovereignty, 37 *sqq.*
Constitutional convention, 4
Constitutional law, definition of foreign country, 95
Consuls not diplomatic officials, 122
Contracts under recognized government, validity of, 67
Counterfeiting, under international law, 76
Country, see *Territory Land*
Court, American in China, 126
Court, Circuit, of Appeals, 117
Court, American in China, 126
Courts, acts of sovereign not to come under foreign, 75
Courts, admiralty, assumed jurisdiction, 111
Court, naturalization proceedings, 140 *sqq.*
Court of Claims, American, British subjects in, 82
Court of Claims cases, 14
Courts, decide own jurisdiction, 112
Courts, duty to decide cases under international law, 9
Courts, enforcement of treaties, 170
Courts, extraterritorial, 126
Courts, federal, enforcement of common law in, 2
Courts, federal, expound international law, 3
Courts, federal, jurisdiction over certain aliens, 23
Courts, government cannot be sued in foreign, exceptions, 83
Courts, jurisdiction in international law, 7
Courts, respect for decision of foreign, 112, 192

Courts, not subject to foreign, 117
Courts. See *Judicial power Tribunals*
Cowen, Mr. Justice, 22
Cuba, date of extinction of Spanish sovereignty in, 94
Cuba, foreign territory during American occupation, 73
Czechoslovak republic, 39

Decrees of unrecognized governments, force of, 66, 71
Denmark, treaty containing "most favored nation" clause, 177
Domicil, 142
Domicil, change of, effecting expatriation, 146
Diplomatic channels, method of a state's treating with citizens of another, 78 *sqq.*
Diplomatic immunity, 119
Diplomatic officials, consuls not, 122
Diplomatic officials of sovereign not suable, 119
Discovery, acquisition of new territory by, 89
Durfee, Amos, 21
Dutch occupation of New York not legal, 89
Duties of states, 74 *sqq.*

Effect of decrees of unrecognized governments, 71
Embargo, 190
Embargo, definition, 190
Embassies as asylums, 123
Enforcement of international law, 10, 27, 190 *sq.*
Enforcement of treaties, 169 *sqq.*
Equality of states, 75 *sqq.*
Expatriation, 143 *sqq.*
Expatriation, conditions effecting, 146
Expatriation, definition, 143
Expatriation, methods, 144 *sqq.*
Extradition, 129 *sqq.*
Extradition by treaty, 130 *sqq.*
Extradition, definition, 129
Extradition, offences under, 132

[215]

Index

Extradition treaties, political offenders exempted, 134
Extradition treaty not guarantee of asylum, 133
Extradition treaty with Prussia, 87
Extraterritorial jurisdiction, 124

Falkland Islands, controversy over title, 43
Federal legislation and international law, 10 *sqq.*
Felony, 5, 7
Felonies, on high seas, in Constitution, 6, 7
Felonies, on high seas, power of Congress over, 7
Force of decrees of unrecognized governments, 66
Foreign country, definition by constitutional law, 95
Foreign country, penal laws of not enforced, 126
Foreign territory, passage of troops through, 114, 123
Forsythe, Secretary of State, 21
France, commercial agreement with U. S., 1898, 45
France, treaty with U. S., 1778, 160
France, U. S. diplomatic rights against, 14
French Government and Claims Commission, 80
French Spoliation Claims, 13 *sqq.*

Garner, James W., 16
German Empire, formation not termination of treaty with Prussia, 87
Government, agency of state, 38
Government agents, responsibility of, 84
Government and state, definition, 38
Government, belligerent rights to form, 73
Government cannot be sued in foreign courts, exceptions, 83
Government, unrecognized, force of decrees of, 66, 71

Government, validity of grants of land by a former, 93
Governments, de facto, 58 *sqq.*
Governments, de facto, validity of judgments of tribunals, 74
Governments, kinds of, and their powers, 57 *sqq.*
Governments, recognition of, 40 *sqq.*
Governments, unrecognized, 58 *sqq.*
Governments, unrecognized, judicially nonexistent, exceptions, 71
Governments, unrecognized, liability of individuals for acts under authority of, 47
Governments, unrecognized, rights of in courts, 62 *sqq.*
Governments, unrecognized, validity of acts of, 67 *sqq.*
Governments, unrecognized, validity of contracts under, 67
Governments, unrecognized, validity of land titles acquired under, 66
Gray, Mr. Justice, 25
  International law part of law of land, 9

Halleck's International Law, 53
High Seas, American Great Lakes as, 103
High Seas, jurisdiction on, 128
High Seas, jurisdiction of Congress on, 18
High Seas, unrecognized insurgents on, are pirates, 55
High Seas, vessels on, jurisdiction, 107
Holmes, Mr. Justice, on supreme law of land, 159

Immunity, diplomatic, 119
Independence and sovereignty, 28 *sqq.*
Independence, when commences, 39, 40
Independence. See *Sovereignty*
Insurance, Russian Co., in New York, 70

[216]

Index

Insurgent government, title to property under, 87 *sqq.*
Insurgents, information needed for judicial proof of conflict, 57
Insurgents, unrecognized, legal consequences of acts, 55
Insurgents, unrecognized, on high seas, are pirates, 55, 56
International comity, statute conflicting is superior, 15
International law, Act of Congress in violation of, 11
International law and federal legislation, 10 *sqq.*
International law and municipal law, conflict, 16
International law and state legislatures, 24
International law and states of the Union, 18 *sqq.*
International law as law of land, limitations, 10 *sqq.*
International law, as part of the common law, 1
International law, changes in, 25
International law, counterfeiting under, 76
International law, definition, 28
International law, enforcement, 10, 27, 190
International law, enforcement by economic boycott, 191
International law, expounded by federal courts primarily, 3
International law governs recognition, 48
International law in Constitution, 3
International law, judicial decision declaring part of law of land, 8 *sqq.*
International law, nature and sources of, 24
International law, not changed by municipal law, 13
International law, part of common law, 18 *sqq.*
International law, part of law of land, 9
International law, power of Congress in sphere of, 6, 7, 16, 76
International law, power of legislature to carry out obligations of, 15
International law, private, 7, 9
International law, responsibility of a nation under, for acts of citizens, 77 *sqq.*
International law, sovereign state not suable under, 33
International law, stabilized by judicial decisions, 26
International law, states as persons in, 28 *sqq.*
International law, statute conflicting with, 11 *sqq.*, 19
International law, superiority over constitutional and municipal law, 11 *sqq.*
International law, U. S. as state in, 29
Interpretation of treaties, 169 *sqq.*

Jacob and Johanna, the Young, case of, 24
Judgments of a foreign country, recognition of in U. S., 112, 192
Judicial decisions declaring international law part of law of land, 8 *sqq.*
Judicial decisions stabilize international law, 26
Judicial power under treaties, 7
Jurisdiction beyond three-mile limit, 105
Jurisdiction, courts decide own, 112
Jurisdiction, extraterritorial, 124
Jurisdiction, maritime, 103 *sqq.*
Jurisdiction of admiralty courts, 111
Jurisdiction of states, 101 *sqq.*
Jurisdiction on high seas, 18, 128
Jurisdiction over piracy, 128
Jurisdiction over vessels in high seas or in foreign waters, 107 *sqq.*, 123
Jurisdiction, sovereign not to come under foreign courts, 117
Jurisdiction, territorial, exemptions from, 116
Jurisdiction, territorial limit of state, 101 *sqq.*

Index

Knox, General Henry, 4

Lakes, American Great, as high seas, 103
Land, validity of grants by a former government, 93
Law, contrary to international law, 11 *sqq.*
Law of land, international law as, limitations, 10 *sqq.*
Law of land, international law part of, 9
Law of land, judicial decisions declaring international law part of, 8 *sqq.*
Law of nations. See *International Law*, 6
Laws, neutrality, 49
Laws of conquered or ceded territory remaining in force, 93, 96
Laws, penal, of foreign country not enforced, 126
Laws. See *Municipal law Constitutional law International law*
League of Nations, economic boycott to enforce international law, 191
Legality of acts of states in rebellion, 61
Legations as asylums, 123
Legislative power of state, 110
Legislature, power to carry out obligations of international law, 15
Legislatures, state, and international law, 24
Liability of individuals for acts under authority of unrecognized governments, 47
Limitations on Congress with respect to international law by Constitution, 16
Louisiana, cession of, 42
Louisiana, civil law, 1

Madison, James, 5
Mansfield, Lord, International law part of common law, 1
Maritime jurisdiction, 103 *sqq.*
Marriage, citizenship in U. S. not lost by, 145

Marriages, recognition in other countries, 113
Marshall, Chief Justice, 24
  Act of Congress in violation of International law, 11
  boundary settlements political, not judicial, 42
  definition of sovereignty, 37
  International law part of law of land, 8
  on retaliation, 191
  on title by discovery, 89
Massachusetts, penal statutes, 127
Massachusetts, sovereignty, 3
McLean, Mr. Justice, 44
McLeod case, 20
Mexican government of Carranza, 75, **76**
Mexican governors, authority to alienate public domain, 94
Mexico, foreign territory during American occupation, 73
Morris, Gouverneur, 6
"Most favored nation" clause, 176
Municipal law and international law, conflict, 16
Municipal laws, courts decide own jurisdiction with respect to, 112
Municipal law, does not change international law, 13
Municipal law, superiority of international law, 11 *sqq.*

Napoleon III, suit in name of, 86
Nation, most favored, clause, 176
Nationality compared to citizenship, 135
Naturalization, 139 *sqq.*
Nature of international law, 24
Nature of sovereignty, 34
Neutrality laws, 49
New Jersey Plan, 5
New York, Dutch occupation not legal, 89
New York Supreme Court, 22
Nonintercourse, 190

Peace Conference after great war, 92
Penal Code, Texas, 127

Index

Penal laws of foreign country not enforced, 126
Pennsylvania, sovereignty of, 4
Persons, states as in international law, 28 *sqq.*, 34 *sqq.*
Personality, continuing, of states, 85 *sqq.*
Philadelphia project, 5
Philippine Islands, question whether foreign territory, 94
Philippines, Senate resolution on citizenship of inhabitants, 176
Piracy, 16
Piracy, definition, 5
Piracy, in Constitution, 6, 7
Piracy, jurisdiction over, 128
Piracy, power of Congress over, 7
Pirates, unrecognized insurgents on high seas are, 55, 56
Political offenders, exempted from extradition, 134
Porto Rico, question whether foreign territory, 94
Power to make treaties in U. S., 156 *sqq.*
Power to make treaties, limits, 158
Powers of governments, 57 *sqq.*
Power of U. S. under Constitution, 20
Prize Cases, 51 *sqq.*
Property, title to, under insurgent government, 87 *sqq.*
Prussia, extradition treaty with, 87
Prussia, treaty with U. S., 161

Randolph, John, defects of Articles of Confederation, 4
Ratification of treaties, 168 *sqq.*
Rebus sic stantibus clause in treaties, 179
Recognition, governed by international law, 48
Recognition of belligerency, 48 *sqq.*
Recognition of factions of civil war, 47
Recognition of states and governments, 40 *sqq.*
Recognition of states political not judicial, 41 *sqq.*

Recognition, until accorded, courts will consider the old order unchanged, 48
Registry of vessels, 80, 81
Reprisals, 191 *sqq.*
Reprisals, definition, 193
Respect for decisions of foreign courts, 112, 192
Responsibilities of states, 74 *sqq.*
Responsibility of government agents, 84
Responsibility of nation for acts of citizens under international law, 77 *sqq.*
Retaliation, 191 *sqq.*
Retaliation, definition, 191
Right of U. S. citizens to prosecute claims against British government, 83
Rights and privileges of aliens, 147 *sqq.*, 152
Rights in courts of unrecognized governments, 62 *sqq.*
Rights of belligerency, 50 *sqq.*
Rights of inhabitants of ceded territory, protection by treaty, 97 *sqq.*
Rights of states, 74 *sqq.*
Rivers as boundaries, 101

Sapphire, The, suit against, 86
Senate, power in treaty making, 168 *sqq.*, 173
Senate resolution on Philippine citizenship, 176
Ships of war, justification over in foreign waters, 123
Ships. See *Vessels*
Society of the Cincinnati, 4
Sources of international law, 24
South American Colonies as belligerents, 54
Sovereign, acts of not to come under foreign courts, 75 *sqq.*, 117
Sovereign not suable, 118
Sovereign, power to sue in foreign courts, 117
Sovereign's diplomatic officials not suable, 119
Sovereignty, acquisition and loss of, 88 *sqq.*

Index

Sovereignty and independence, 28 *sqq.*
Sovereignty, constitutional theory of, expounded by judiciary, 37
Sovereignty, definition, 37
Sovereignty, limits of state, 34
Sovereignty, nature of, 34 *sqq.*
Sovereignty, nature of from constitutional viewpoint, 38
Sovereignty of colonies, 3 *sqq.*
Sovereignty of states, 20, 24
Sovereignty of U. S., constitutional limits on, 39
Sovereignty over territory, recognition of, 40 *sqq.*
Soviet government, acts of, effect of in U. S., 68
Soviet régime, 66
Spain, grants in disputed territory of Louisiana, 42
Spanish sovereignty in Cuba, date of extinction, 94
Spoliation Claims, French, 13 *sqq.*
State and government, definition, 38
State, definition, 29 *sqq.*
State jurisdiction, territorial limits, 101 *sqq.*
State legislatures and international law, 24
State, limits of sovereignty, 34
State, method of treating with citizens of another, 78 *sqq.*
State, relation to citizens in U. S., 79
State, sovereign, not suable by international law, 33
State, territorial limit of legislative power, 110
States as persons in international law, 28 *sqq.*, 34 *sqq.*
States, boundaries, 101 *sqq.*
States, continuing personality of, 85 *sqq.*
States, equality of, 75 *sqq.*
States in rebellion, legality of acts of, 61
States, jurisdiction, 101 *sqq.*
States of the Union and international law, 18 *sqq.*
States, recognition of, 40 *sqq.*

States, recognition of political, not judicial, 41 *sqq.*
States, rights, duties and responsibilities, 74 *sqq.*
States, sovereignty, 20, 24
Statute, conflicting with international law, 11 *sqq.*, 19
Statute, conflicting with international comity, 15
Story, Justice, definition of sovereignty, 37
Stowell, Lord, 24, 25
Supremacy, national, effects of, 110
Supremacy, territorial, legal effects of, 109
Supreme Court, definition of belligerency, 50
  definition of citizenship, 135
  definition of international law, 28
  definition of a state, 29 *sqq.*
  definition of United States, 31
  effect on of commentators on international law, 25
  effect on of decisions of foreign courts on international law, 26
  extradition treaty with Prussia, 87
  international law part of law of land, 9
Supreme Court of New York, 22
Supreme Court, on action beyond three-mile limit, 106
  on constitutionality of treaties, 161
  on effect of war on treaties, 183
  on power of Congress to punish piracy, 16
  on supreme law of land, 159
  on treaty power, 163
  on Virginia debt, 92
  right of sovereign to appeal to, 117
  statute, conflicting, superior to international comity, 115
Switzerland, treaty with U. S., 160

Talbot, Lord, international law part of common law, 1

[220]

Index

Tampico, foreign territory during American occupation, 73
Tennessee, bank-note amendment, 85
Termination of treaties, 178 *sqq*.
Territorial jurisdiction, exemptions from, 116
Territorial limit of legislative power, 110
Territorial limits of state jurisdiction, 101 *sqq*.
Territorial supremacy, legal effects of, 109
Territories, acquisition, 88 *sqq*.
Territory, abandonment of, 92
Territory, acquisition by accretion, 90
Territory, acquisition by adverse possession, 91
Territory, acquisition by conquest and discovery, 89
Territory, acquisition by treaty, 91
Territory, conquered, conqueror's acts therein valid, 72, 73
Territory, conquered or ceded, laws remaining in force, 93, 96
Territory, foreign, definition by constitutional law, 95
Territory, foreign, passage of troops through, 114, 123
Territory, power to incorporate into U. S., 162
Texas Penal Code, 127
Titles to property, acquired under unrecognized government, 66, 87 *sqq*.
Treaties, 156 *sqq*.
Treaties as law of land, 171
contract nature of, 174
effect of war on, 183 *sqq*.
enforcement and interpretation, 169 *sqq*.
enforcement by courts, 170 *sqq*.
extradition by, 130 *sqq*.
judicial power under, 7
legality of, 161
limits to power to make, 158, 162 *sqq*.
method of construing, 175

Treaties as law of land, modification by later laws, 181
money payments under, 166
"most favored nation" clause, 176
negotiation and conclusion of, 168
power to compel action by a state, 167
power to make in U. S., 156 *sqq*.
power to ratify, 173
purchase of Alaska by, 167
rebus sic stantibus clause, 179
self-executing, 165
state statute inferior to, 182
supreme law of land, 7, 158, 182
termination of, 178 *sqq*.
violation, 170, 180
when effective, 173
Treaty, definition, 156
extradition, with Prussia, 87
necessary to acquire conquered territory, 91
obligations, enforcement of, 6
of peace with Great Britain, 6
protection of private rights of inhabitants of ceded territory by, 97 *sqq*.
Treaty. See *Extradition Treaty*
Tribunal, arbitral, decision of final, 188
Tribunals, arbitral, do not have power of judicial tribunals, 189
Tribunals of de facto governments, validity of judgments of, 74
Troops, passage through foreign territory, 114, 123

United States as a state in international law, 29
constitutional limitations on sovereignty, 29
definition, 31
diplomatic rights against France, 14
right of citizens to prosecute claims against British government, 83

Validity of acts of unrecognized government, 67 *sqq*.

[221]

Index

Validity of contracts under unrecognized government, 67
  of grants of land by former government, 93
  of judgments of tribunals of de facto governments, 74
  of land titles acquired under unrecognized government, 66
Vattel, acts permitted in war, 53
  definition of state, 31
  on civil war, 52
  sovereign state, 33
Versailles treaties, 92
Vessels, armed merchant, 129
  as asylums, 123
  belligerent right to search, 128
Vessels, on high seas or in foreign waters, jurisdiction over, 107 *sqq.*, 123
  registry of, 80, 81
Virginia Convention, 5
Virginia, debt of, 92

War, effect on treaties, 183 *sqq.*
Webster, Secretary of State, 21, 151
Williams, Senator John Sharp, on treaty power, 167
Wilson, Mr. Justice, 6
  definition of state, 29
  international law part of law of land, 8

Date Due